The Healing Hands of Love
A guide to spiritual healing

Tarajyoti Govinda

The Healing Hands of Love: a guide to spiritual healing
Govinda, Tarajyoti, 1958-1999
Copyright Govindamurti, G. A. 1999

First published 1997. 2nd. ed. 2016

Deva Wings Publications
www.devawings.com
Daylesford, Australia

All rights reserved. No part of this book may be reproduced by any process, nor stored in a retrieval system, transmitted, translated into another language, or otherwise copied except for brief passages quoted for the purpose of review, without prior written permission from the publisher.

Cover:
   Artwork by: Henning Klibo
   www.artalexander.com

National Library of Australia, Cataloguing-in-Publication

Govinda, Tarajyoti, 1958-1999
The Healing Hands of Love: a guide to spiritual healing
Bibliography.
ISBN: 978-0-9587202-5-0

1. Healing - Religious aspects. 2. Spiritual life. I Title

'This is my Light that I give to you. Shine it, that others may see and be illumined also.'

Jesus

I could see the task up ahead -
lifetimes, two or three -
that behold a love and purpose of heart,
that speak of eternity.
The past, the present, the future merged,
the omnipresent now
when all are being prepared
for what is to come.
The beginnings and the endings,
the changes, through and between
give insight and clarity to the perennial theme -
Love,
it waits for us to open to its sound,
to let our hearts ignite its fire - newly found.
The Son -
He merges with the Earth
and takes us to the sky
where we can feel the power of our wings
as we soar through the sky.

This book is dedicated to Lord Jesus for awakening me to God's Love; to Ananda Tara Shan, my Teacher - for her eternal gift of Higher Teaching and Love; Gregory Govindamurti, my beloved husband - for his heartfelt support and love; Frank Brew, my father - for his love and honesty; Laurel Brew, my mother - for her dedication, commitment and perseverance; Stephen Brew, my brother - for his protection and companionship; Right Reverend Shri Bent Mundt, my healer - for his trust, peace and calm; and Shri Ishwara Sarma and Priscilla Lindsay, my dear friends - for their friendship and the memory of union in Spirit.

Contents

SPIRITUAL HEALING	7
THE ANGELIC HELPERS	37
THE HUMAN STRUCTURE	75
THE CHAKRAS	101
THE AURA AND ITS COLOURS	129
THE HEALER	159
REINCARNATION	175
KARMA	199
THE UNCONSCIOUS	217
REGRESSION	233
GUIDED IMAGERY	253
ALCHEMY	289
SPREADING THE LIGHT	305
REFERENCES	307

Foreword

Dear Reader,

Like many, I felt very much in touch with Spirit as a child. As life moved on, as a river with its many twists and turns, sometimes meandering, sometimes flooding, I slowly lost that touch until I dared to search for that touch again. It came then like thunder through the vehicle of karma, disguised as trauma and pain, as horrific experience in the brutality of humanity. Over time, and with the help of the angels, through a spiritual awakening and death experience, I came to uncover Spirit's disguise and feel the fullness of truth, life and love once more. In my first book *The Language of the Heart Is Spoken All over the World* I have told something of these experiences and the gifts they have brought, gifts that are the wisdom of Spirit, the essence of life. By opening my heart in trust to Spirit I have come to know The Healing Hands of Love. The Healing Hands are the hands and touch of the Divine which come through the Divine Vision or touch of the angels' wings, where heart meets heart and we find the angelic healing we all seek, in union with our divinity.

My awakening was seemingly sudden. Like Lazarus resurrected from the grave, I saw the Glory of God's Kingdom. It came in three stages. Firstly, in facing my death in war, rape and violence, the recognition came that there was indeed a God who was symbolised and embodied in the Light of the Sun. Secondly, in the simple act of praying to Jesus after this crisis in war and rape, I came to recognise that I too am Light. Thirdly, through the sudden collapse of both lungs I experienced my death and rebirth in the glory and splendour of the inner worlds. Had it not been for some simple yet curious twists of fate, I may have been added to the large figure in statistics where death is attributable to being shot in the war, raped and murdered or death by asthma.

After the death experience I lay in a coma for two weeks and I regained consciousness as never before. I brought back with me the memory of that experience and the knowing that heaven is in our hearts, the Light is here; we need only choose.

That was 1984. It is now 1997 and it is much more acceptable now to speak of such experiences of the Light. Like others who have had such experiences, I went through the tunnel to the Light and was greeted by many angels. One in particular met me then and is still with me to this day. When I dare to open and listen, it gives me the Divine guidance that I need, to stay in Light. The angel showed me a series of past lives, and some future ones. I could see what I had not understood, what I needed to redeem and change and what I would need to do should I choose to enter the Earth plane. For me there was no choice. I so wanted to tell others about this great Glory - this great Light that is God's Love. I felt as though I had just been born into a twenty-four year old body and I had first to learn to work within it. *First you must learn to love yourself and honour the body as a temple in which your Spirit lives.* This was my first task. In the weeks that followed I tried to understand what had happened and what was happening to me. My values and beliefs had been turned upside down, as had the relationships I had with others. I could not remember how long I had known people or their relation to me. Slowly I discovered that the person I had been was no longer. I was someone else. I had a whole new consciousness. Reincarnation was no longer just a possible theory, it was my reality. Quickly I needed to re-establish a life: throw out what was needed and create anew. The weeks that followed turned into months and years. I wanted to know more.

Some months after leaving the hospital where I had been for some time, when I was starting to be well enough to drive and socialise, I went along to a spiritual fair where I met my Teacher, Ananda Tara Shan. At the fair people were giving aura cleansing and spiritual healing. I realised then that through spiritual healing this great Light could be transferred to others to awaken them, and that not everyone needed to go through experiences as traumatic and life-changing as mine had been to transform. Ananda was teaching people how to heal with the great Light, and in so doing to awaken it in others. So I went to her to learn. I related my experience to her, and throughout the years that have followed she has helped me to open to the wisdom and experience of that great Light that is Theosophy or Divine Wisdom. Theosophy reveals the way to the inner worlds. It reveals the way that we can walk on Earth and find heaven in our hearts. The Light of Theosophy is eternal and reaches towards infinity.

The Healing Hands of Love, therefore, though different in form, becomes a welcome sequel to *The Language of the Heart Is Spoken All over the World*. It gives to us the next step in understanding how we can open our hearts and live in love, with the help and guidance of the Healing Hands of Love. The Healing Hands of Love are everywhere, about us and within us, in the wings of our inner angel, our Christ-self. In *The Healing Hands of Love* I have striven to provide the knowledge we need to heal. When we open to the inner worlds, we open to a well full of everlasting wisdom and love. I hope you enjoy reading this book as much as I have enjoyed creating it. May the angels and beings of Light bless you on your way.

Introduction

Spiritual healing, simply stated, is the healing of the spiritual aspects of human nature. It is also the process of working with Spirit in a way that will help heal ailments of the human condition that are in some way attributable to a spiritual cause. It deals with the subtle bodies of a person, inviting movement away from stress and congestion, towards harmony and balance within. When we embark on a journey of spiritual healing we begin to open the doors to a wondrous and expansive world which is known as the inner world. It is a world that many live their lives unconscious of, while others spend life enjoying the richness and fulfilment that comes from knowing it. As we venture within we find the truth of what the inner child has always sought to know - is there a God? Or is God, like Santa Claus, the Easter bunny and the tooth fairy, just another adult creation? Yet even as children we seem to know that God is somehow different to the other mysteries we are asked to believe in - somehow greater, and even more unknowable. That is what makes God such a powerfully present Mystery. If we are lucky and have the karma, we come to know that we can find God in Spirit, and if we are still luckier, we come to discover that Spirit lives within us - that we are born containing a spark of God. It is with that spark that spiritual healing works. Spiritual healing aims to awaken us to that spark in us all. The healing Light heals us from the inside out, and drives away all that is not of God from within us.

Spiritual healing awakens us to the Glory of God, to the knowing of the existence of the soul and Spirit. We discover that there is much more to the human being than the personality self we are most familiar with. The human aura and the chakras, which form part of our subtle energy bodies, provide us with the keys and the doorway to the inner worlds into which we can enter and heal ourselves. Spiritual healing also awakens us to the spiritual

Laws - to the reality of karma and reincarnation. Through spiritual healing and regression we come to know ourselves as the summation of all our past, and we discover the potential of the future within us. We see the aspects of our nature we need to purify, transmute and redeem. We come to understand some of how the universe works and find our soul's purpose within that universe. We discover that we are Light and can open to the inner worlds, sharing in the glory of that Light. We also discover the enormous help available from our angelic friends who live in the inner worlds and communicate to us through colour, light and symbol, as we dare to open to their world, through meditation, guided imagery and healing. The angels are God's messengers and they reveal to us the Divine Plan.

Spiritual healing provides us with a means for deep inner change, change that we can tangibly identify as alchemy - spiritual transformation. Through it we spread the Light and make a greater consciousness available to all who seek it from a pure heart.

Spiritual Healing

Spiritual healing is a practice that has been used for millennia. From ancient civilisations such as Atlantis and Egypt, and medieval England and Europe, China, India, Africa, etc. to countries worldwide in modern times, healing has spread in a variety of forms. Indigenous peoples have worked with spiritual healing for centuries and pass the wisdom from generation to generation. Today, when technology is advancing in the West and the East, a simultaneous growth is occurring in the awareness of spiritual development. We may see spiritual healing as an alternative method of health care, but slowly it is becoming more mainstream. Its practice is spreading to hospitals and other places where there is a need.

Since the development of air travel and its more common usage for a larger number of people, many more westerners have spent time in the East and have brought back practices of eastern traditions. Spiritual healing has always existed in the West, but society has confined its use to a small minority of the population. This is rapidly changing with the growing awareness of spiritual concerns in our daily life, and it marks the beginning of a needed education, world wide.

Some people associate spiritual healing with particular religious beliefs or groups, and some groups and organisations claim that only they have access to the true Light. The Light of the Holy Spirit, which is the Light behind all true healing, is not owned by any group or organisation. It is a universal energy that is given from the Heart of God and given freely to all who call for it from the purity of their hearts. It does not discriminate according to race, colour or creed. It does not matter which religion a person follows; if he or she wishes to work from the heart in a way that benefits humanity for the good of the whole, the Holy Spirit will come. The source of spiritual healing is the Light and Love that is behind all true religions. It is the Holy Spirit which is given to us from the Lord of Love.

The Teachings of Jesus in healing

The Lord Jesus spent part of His mission teaching about healing. He did this by example and by explaining to some of His more intimate followers the philosophy and science behind healing. He healed through touch and through offering words of comfort to those in need, giving as much as they were able to receive. He also taught us about the Path, the way to walk to increase our consciousness of the Light, and of qualities such as purity and love. The way He gave, as evidenced in His Sermon on the Mount, gives us a guide to healing. He taught us about forgiveness and the desire to acquire soul awareness through the vital restoration and sanctification of our inner being.

Healing brings alignment with the inner life and brings the wholeness that comes when our consciousness rises to touch the indwelling Presence of the Christ within us. Healing comes for those who are prepared to open to the Light and to follow it. Through compassion and love, we bring about healing.

Jesus taught that the source of His power was the Christ, the Lord of Love. In order to open to that source of power that was in Jesus, we must open to the Lord of Love also. Jesus' message is a message of faith, and through that faith we come to see it also as a message of Love. The faith and Love bring to us a heavenly perception. They give us a vision and help us to understand that vision. Jesus taught those around Him, who were close to Him, how they could transfer the healing Light and showed how even He was simply a vehicle for the Divine Love. Through example

He taught the need to constantly align ourselves to the quality of humility and to apply the principles of loving thy neighbour, and of truth, to our daily life. In this way we too can learn how to radiate the healing Light, how to radiate love, and in so doing become healed ourselves. He counselled many about how to purify themselves through becoming conscious of being honest, righteous and just and to let go of arrogance and hate. He asked that we do this not by proclaiming it but by living it and by becoming gentle and tender, righteous and loving, humble and willing, honest and pure. These simple suggestions are the keys to the healing of the human race. The practical application of the higher principles is necessary in order for us to bring Spirit into matter and to manifest the Kingdom of God upon the Earth.

Jesus taught the quality of selflessness, for without this a healer cannot radiate the Divine Light nor can he or she open to be a vehicle for that Light. Here we see the need to not attach ourselves to the glamour of being a healer, or to live in the illusion that being so we are somehow special. We realise that humanity cannot heal by itself and that the power of Light and Love, given by the Lord of Love, is the only power through which we can truly heal. It certainly is the only power that will heal the soul and therefore ultimately the only power that can heal us.

In his book *Spiritual Healing*, Reverend J. Todd Ferrier talks about the healing of doubt, inward pain, soul hunger, aloneness and soul travail. He suggests that the only ways to heal ailments are through the vision of the Presence or the touch of the Divine Hand. He says, "when the Light of that vision falls upon the mind's shadows they are chased away" (1984, p. 101). The Divine Hand similarly touches the suffering mind and generates "an atmosphere of peace" (1984, p. 100). The consciousness of His Presence heals the pain of the soul. Often during healing people receive comfort through the simple knowing that they are not alone. This inner knowing gives strength and courage that will help us through the most intense inner and outer struggles and seems to provide all with a sense of inner conviction to persevere. It is for us to remember that we are not alone and to hold the memory of the vision and the memory of His Presence. When we do this, life is instilled with a serenity and peace unknown. The following story illustrates the power of the Divine Vision, the Divine Presence and Divine Touch. It also gives a clear indication of what healing really is. It is written from the perspective of Lazarus at the time of Jesus.

Resurrection

"Come Lazarus, come", Master said. "There is work to do".

I could hear His magnificence in His voice. He seemed so pure, so full of Love and He treated me like a brother.

"Lazarus", He said. "What is it?"

"When you speak My Lord, You treat me with reverence and this is difficult for me to comprehend. You seem so great and I so little. How can I do Your work when I am so unworthy?"

"You are My brother, Lazarus, and together we work for the Father. Work with Me and I will lead you to His Kingdom. It is easier to work with one who has low self-esteem for then I have the keys to the doors within. When one is full of pride and ego centred, the doors are closed to Me and the Father. Why do you choose to stay in the darkness when there is so much Light? Come Lazarus!"

The sound in His voice was so full of Love and honour. It held within it a purpose and a brotherhood for which I was yearning. I felt I would give anything to be with Him, and He was calling me. I could understand

why I was calling Him but not why He had chosen me. I remembered when He showed me the Glory of God.
The yearning and desire for Him in my heart propelled me forwards.

"I am coming, Master", I said, and within moments I was in Light.

Master continued, "My people cannot always come to you, they have not always the means. Sometimes you must go to them."

Then, as if transposed between worlds, I found myself with Master in the streets of Jerusalem. The streets narrowed as we walked and we entered into a cold and musty cellar. Seated in the cellar was a blind person who appeared full of need. Master gave him a walking stick.

"But doesn't he need vision, Master?"

"He wants vision but that is not what he needs. He needs a walking stick to help him climb from the cellar to the Light. You must remember this. You cannot give people what they want. All want different things and thousands of conflicts arise. Sometimes, though, you can bestow what is needed. It comes as a gift of Grace from the Father, like this walking stick for this blind man. You can't control what he does with it, but you can give it with the Father's blessing. The blind man might get angry and throw it down and never find his way from the cellar but that is his process and you cannot interfere. You can merely try to help him see the gift the Father has given. Whether he uses it or not is his choice and not one that you can make."

The blind man took the stick and though his eyes still could not see in physical life, a Light came into them, of understanding and of hope.

"Our work is done," Master said, and we left the person to his own devices.

Certainly an enormous energy of Peace and Love was present in the cellar and the musty smell had transformed to the fragrance of a rose.

"Come, I have more to show you."

I followed Master through the narrow streets with my head down watching the patterns of the cobble stones as I walked.

The streets became narrower and narrower until we entered into the bazaar. We passed stall after stall until finally we stopped in front of one where a person stood alone. I could see just by looking at her that she was perceptually blind. Her eyes were large and clear but had no depth. It was clear she had no consciousness from where I was looking. Jesus placed his hands on her head for some moments. It was as if she came to life. Suddenly she could see. She looked around her. She was wondering what she was doing there. Within a very short time she started to pack some satchels and move away from the bazaar along the narrow streets into the wider horizons. She had entered a life of purpose.

"This is true healing," Jesus said, "when one previously unconscious becomes conscious and chooses."

We continued walking away from the bazaar to the slightly wider streets of the township. I noticed that the patterns of the cobblestones had become more square. Master pointed to the thirteen stations of the cross.

"People are arguing about where I walked. This is the greatest insult to Me and My Teaching. People are using My name to fight, creating belief systems as the cause of battle. I have taught you to love one another from the heart, regardless of colour, race or creed."

We continued to walk. Many lined the streets to await Master hoping in their hearts He would heal them. I watched in awe of His Presence, the effect He had. There were some that He touched as He had the person in the bazaar. There were others that He walked by, so many *distressed faces. It was as if all the pain, suffering and grief of humanity had risen up to greet Him. I caught sight of a distressed person who appeared angry as Jesus passed her by. Her face showed the anguish of her lifetimes on Earth. Jesus was up ahead touching someone else by now. I watched the anguished person and noted that slowly she could be angry no more. She had been touched by Master's Presence and it was bringing an unknown peace into her aura. It left her in a state of confusion intermittently interchanging with the new-found understanding.*

Master was now a long way ahead and the crowd had certainly been transformed by His magnificence. I looked again at the distressed person and I noticed a vision of Lady Mary. I could see many images of Lady Mary throughout the crowd now. The Light of the Mother was helping many people assimilate the Christ Light to bring it into all levels of existence, the mind, the emotions, until no gross matter was left. The Lady Mary had many helpers on all levels of existence to help this take place. Her helpers were replenished by the Love of the Mother. The only ingredient necessary was the desire to serve the Divine through a loving heart. I began to see how the Light of the Hierarchy comes to us - through the Light of Christ, transformed to all levels of existence by the many great beings and helpers who worked selflessly for the Light.

Jesus seemed to create a path now into the heavens. I felt myself left on Earth ready to speak in His name, filled with the Glory of the Light, ready to work for lifetimes ahead that all may come to know God's radiance.

It was not long after Jesus left that the townspeople became angry, wanting to find and kill Him. They came for me and stoned me in a relentless and intrusive manner. Master's voice resonated in my ears, "send them your deepest love and compassion for they have not seen the Light."

I could feel no resentment, only love, compassion and gratitude for the knowing I had been given.

Word came quickly, "The King is dead, the King is dead!" I felt for a moment the pangs of enormous grief. They were pervaded, however, with the knowing that He was indeed not dead. He had risen and created a path for us to follow to His Master, the Lord of Love, the Lord Maitreya. Jesus' Presence was felt through the Presence of His Master, the Lord Maitreya. A glorious impregnation of Light and Love entered the Earth as the Christ came closer to humanity.

"Wherever you go," I heard Master's words, "I will be with you, you are not alone." I knew in my heart the truth of these words. He is always there for those who wish it.

Jesus comes when we call, constantly resurrecting us from our illusions of hopelessness and despair. His Presence fills us instead with hope and faith, constantly serving as a true example of the healer, the counsellor of love.

What is spiritual healing?

Spiritual healing is the transmitting of Light and energy of a high vibrating matter into the auric field of another being, be it another human, an animal, a plant or the Earth itself.

In spiritual healing we identify and separate the dense matter which we wish to purify. Through magnification and multiplication of the sacred fire we burn away the dross (negative matter) and then unify the remaining substance of Light with the whole. The new substance becomes an integrated part of that whole. For example, if someone comes for healing to work with a negative quality such as selfish ambition, the surrender of that quality to the Light enables the Light to enter into the dense matter, multiply and transmute that matter. The ambition is therefore alchemically changed by this process and is transformed to become, perhaps, the desire to serve selflessly. This desire to serve selflessly is then reunited with, and integrated into, the person, who through the experience is changed and made whole.

> "To heal truly is to get at the cause, which is usually deep seated in the mind or in the emotion of the individual, and by a true spiritual pathology to proceed from here outward, driving the trouble out of the vehicle through healing the cause of it in the mind, or in the emotion, or, it may be, in the love principle, or even in the higher will."
>
> (Ferrier, 1984, p.12)

We often think of ourselves as we appear in the physical. However, we are more than that - we also consist of our astral (emotional) self, our mental (thought) self, our soul and our spirit. The chapter *The Human Structure*, will explain these selves in greater detail. When we work with spiritual healing, effects can be seen in our physical, astral and mental bodies. With some methods of healing which work with the Holy Spirit, effects are given to the higher bodies, assisting the development of soul. Healing can take place on all levels of our being whether it be in our physical body, our emotional state or within the ramblings of our uncontrolled mind. As with the chemist, the result of the healing depends upon which chemicals we use and what compounds we are trying to create. For example, help can be given on the physical level where the healer works to heal a particular disease, an organ within the body, or perhaps a limb or bone. In such cases the healer can assist by visualising the organ such as lungs as healthy and by multiplying the fire until vision of the healthy Light-filled lungs is possible. For instance, the healer may initially see a person's malfunctioning lungs as brown in colour. If healing is sent to the lungs of that person, through the multiplication of Light entering the lungs, the visualisation changes to a white vibrant pulsating Light within which the lungs start functioning normally.

In our daily lives we are often weighed down by our fear, guilt and anger, especially when things do not go as we would wish and we have conflicts with people. We sometimes hold on to these conflicts as a grievance towards another. This holding on creates a congestion of astral (emotional) matter, which is a stored knot of emotion. The congestion can be experienced in a number of ways, for example, as a feeling of unease when we meet with, or think about that person. If the congestion is left for too long without being cleansed, it can transfer its effects to the physical body and become disease. Holding a grievance towards another can limit us when we try to contact the higher levels, as we are not open to the energy of love. We have closed down to it by not extending that love to those around us. In this case spiritual healing, working with the Light of the Holy Spirit, can help us to release the stored knot of emotion. The stored knot of emotion or the grievance held takes the form of dense matter. When Light and energy are transmitted into the body in which this dense matter is held, it has the effect of untying the knot, loosening it and raising its vibration. This enables the person being healed to re-experience the contents of the knot. The way in which it is re-experienced will vary. Some will have vision or understandings that transpire; others may experience it on a feeling level; and some may not even notice its release, but will feel lighter and clearer afterwards. Through this re-experiencing, the knot is released. In spiritual terms, the energy is transmuted. This means it is lifted in vibration from one of darkness to light. To transmute is to change the vibration of matter from a negative and involutionary, or downward, path to a positive evolutionary, upward one. A deeper knowledge of healing shows us that this takes place through the chakras, where the dense matter is lifted from the lower chakras to the higher and transmuted in the process. An understanding of the chakras and the inner bodies and their function is paramount to understanding the effects of working with the Holy Spirit in healing. For an explanation of the chakras see chapter: *The Chakras*; for a description of the inner bodies see chapter: *The Human Structure*.

Healing is a science

Spiritual healing is based on the science of and mysteries of Nature, and it deals with matter in the physical, etheric, astral, mental, psychic and spiritual realms. Its scientific nature is clear and evident in the miracles it performs. We know through chemistry that certain chemicals placed with other chemicals will create specific compounds, and if we alter one of the chemicals involved, we will create another compound. Similarly, with spiritual healing we work diligently with Light and energy to create a specific effect. It is a science based on the principles of alchemy, and it works with the Sacred Fire of the Holy Spirit.

Spiritual healing is often ridiculed for being "airy-fairy." However, it is an extremely thorough science. It utilises the elements and the attributes of soul, as well as the Divine potencies that we can access within us. The alchemical nature of the work reveals how working with the Holy Spirit in healing can take anxiety and turn it into peace; can take grief and turn it into yearning to be with, and the joy of serving, the Christ, and can take anger and turn it into forgiveness and compassion. The Holy Spirit lifts the vibration of the client. It helps transmute fear to love; guilt to innocence; egoistic attitudes to humility; low self-esteem to a balanced sense of self; and rebellion to obedience to appropriate inner authority. Those who heal work alchemically with the Holy Spirit. The Holy Spirit knows the exact process and requirements for this transformation to occur. The process of spiritual healing by its very nature is transformative. It can heal ailments that are centuries old that we have carried with us from lifetime to lifetime. In order for the healing to take place, however, we must be willing to surrender our negativity, grief, hurt and anger, and be prepared to open to the Christ Light and allow the healing. To allow the healing often requires the letting go of that to which we cling - the old and the familiar - and the preparedness to open to the new and unfamiliar. Many live in fear of healing because of this risk. We must let go of what we think we are and open to what we really are, allowing our inherent goodness to strengthen and come to the surface. We are thereby healed through outward motion from within. We must let go of our arrogance, pride and ambition and replace it with faith in a greater Plan. The humility that comes from having faith allows us to open to doing what is required for us to heal. Often in healing we become aware of what the next step is for us to draw closer to our healing. It is up to us to follow that step and to put into practice what we have been advised on the inner. When we have faith enough to follow that step and to put it into practice, life changes and we are lifted. This inner advice can be given in a variety of ways and forms and through it we can be sure that our healing will unfold as it should. The willingness to follow the Light, and the steps we are given, helps take us to a point of healing. It is through our willingness that the Light can enter us and do its work. Healing is a sacred science that takes place through the healing power of the Holy Spirit.

The Holy Spirit - the secret fire of alchemy

Through ritual and symbolism, humanity can share the work of God the Holy Spirit and the work of world creation. Through the secret fire of alchemy, which is the Holy Spirit, the Divine Creative Forces that are responsible for our creation can be transmitted to the world around us. When we work this way we become co-creators with God. We can experience the teachings as a reality in our consciousness and can benefit psychologically and spiritually from the effects. It enables us to bring down the higher energies to a form with which we can work and can manage. The transmitting of the Light and Love of the Holy Spirit is a form of spiritual healing or energy work that creates alchemy. Alchemy is the science of the work of the Holy Spirit; it is the science of Nature pertaining to the chemical elements and their interaction. It is the Divine chemistry that takes place when working with the creative power of the Holy Spirit. Alchemists have knowledge of this creative power. They work to affect transformation in nature and humanity. Transmutation is the process of transforming a low vibrating energy or matter to a more highly vibrating one. This can be carried out through the chakras in healing.

The Holy Spirit is the energy through which the healing Light comes to us. It is the Holy Light, the Spirit, which is transmitted so we may heal. The Holy Spirit is the Breath of Creation that gives life to all forms. It is the Giver of Life, the Great Comforter. The Holy Spirit brings peace and protection, nurturing our growth along our path to perfection, and stimulating the Light and life within us. We find the Holy Spirit in nature, in the beauty and fullness of a forest walk, in the Light that pours forth from a flowing white waterfall. It is the Breath of the Universe; through our breath we can go within and contact it. It is the Light that the angels bring forth to help us come to know the Kingdom of God. It is the Active Intelligence. The Holy Spirit is Love. The angels use it to imbue us with inspiration and enthusiasm, inspiring us to write, to paint, and to create pieces of art. It inspires us with new ideas and helps us to link with God's Plan. Through the Holy Spirit the Christ Spirit comes to Earth bringing Spirit into matter. When we open to It we begin to experience the gift of Spirit It brings us. We find enthusiasm for life and a positive attitude towards others and ourselves. We begin to look for the goodness around us instead of the problems and to recognise the goodness in others instead of their faults. Our world-view changes; resentment, blame and bitterness leave as we open to the abundance of love and joy that is ever-present in the Light of the Holy Spirit. We begin to see that we are not separate, but united in the Divine Light. We see that there is only one race, the human race, and only one Spirit, the Great Spirit in whose Heart we are all loved.

In many religions the third aspect of the Holy Trinity is called the Holy Ghost or Holy Spirit. In Egypt the Trinity is seen as Ra, Osiris and Horus, or Osiris, Isis and Horus; in Christianity - the Father, the Son and the Holy Spirit; in Hinduism - Shiva, Vishnu and Brahma; in Northern Buddhism - Amritabha, Avalokiteshvara and Mandjusri; and in Southern Buddhism - the Buddha, the Dharma and the Sangha.

The Lord Jesus gave the energy of the Holy Spirit to His disciples at Pentecost two thousand years ago. He has continued to send the Holy Spirit that we may, through It, come closer to God. It makes active in us what is called, 'the Active Intelligence', raising our consciousness towards the Kingdom of God. The Holy Spirit is full of Love. Its Presence and energy come to us when we call on the Christ from a loving and open heart. It does not matter how developed we are, He does not discriminate as we might. If He is called from a pure heart, His Presence will come and aid us as we need to be aided.

In the early days, through Christ, the Holy Spirit was evident in Christianity, as Christ conferred that power unto others. Some Christians, however, concentrated on God the Father, and others on God the Son. The Trinity is a threefold function of consciousness. Through the Will aspect we approach the Father, through Love and Wisdom we approach the Son and Daughter or the Christ Consciousness, and through the Divine Mind or the Active Intelligence we approach God the Holy Spirit, which, in Theosophy we refer to as God the Mother. To find God, Ananda Tara Shan (1993, p. 95) has written in *The Living Word of the Hierarchy*:

People ask, "How can we find God the Father?" I would answer, "become acquainted with the Son and the Holy Spirit - Mother and Grace." The Son is the Second aspect of the Logos represented and radiated unto humanity by God's Great Sons, Gautama and Maitreya, Jesus, and others like Them. When you feel Their Compassion, Their Understanding of your plight and your suffering and when you know Their Wisdom which teaches the Law to you, when you feel Them moving around in your mind and heart, then you come to know God through Their Presence. When you open up to the Holy Spirit Who is God the Mother and feel Her moving lovingly within you, then you will come to love Her, and through Her, the Father who is the Power and Creator in Son and Mother. If you really want to find God, then give yourself to the Son and the Mother, for They will bring you to God the Father.

As the Mother Christ manifests more on Earth we can look forward to a humanity that is more full of compassion, hope, inspiration and idealism. If we wish to work to help this shift in consciousness take place, we must make this the centre of our life and work so that the Holy Spirit can inspire and guide us to that task. As the Holy Spirit inspires us it is possible to become lost in the inner beauty and lose touch with the daily world of matter. If we do this we are not of much help to the Christ and cannot help manifest the vision. To hold the vision and help it manifest, it takes concentration and practical ability. We need to learn from the eagle, a noble bird with great ability to fly sky-high and yet return to Earth with a solid grip. It has wings of great expansion and leg muscles and claws which allow quick grounding of spirit into matter. To be able to go high and gain perspective, yet return quickly and attend to detail where needed, the eagle has the key. The Mother can help us to open to that key and bring spirit into matter or form. When the Holy Spirit begins to manifest, we have the opportunity to begin to trust life. We can bring forth the Light of the Holy Spirit when we exercise trust and compassion in our lives. If we are to look at ourselves honestly, by aligning to our goodness and purity, we can recognise when we fail to live in compassion and trust.

The Holy Spirit empowers us in our thoughts and speech. It can be easily recognised because the words of the Holy Spirit are full of love and tenderness, and at the same time are integrally aligned to the Divine Plan. The words are filled with determination and passion, speaking the truth in such a way there can be no denial. Regardless of whether it may bring suffering or joy to the individual, it will always also bring comfort. With the words the individual is given the necessary energy to carry out the Divine Purpose whatever it may be. The energy is silent, yet fiery and full of grace. The Holy Spirit gives us strength.

According to Van der Leeuw (1987) in *The Fire of Creation*, the gifts of the Holy Spirit are inspiration, enthusiasm and idealism. Our lives are transformed by it. It brings us Reality: Inspiration comes when we are touched with the power of the Holy Spirit, that creative power that makes us one with God. It is contact with higher reality. It influences us into action; to get the vision of perfection and future development and to be inspired enough (by the creative energy) to make it happen. Inspiration influences us to become the living organism through which the Divine Life can express itself. When we are inspired we become enthusiastic. *Enthusiasm* "is to be filled with God" (p.81). The enthusiastic person receives an influx of Divine Life and "is for the moment, God" (p.82). *Idealism* is willingness to dedicate ourselves to the service of the Ideal and to sacrifice to it all we have and are. It is a power which possesses us but which we cannot possess. Through it we become subservient to the greater reality of life and Light.

It is the Holy Spirit which inspires us to do great works and which, when we open to It, reveals the next step in the Great Plan, assisting us to know what our part, no matter how small, may be in that Plan. The Holy Spirit brings new life and new hope to those in need. It is the Breath of Creation that gives life to all living beings. It is a great gift given to us, one that enables us to be sanctified and redeemed in the Light of Christ. The Holy Spirit permeates the third aspect of all true religions and permeates also the true healing Light. It brings to us the much needed Love of the Mother and bestows upon us the compassion of the Heart of the Lord Christ. It gives us the strength and courage needed to begin a new life, one that is guided by the Holy Spirit and the Christ.

We do not have to be clairvoyant or highly sensitive to feel the healing effects of the Holy Spirit. While we may find that the Christ's energies are not felt easily, the Holy Spirit healing can be felt with our ordinary consciousness. It is often reported that it is felt as heat, a gentle pulsating warmth, an electrical sensation or a beautiful peace and stillness. In Holy Spirit healing we surrender, when we give ourselves to the flow of the Great Breath. In surrendering we allow ourselves to be permeated by the Peace and Love of Father-Mother God.

Who heals?

Spiritual healing allows us to find our humility in knowing that there is a God, the glory and greatness of Whom we can come to know through the Love and Light of the Christ.

Ananda Tara Shan (1995, p.1) tells us in her booklet *Spiritual Healing*:

The Healing Light comes from the Heart of God into the Heart of Christ, and then it is further transmitted through an angel of the Christ to a human being, either directly or through the inner bodies of the healer. In rare cases the Healing Light is given directly to a person by a Master of Wisdom or by the Christed One Himself.

It is important for healers to always remember it is not us who heal, it is the Christ through the Holy Spirit Who heals through us. To be a good vehicle we must in essence forget ourselves and become the Light. In that way we are witness to His Great Work, and that is the greatest joy any human being can ever have. The Christ Light comes to us through the Holy Spirit. The healing Light radiates from the Heart of Christ. It often radiates through the intervention of an angel. The angel acts as a transformer or mediator, bringing the Light in a capacity with which we can deal. Generally, the Christ does not come to humanity directly as the intensity of His Light would cause too much disturbance and disharmony, because most people do not have the spiritual consciousness to deal with it. He therefore has many helpers on all levels of existence to help bring the healing Light into even the grossest of matter. He is like a brother to humanity, attempting to heal a whole world of imbalances.

Healers should not look for praise or recognition for their works of healing due to the realisation that they are nothing without the help of the Christed One. In such cases where a client praises or gives recognition to the healer, the healer learns to deflect this praise to where praise is due, for example, to the Holy Spirit or the Christ Himself, forever remaining humble. The healer's consciousness is not one that seeks praise, but rather the Divine Light and the Divine Love, where praise is not needed nor understood.

When individuals and group healers do not acknowledge the Christ, and say the healing comes from them, or another human being, people are in some way robbed of their relationship to the Christ. If we acknowledge the true source of the Light, a relationship will develop fostering faith and trust in Him. Nothing of healing exists outside Christ. A good healer must have and must develop that connection. When working with the Holy Spirit, we cannot avoid the connection with Christ.

Reverend J. Todd Ferrier (1984, p.4), in his book *Spiritual Healing*, emphasises that Divine Love alone is the source of all true healing.

> The Great Healer is Love - Divine Love. The true medicine for all disease is Divine Love. The true way of healing all manner of tribulations, to which so many think themselves heir, is to give the phial of Divine Love. That Love is the solvent which disintegrates evil conditions, separates the elements, heals the substances by purifying them and restores the various powers of the Being to equilibrated states. It heals the mind and fills it with Peace. It harmonises the emotions and brings Divine Comfort. By it are all feelings made beautiful and the body whole. The deep problems of Life are solved by its coming and the Mystery of Being is unveiled.

What can healing achieve?

Through healing we can strengthen the link to the Light and overcome many of our limitations. We can begin to radiate love and hence heal ourselves and others. We all have the potential of healing within us. When we gain courage to work through our anger, fear and guilt, resentment, rebellion and projection that we store like knots in the aura, we can gain deep insight that can help us in both our daily lives and in our overall life patterns. Hereditary "dis-ease" ceases to exist when we make different choices to the patterns of our ancestors - provided we are aligned with the soul in our new choice. Through meditation and healing we can strengthen our link to soul and begin to get guidance on how to actualise our true potential and move out of our limiting patterns.

When we come into the vibration of a healer, or when we heal, our vibratory rate increases. This breaks up the knots of stored experience and emotion that sit like a weight within the aura, causing us discomfort and pain. We are open then to "seeing" these knots for what they really are. With faith and trust in the healing process, by allowing ourselves to feel these knots, and by looking for their underlying meaning, we can transmute them to a smoother vibration and pattern. A joy, an inner feeling of knowing, that is peaceful with wisdom and love, emerges. Life changes.

Through regression and past life therapy, guided imagery, looking at the role of the psyche, contacting higher guidance within, attuning to Christ and the Holy Spirit and working with the great streams of healing Light within the Seven Rays, change is not only possible, but imminent - as is the liberation of soul. These methods enable us to get in touch with whatever is holding us back. We can find out what it is, why we have it and what lesson we must learn to let it go. With the help of the Light, we can open up the knots within us and find the reason for their presence in our lives. We learn the lesson and move on. We can work directly with the particular issue or block that we may have. Release can occur on all levels, spiritual, mental, emotional and physical, depending on where the individual need may be. It may occur on any or all of these levels through tears, physical release, a mental understanding or a knowing within, giving new insight and meaning to life as it is now.

Healing can help us to grow psychologically. It can help us let go of attachment to others and help us to deal with our fear, guilt, resentment, and rebellion. For example, if we have an unhealthy need to be right or a tendency to blame others for all that is not manifesting in our lives as we think that it should, we can, through healing, learn to deal with this. By opening to Spirit in our lives we are opening to a humble respect for all that is unknowable in the universe and are opening our hearts to forgiveness and unconditional love. Love is the power that heals. When love is linked with pure motive of heart and aligned to Divine Will, healing must and will occur.

Will spiritual healing cure me?

Having healing is no guarantee that we will be cured. However, we may be, depending on our karma. Spiritual healing helps us to deal with our dispositions more constructively. We may receive insight as to the learning that our "dis-ease" has for us. It can even make Transition (dying to the earthly world and passing over to the inner worlds) easier. We chip away at all that exists in our life which prevents spiritual flow, until that flow returns, provided we, at some inner point, wish this healing to occur.

Whether a person is cured from a disease or not depends upon his or her karma. However, even if a situation is karmic, it does not mean that a person will derive no benefit from working to heal that disease or situation. Quite the contrary, working with the Light of spiritual healing can help us to understand the reasons for our karma and come to a point of acceptance that helps us live with that karma. For explanations about karma see the chapter on *Karma*. The healing Light will always help lighten our burden whether we are aware of these effects or not. We are healed of many of the traumas we carry with us in the process. Ananda Tara Shan (1995, p. 2) in her booklet *Spiritual Healing* tells us:

Karma determines each outcome of a healing. People have no idea of how many traumas and difficult patterns they have brought into the present life. They are unaware of how the Holy Spirit works wonders and miracles in the removal of such traumas and patterns from past lives and present life. A healing is not a failure just because a person may be unaware of the effects created in the healing. In the hands of a skilled healer and counsellor, healing is the greatest psychotherapy ever created. True healing facilitates the flow of soul life in and through the lower bodies.

New ways of healing are coming. Spiritual knowledge is descending and new techniques that combine the Divine Laws of Health, orthodox medicine, psychology and spiritual methods are leading to an entirely new approach. Personal responsibility is more and more emphasised.

If we are to move forward into the New Age, we must first take the decision to heal so that the Divine energies can help us. Having done this, we can then let go of all that is not in alignment with this choice. In so doing we open the way for more love, compassion and joy to enter our lives.

Acknowledging our shadow side

When we open ourselves to be healed and to be a healer working with the Light of Christ, we open to the Will of God in our lives. Through this act we invite change, and the material within us that is not of God becomes threatened. We are made up of shadow and of Light. The shadow self, sometimes referred to as "the little self," has the tendency to cling to life as it desires it and manifests as a selfish energy instead of a selfless one. When we invite healing, we open ourselves to become selfless servers of God. The denser matter within us is open to be cleansed and purified, transmuted and transformed. In this process we often become aware of our darkness, which can prove to be a shock to us particularly if we generally deny its existence, or alternatively, repress it.

It sometimes happens that when people begin the path of spiritual healing they get such a fright in what they see in themselves that they cannot contend with the difficulties. They may run off to avoid facing what they have found inside and may convince themselves that the healer or the healing process is dark. Because they cannot cope with the darkness, they project it onto what or whoever is around. Such experiences can be curtailed by sensitive and aware healers who educate their clients in the processes that may occur in healing so that the clients are not so surprised. Such healers will gently assist the client in taking responsibility for what the client sees, senses or feels within, and help the clients know that they are not alone in battling the inner darkness.

We all have a shadow. Healing comes when we accept that and begin to deal with it. If we do dare to begin to deal with our shadow, our first focus is often in identifying the shadow and how it manifests. The shadow self is clever. Sometimes it manifests through fear, guilt, anger, resentment, rebellion, resistance, projection, wilfulness, jealousy, ambition, pride, greed - the list goes on. These ways are probably the most easily identifiable. At other times it can clothe itself in Light and appear to be loving, warm and kind when it is really manipulating a situation for its own ends. The shadow can utilise the lighter aspects of our personality to fulfil its ends. However, if we look closely enough and are persistent in shining Light upon ourselves, we will come to see the motives behind our supposed goodness and so uncover the shadow.

When we shine the Light, the darker parts of ourselves run for cover and wait until we relax a little and forget. They then take the opportunity to step in and take over. It may seem like a fruitless exercise to try to win the battle, but with constant effort and mindfulness we can play sleuth upon ourselves and eventually come to spiritualise the denser matter within us and impregnate it with Light.

Healing changes our perceptions of the world. We get another perspective on life, the universe and how it works and come to see ourselves as we truly are. In the process we go through stages of seeming imbalance. Sometimes this is necessary to find balance again. The Holy Spirit works to decongest the chakras and transmute and transform the negative energies within them so that the kundalini can continue on its upward path and eventually lead us to enlightenment. Before we can reach enlightenment there are many negative energies within us with which we must deal. It is in the process of dealing with these energies that we may become imbalanced.

We must keep our common sense with us when we are dealing with the shadow self and create an observer self which stands steady in the outer world to give us balance. This observer self becomes a good friend we return to repeatedly in our darkest hours. Sometimes we choose a healer or therapist to take this role for us. That can be useful. It can also be a relative or a friend. If we are prepared to accept the truth that we consist of darkness and Light, and aspire to become more and more one with the Light, and if we are prepared to put in the work required to deal with the many aspects of ourselves that spiritual healing brings to our attention, we will grow both personally and spiritually. We must act on what we find and work to purify our minds, our feelings and our actions. Only then can we become illumined.

Spiritual healing helps us to identify many aspects of ourselves. We come to know ourselves as Spirit and soul working through the personality self. We come to see ourselves in this incarnation as a drop in a great ocean. We find humility and conversely, the value and significance of ourselves. To explain this more clearly we can look at the following phrase: "I am nothing. You are Everything. You are in me, so I am Everything." We are taken out of ourselves and come to see ourselves in a proper perspective. We begin to yearn to live as soul and to see from the soul's perspective, to unite with the higher life. We are freed from the trappings of the lower mind and liberated from the insidiousness of our lower emotions.

Through spiritual healing we learn to bring the lower mind and the lower emotions into balance, stilling them so we can again find peace. This does not mean that we cannot express our innermost thoughts and feelings that may be negative in nature. Sometimes such expression is needed to release them. It does mean, however, that we should strive to do this consciously and in a balanced way so that we can rise above and transcend the negativity. Our lives then are not ruled by our lower nature but are guided and inspired by the higher forces of love and Light.

The process of dealing with our shadow side helps us to purify our inner bodies. Rising to the challenges that come in the process of healing equips us with the wisdom of experience that we need to help others. For example, if someone who comes to us is angry or in grief, through our experience we are able to develop true compassion and empathy. We must never forget, whether we are the client or the healer, that we are human beings alike. That alone gives us the potential for empathy. We begin to develop an energy of loving kind-heartedness which helps to lift our thoughts, feelings and actions to a higher place.

Can we forgive ourselves that we are not perfect, yet still try to be that and do our best? We are loved by God, the Father, the Mother, the Son and the Daughter and can learn from that Love. We are human beings with strengths and weaknesses. Where we are weak, we can work to become strong. Where we are strong, we can give strength to our weaknesses through love and develop trust and compassion in ourselves, for ourselves and others. In loving ourselves we open to God's Love and to loving others, for then the Father-Mother may love through us and we can become true vehicles for that love. The compassion of the Christ is never-ending, for the Christ has walked among humanity for thousands of years. We must learn to trust in the Christ and trust the inner Christed One in us. We find the Love and Light in our hearts if we look within.

If we choose to look for faults in others and ourselves, we will find them. When that is our main focus, we lose sight of the overall picture and sink into dissatisfaction, blame and complaint. This is not to say that we should not look to see where we can better ourselves, or even point out to others something we may notice that will help them as they try also to better themselves. Our motives need to be clear and, what we say must be truthful, kind, necessary and timely. We can try to cultivate qualities that see us looking for the goodness in life and others. Focus on what the Buddha calls Right Remembrance, that is, not remembering and holding on to the "bad" things: harsh words said; our grievances towards others. Instead, we should remember the good things, the positive things said, and the love. In doing this, we begin to embody the qualities needed to manifest the teaching of Jesus, to love our neighbours as we love Him. We can also remember the "bad" things, but not in a negative way, but rather to learn from them to see and understand what made us do them and how can we not repeat them. We are all part of the human race and are all unique. We are children of God, created in God's image. To honour God, the Father-Mother, to honour the Christ, the Son-Daughter, and to honour the Holy Spirit in unity, we must learn to honour each other and ourselves. We must come to learn what it is to truly love. To truly love you may say is quite a task and not one so easily accomplished in one lifetime. We must start somewhere. That somewhere is with ourselves and each other. To do this we can affirm, "Let there be love and peace and let it begin with me." Create loving relationships, bring honour and respect into your life. Invite the Holy Spirit to set you free.

The Native Americans talk of the necessity of becoming pure of heart. When someone is pure of heart and is deciding to choose heart, when attraction to the glamours and illusions is no longer present, that person is called a one heart. The person has chosen goodness, and there is a purity within. On the other hand, a person who may choose goodness some of the time, but who is not opposed to a little indulgence of his or her shadow nature, who may sometimes lie or cheat if it will cause some sort of self-gain, is called a two heart. Such people serve others when it suits their purposes and may appear friendly, even kind. The inner motive is selfish and they are not pure of heart. They do not care about cultivating virtues of harmlessness, justice and loving kind-heartedness. We decide what we will be - a one heart or a two heart. Through our choices over many lives we strengthen the positive or the negative qualities in ourselves. Each time we choose the negative we strengthen that in us, and the positive likewise. Let us think about this. Which one would you prefer to be - a one heart or a two heart? How can we become a one heart? Develop purity of heart. How can we do that? The Native Americans say that we must open to the Great Spirit and let our lives be guided by It. Let us do that now and let us pray that the Great Spirit, the Holy Spirit becomes the guiding force in our lives. Let us choose the Light and become one nation, one mind, one purpose and one heart.

The sundance

The plains stretched far and wide across the American continent. My people had cultivated some of the land and the community life was thriving. The tribe had some years of peace. The land was fertile, as were the female members of the tribe who had produced many new sons and daughters. I was old with long grey plaited hair. I had seen many suns and many moons. My name was Lightning Bear, given to me for my ability to hunt bear, being very fast on my feet in my younger years. I had many good years behind me and had become a well-respected member of my tribe. Over the years the inner wisdom had grown considerably, assisted by those before me who had demonstrated the wisdom. It was my turn now because of my standing in the tribe to partake in the ceremony of the Sundance. I had fasted for some days and was ready, being at a point of peace within. Other male members of the tribe were dancing around me and I was preparing to be lifted by the structure of wood and hide.

My chest was pierced and the wood inserted through so that I could be easily erected into position. Within I was chanting to the Great Spirit. My inner heat soon overcame me. The voice of God filled me through vision and communion. I came down to the ground to speak the vision. I saw floods and fires, destruction of tribal life and laws, violation of the Sacred Life and Laws - invasion by the dark forces. There were black lines like strips continuing, taking up the land. It all seemed very foreign to me as if aliens had attacked. I had fear for my people. I looked to the sky and the sun, asking Father Sky, "Why?" I did not comprehend why the Great Spirit would let this happen, but I could not doubt and did not doubt the vision. I felt the needed lessons, the karma of humanity for the greed and ambitions spreading all over the earth. I sat with one foot in the heavens and one on the earth and I asked my Father,

"What can I do?" The answer came,

"Heal the Earth and all life on it. Spread compassion. Where there is darkness, bring Light; where there is doubt, bring faith; where there is hatred, bring love. Sow the seeds for the new humanity."

In the midst of the Light I could see scenes of destruction. Men in uniforms on horses were shooting, looting, burning tepees, killing many. Only a few remained that had the Sacred Knowledge. There was only a handful of people left who gathered and followed the buffalo and relocated. There was more vision of the black strips covering the land. I held the vision deep in my heart and I knew the dark forces were invading.

I am now young again, having been in another baby body growing up with my brothers and put into a reservation with some of my tribe and some of other tribes. Others have taken the power and the land and I feel great restriction and pain. I hold the vision still in my heart and I know that the pain is not forever, yet it is for a long time. Inside I am still on the hill near the plains. The power of the land is in my heart. The vision gives me hope and faith in God's plan and enables the song in my heart to sing.

Person after person stands up one by one. The people are remembering who they are and they join to reclaim the land, the heart of the land. The sun is shining above. The eagle is flying higher and higher.

Lotus Eye stood at the top of the hill, his moccasins worn from the many miles he had travelled. He gazed across the horizon and could see the mountains all around him. He stood level with their peaks, and many a wearied traveller had stood as he did now, open and ready to take in the great perspective. An energy of peace filled his heart as he remembered what it had taken for him to reach this destination. The destination was the beginning of being and every step it had taken had awakened more of his inner knowing, more of his inner peace. He could see the eagle flying above, the Great Spirit calling. He had come home. After some moments of silence, he took a breath and began again on his way down the mountain towards the next. The journey was eternal, the sun beat upon his brow and beads of golden sweat formed around his ear lobes, mixing with the whiskers on his cheek. Lotus Eye was content. He was flowing with life, its joys and sorrows, its challenges and pleasures. All this he could behold within and as he took each new step. For he knew he was guided by The One, the Son of the Sun and the Sun God would make for his way.

A prayer to the Great Spirit

Spirit of the Sun

*Oh Great Spirit
Spirit of the Sun
Forever shining
Forever one*

*Be my guardian
My shining Light
Take care of me by day by night*

*Help us find
the way to peace
help give our hearts release*

*You are the Eagle
flying high
Wandering Star passing by*

*If we dare
follow Your Light
We will be given new sight*

*Oh Great Spirit
Spirit of the Sun
Forever shining
Forever one*

The Angelic Helpers

The angels' wings are the healing hands of love. The angels teach us how to heal, and to those who are open to them, they become constant companions in life, always helping to lift and make light of our troubles and burdens, guiding and guarding the way. Angels are our mentors, teachers, and friends in Spirit, who help us to unite with Spirit and find unity and oneness in our hearts and minds. In this chapter we will look at the angelic kingdom and try to understand something of the angels inner nature.

The angels come to us as messengers of God. We are blessed with angelic guidance and with guardians who seek to assist us in our spiritual development. The angels may warn us when there is disaster, and assist us in our process of birth and death, in our daily life on Earth, and in the after-life, where some of us walking the Earth now may then function in the angelic form. Many people are not conscious of the love and assistance the angels give them. Yet for many the veil is being lifted and the help and vision of the angels are becoming evident. More of humanity is being awakened to the beauty of a life lived in conscious awareness of angelic help and the cherished companionship they give. Once we discover this contact, we know deep in our hearts that we are never alone.

We must ask for help to be given help. That is the Law. I have been working as a spiritual healer for many years. In that time I have not ceased to be amazed at the wondrous efforts of the angels. They bring insight, revelation, faith, hope and forgiveness to many a needy heart. They help us to lift out of our more negative nature and see the world in a new Light, bringing vision and trust, restoring us to a state where we can reconnect with God within.

Angel Love

*Joyous whispers of golden light
shower celestial sounds,
Lords of the Flame
Grace us again
and bring forth the angels' crown.*

*Angels of Love and Mercy
send us your prayers of hope.
You are the legends of the sky
that lift us to the Light.*

*Angels oh angels -
You show us the path of love,
lined with star like rays of fire
and thousands of petalled doves.*

*We follow you to the heavenly worlds -
Your love it lights the way,
You grace us with your freedom
and shine the new light of day.*

*Angels oh angels -
on wings of love you fly,
bringing us the peace and joy
of God's sweet lullaby.*

Angels oh angels -
The Christed Ones of heart,
You lift the New humanity
into Maitreya's Heart.

Your wings of Lighted Spirit
transform all they touch,
healing humanity
with God's Love.

Angels oh angels -
Hope, truth and faith,
Help us find our way again,
Help us through the gate
that opens to the heavenly worlds,
Lifting us to Him,
The Lord Maitreya is here again,
Teacher of Angels and humanity.

The angels live on the inner levels and work with colour, Light and symbol. They communicate through the language of the heart, expounding the virtues of goodness and all that is holy. In their Light we are lifted to the Love of God, and experience the sense of unity that brings. We can ask the angels to help lift us to their special vibration where they can communicate with us. When we are down, we can ask for their help to lift us and they will give it readily. In their Light we may receive messages of a joy and peace we never dreamed possible. Let us open to the angels and their special message. Open now to their message for you.

The form of the angels

The angels have no physical body as humans do. They have a body of Light which enables them to move and function swiftly in the world of Light. They are normally unseen by the human eye; however, when the veil is lifted and clairvoyant or clairsentient faculties are used, they can be seen and felt. The angels are on a path of evolution, as we are. They are working towards unity with the Divine as we walk towards unity on the Path to Perfection.

We are both children of Father-Mother God. The angels live to serve the unfoldment of the Plan, while we in our denser matter strive to consciously cooperate with the Plan, and aspire to serving in a similar manner. When we look through our inner eyes, the angels become visible to us. The air about us is full of them. They live in Nature, wherever there is Divine life. They evolve through their inner work. Some dwell in crystals, in the woods and gardens, some are attracted to the elements of water, fire, air or earth. There are angels who have the task of assisting human beings in their evolution, and guardian angels who are angels protecting us as we walk the spiritual path. It is our guardian angels who help us to align to the will of the soul. The guardian angels are the angels who guide us and are our guardians helping us to lift our consciousness and vibration to that of Light.

Angels move so freely in the world of Light, flying with the speed of Light. They do not have feathers as they are sometimes depicted as having. Their wings are a concentrated mass of Light that is part of their bodily existence, and which, when we look through the inner eye, may appear like wings. Their inner form is radiant, colourful and made of particles of Light. Through their Light and their colour, they communicate with us, making symbols through which we can discern and comprehend their message. The colour may vary; for example, when looking at the army of winged healing Light beings assisting the Archangel Raphael, the wings at first appear to be a deep emerald green. On looking more closely at the concentration of Light evident in the wings, the richest violet can be seen, depicting not only their healing nature, but their ability to transform all that they touch. We may say that they are so richly emerald green they are violet. To find something to illustrate this on the physical plane, perhaps we could liken it to the richness of the colours of the feathers of a peacock, which have a luminous quality and profound depth and beauty.

The people in the East have often called angels "devas" which means "the shining ones." Angels have a very dynamic energy and a vividness of consciousness and of life. It is said that angels may even guide the artists into drawing the angels as they are. Sometimes the faces may appear human but on a closer look they are not; sometimes the eyes may be full of Light. Such Light is rarely seen amongst human beings.

How can we recognise them?

When angels come, people often feel the love and the sense of self-acceptance and inner peace that is given, and feel recognised and deeply cared for. They may simply have a tingling in their hearts, and they will feel themselves becoming more open-hearted than is their normal state of being. Of course, the physical signs sometimes come, such as goose bumps, tingling at the back of the neck, tears, heightened clarity of vision or a beautiful fragrant smell.

In the theosophical view, the Archangels are the head of the angelic kingdom. Christianity also speaks of the ranks of angels: Thrones, Dominions or Dominations, Principalities, Virtues, Powers, Cherubim, and Seraphim. According to Geoffrey Hodson (1987), in *The Kingdom of the Gods*, to each of these types of angels certain qualities and activities are assigned. "Archangels are sent as messengers in matters of high importance," as we have seen through Gabriel, Raphael, Michael and Uriel. "The Cherubim excel in the splendour of knowledge;" Seraphim "inspire with Divine Love;" and the Thrones are known for the "glory and equity of the divine judgements." The Cherubim enlighten through wisdom; the Seraphim motivate with love; the Thrones teach us to use our discrimination and judgement. Dominions "regulate the activities and duties of the angels," and the "Principalities preside over people and Provinces and serve as angelic rulers of nations of the world." Devas of particular countries, national devas we call them, come into this last category. "Powers keep a check on negative energies. Virtues have the gift of working miracles" (p.158).

The nature of the angels

The angels are by their nature tuned in to the Creative Intelligence, and love to create in a light and heartfelt manner. They are Light and their nature is Light. We may call it lighthearted. The ability they have to be joyful and bring humour can help to lighten up what might seem like the darkest of situations. They remind us not to be so serious in our quest, but instead to allow the universal forces to assist us to go through life in rhythm with the universal flow. Their symbolic language, when understood, provides insight from a high intelligence. They have a sharp mind and wit which help us to perceive their higher meaning.

The angels look from above and have the objectivity that we in our subjective feeling and thinking states lack. It makes sense, therefore, that if we truly wish to rise into the lightness of their vibration, we should call on them for help. They can lift us, they know our weak spots and are aware of our virtues, helping us to strengthen them, so that we can cooperate in the work for the Light.

Contacting the angels

To talk to the angels, we simply need to come to an open-hearted space. This may not sound so easy to some who have difficulty contacting their heart and to others who are hampered from contacting the angels through their negative inner voice. The angels do not resonate in unison with the negative ego which expresses itself through harsh self-criticism or blown up feelings of self-importance. If we feel that we have become arrogant, we can ask the angels to help us find humility again. If we feel we have become too self-denigrating, we can ask the angels to help us to find self-acceptance. When we go into negative mind and feeling states, we have to learn to be able to release the negativity instead of holding onto it. If we have difficulty letting go, we can call on the Angel of Release, who is an angel who helps us to let go of what we need to. I often think of it like this: if we fill our minds with worry about what may or may not happen in the future, or about what did or didn't happen in our past, no space is left in us to experience the present now. Similarly, if we hold on to grievances against others, our fear, our guilt, and our pain, no room is left to experience the joy, peace and love.

Worry and stress make it difficult for angels to contact us. Our astral bodies bloat up and our inner senses are thwarted. By maintaining calm and working at keeping our thoughts and feelings in balance and harmony through meditation, contemplation and healing, or simply by using positive thinking in our daily lives, we make it easier for the angels to connect with us. So the message is, lighten up and you too may be able to fly!!

Listening to the angels and opening to contact

If we want to hear the angels we need to stop and listen. This is also something that many of us are not good at. It can be learned and must be practised. Be still and listen to the silent voice within. The throat chakra is the chakra connected with clairaudience and is our energetic centre of communication. If we wish to hear on the inner, we can still ourselves and listen to the silent voice. It may be heard from the heart centre, or we may sense it around the throat centre. It is audible not with our ears but from between them. We can affirm mentally, "I open my inner ear and my inner eye." This enables the angels to contact us in whatever way is most suitable. We become a receptive vehicle through this affirmation. Sometimes people align to the angels by feeling an expansion within the inner bodies and by coming into a deep resonance with the silence in which the angels speak.

To stimulate our throat centre, inner ear and inner eye we can use a song or chant that will help us align, provided we do it through our heart. The act of singing helps connect the heart and throat centres. We can even practice making vocal sounds until our body hums with their different tones. If we practise such exercises for the purpose of communicating with our angels, our angels will know it and will assist us to help find the answers we need.

Every effort we make to contact them will be met with enthusiastic response by them, as that is their nature. The intent alone is enough to initiate communication. When we communicate with our angels, it is as though our senses have heightened and we will be aware of moving to different levels of receptivity. The physical world may appear different when we return to it. Colours, shapes and sounds are heightened, or perhaps everything will appear less distinct. This awakens us to the knowing that there has been a shift in our vibration, and we are changed from the communion.

Creating a dialogue with the angels

When your angels come, you can talk to them as you could to another human being who you are beginning to know. They are different from human beings in the sense that they have great wisdom and know all there is to know about your path in life. You can ask them their names; you can ask them to help you find your purpose with questions like, "What is it I need to know now?" "How can I best serve?" It can be useful when interacting in this way to either have another person write down the information you receive or to have a pen and paper yourself where you can write it down. This helps you remember when you return to your usual state of consciousness. If your angel says its name is Raphael, Michael or Gabriel, it does not mean you are communicating with the Archangels; however, it may mean that the angel comes from Gabriel's group or Michael's army.

You may even wish to have a tape-recorder nearby where you can speak and record the messages, or you may sit at your computer and type what you hear. The deep connection that comes with the angelic being can provide a great source of comfort and of pleasure. It can also bring illumination when you connect. The connection may come in a quiet moment. When you become aware of your breath and your body, the sounds of the outer world and the roles you play in it are minimised. You are given time out for a moment, to connect to the higher life, gaining insight and objectivity that has a sacred space, the space where God can be found.

As you practice, the communication can be lengthened, trust grows, and you are receptive to more help. The practice helps you let go of the need to be right and helps you know that there is a realm where more is known than you know. When you acknowledge that you need to learn more, you can, because you are open to it. When you think you know it all, you are incapable of learning more and the doors are closed to the higher knowledge.

Angels and our childhoods

Many of us had imaginary friends as children and were in a lot of contact with the angelic kingdom. The angels love children as they are open and receptive, innocent and believing. They like to be called upon to guard over children and they respond easily to their playful natures. Many of the female Masters (Masters are great Beings who have walked the Lighted Path before us) such as Lady Nada, Lady Portia and Lady Yasodhara, and also the White Tara (who is a cosmic Being, an Avatar of Light) have angels assisting Them to bring the qualities of joy, compassion, acceptance, love and protection to children. By contacting our own inner child we too can become as receptive to the angels as children, letting angels in to help and guide us, making joyful and heartfelt connection.

Many children these days are more able to recognise the fairy or angel world. Often in the past, adults have taught children that this is not a real world. Perhaps now the adults can begin to learn from the children, to see and feel the angels in all their beauty and splendour.

The angels and their role in healing

Angels are on the path of evolution as we are, whereas elementals are on the path of involution or the downward path. If we wish to create a better atmosphere in our workplace, in our homes, and in our rooms, making our environment harmonious and pure, we can call upon the angels to drive away any negative influences. We need to use our own will and the help of the angels. They will help us charge the atmosphere with living Light and power. If we wish, we can ask them to stay and guard where we are cleansing, and maintain the purity and harmony which has been produced. If we could become aware of this ability that angels have, to help us purify not only our environment but also our minds and hearts from negative thoughts and feelings that often lead to negative actions, we could do a lot to help lift the consciousness of the Earth and many of the groups on it.

In *The Brotherhood of Angels and Men*, Geoffrey Hodson (1988) talks about the angels of power, the angels of the healing art, the guardian angels of the home, the angels of nature, music, beauty and art. He suggests we begin to cooperate with these angels to help with the unfoldment of God's Plan. To do this he suggests we develop purity, simplicity, directness and impersonality. Hodson also tells us, in his book *Angels and the New Race*, if we are to uplift the human race, we need to "bring the two branches of the infinite family of God into close cooperation."

As a way of invoking and calling upon the help of the angels, we can meditate in groups in a one-pointed and united effort. We can ask the angels to help with the special purpose we have in mind, provided it comes from a pure heart, a pure mind, and has good intent behind it. We can sit in the sacred symbol of the circle and direct our thoughts to the harmony and unity that we wish to create, until we feel ourselves become one with the angels. We can go to the inner planes to do the work, visualise it happening and visualise the angels at work. This helps us all to evolve.

Geoffrey Hodson in *Angels And The New Race*, gives this beautiful prayer:

> Oh Holy Lord of Love, Teacher of angels and of men,
> We invoke Thy mighty power in all its splendour,
> Thy undying love in all its potency,
> Thy infinite wisdom in all its perfection,
> So that they may flow through us in a resistless flood into this place or person.
> Before the living stream of Thy resistless power all darkness shall melt away, the hearts of all men shall be changed, and they shall seek and find the way of Light.
>
> Amen.

Hodson tells us that after such a prayer, the silence and meditation which follows brings forth His glorious power. The group which is meditating can project the power of love with all the force and concentration of their united wills upon the place or person chosen as the recipient of their aid. The angels can be directed to act, to send the energy for the cause for which it was invoked. It is good to ask that the energy be sent to where it is needed most and leave where to the Lord of Love to decide.

The amount of love and peace and Light that is available is endless; it is an eternal well, available to those who have a pure heart. There is no limit to what this energy can do to help people who are suffering. If our hearts are open to the sufferings of people and we practice cooperating with each other and with the angelic kingdom, we will really increase our usefulness in the world.

To get to a point of being prepared and ready to do such work, we have to go through a purification process. In this individual healing process the angels can help us. We can call upon the angels of cleansing, the angels of purity, the angels of transmutation, the angels of courage and the angels of healing. We can also call upon the angels of the Christ to help quicken the process, provided we are ready, prepared and willing to do what needs to be done as a result. The evolution of the heart helps us to overcome the negative influences, and we can move towards helping the world become a Star of Light, which is its destiny.

The angels move quickly in the world of Light and are set in motion by the Will of God and the purified will of humanity. We can work to create a world which fulfils the purpose of our souls and one which brings forth the Light, Love and Plan of the Lord of Love, the Teacher of angels and humanity, the Christ. It is with the Lord of Love that God shall become known to all on Earth.

The angels, the shining ones, are experts at service. They can drive away suffering and depression, and can exorcise the powers of darkness and disease. If we work regularly with them, they become a reality to us, and when we call on them, they come. With their help we can become radiating centres of Light and open to spiritual life. When our motives are purified, when we will to serve, and when from our hearts we want to bring forth the Will of God into our lives and the lives of those around us, then we are ready to invoke the help of the angels. If we should try to use our will in a negative way, for example, with intent to harm others, or for purposes of selfish gain, then instead we create negativity and destroy any good work. We must learn to pray the ancient prayer, "Not mine but Thine Will be done."

When we call upon the angels, we can experience an increase in vitality beyond our normal capacity. Working in a way that is spiritual, mental and moral brings the angels to our aid. The angels inspire and strengthen our efforts. As we link ourselves with the power and presence of the inner worlds, we open to the guidance of the beings within it. We receive their help and their strength and are able to heal disease and relieve suffering. We move out of our ignorance about disease and suffering and recognise the reasons for it. We can help to dispel our ignorance by calling upon the angel of education, the angel of wisdom, the angel of love and the angel of higher understanding to help us.

If we really wish to help someone who is sick, it would be wise to call upon the angels, because they will bring the needed vitality to help the person become well, and will work in accordance with the karmic condition of that person. When a person has a karmic condition which may come as a disease, the angels can help by giving that person acceptance, peace of mind, a bright disposition, and the vitality he or she needs to do the tasks at hand. With pain or sickness, which is nature teaching us the Law, we can correct the errors of thought and action which have brought the suffering. We may even come to understand the reasons for our disease. We can pray to the Lord Christ, the great Healer and Counsellor of humanity with all of our heart and ask that He send His healing power to those suffering. The help may come on the inner rather than on the physical level, or it can come on both. It won't fail to come. We can mentally call upon the healing angels for their help, and ask them to be vehicles of the Christ Light and remain with the person until that person has returned to his or her health or wholeness, or has entered into his or her true dharma in life. This method is adopted by spiritual healers all over the planet and has been so for many ages. Only some recognise or acknowledge the presence and help of the angels in this work. When we consciously cooperate and acknowledge the Christ, there is an enormous increase in permanent result.

When people are depressed, we can ask the angels to lift the fog around them. We may try to invoke the person's good qualities. We can also, once we have done the healing work with the Christ Light, call upon the angels to rejuvenate and replenish the person's inner bodies with their radiant Light until the person is full of joy, Light and happiness. We can ask the angels to remain with our clients when we have finished our work, to help them in their daily lives until they have overcome the issue or problem. This is very often done with the angels of the pink Light. Lady Nada (one of the female Masters who works closely with the Lord Jesus) has millions of angels at her command. When we pray for healing, the angels are able to stay with the sick person and give him or her the courage and peace needed to get better.

The angels' role in the process of birth

The angels help in the process of birth and in helping to create the astral, the etheric and the mental body of the incoming soul. An elemental works to create the etheric double, and the nature-spirits work with the etheric energy of the mother to create the etheric body. The astral angels work to create a safe environment for the mother and child during the pregnancy and birth, and to stop negative influences and harmful effects, according to the karma of the child. The mental angels have the knowledge of the karma of the individual, and within the aura of the mental angel the incoming soul's past lives can be seen. The nature spirits and angels work with and cooperate with the soul to help build the physical expression of the human being.

The angels' role in the process of death

The angels play a major role in helping people in the transition from the earthly world to the inner worlds, and from the physical level to the etheric, astral and mental levels, depending upon what level they will reside on before they return to the next incarnation. Where necessary and where we have earned the karma for it, they can assist us to continue our work for the Light when we pass over.

The merging

We are coming to a time when the blending of angelic and human life and consciousness is beginning to take place. This is part of the plan of the coming New Age. A very great flood of new life is coming upon the Earth through the Spirit of Resurrection. The Spirit of Resurrection is a great Light full of Holy Spirit and great heart. The Spirit of Resurrection is merging with the Light of Christ to bring forth the blending of angelic and human life and consciousness. As the Spirit of Resurrection sends its Light, a new form of human being comes forward in the form of the winged healer. Many of the old forms are swept away and new forms of beauty are coming. Humanity will have virtues that will make them more God-like; the principles of Right Human Relations will be lived. These are the principles of love and truth, justice and harmlessness.

The grace of coming to know the angels

You may be aware that the angels are more closely connected with us now, because the veil between the inner and outer levels has lifted. There is a great deal of pain and suffering that humanity must yet go through. The grace has been given for the veil to be lifted so that we can become one with the angel kingdom and awaken our consciousness to that of the angels. It is time for us to wake up. As we have seen throughout history, angels come to warn of pending disaster, and they come now to do the same. It is time for us to listen, to wake up and change our ways, opening our hearts to love. Certain Masters and Archangels are working together with the Lord Christ, the Lord of Love, the Teacher of angels and humanity, to help us merge with the consciousness of the angels. When we do this, we become the new humanity, a group of people who will to live by the heart and prepare for the Lord of Love to come in about five hundred years. If we are to become the new humanity, we must open our hearts to our sisters and brothers in human and angelic form. The angels can help us clear the path and point out the way. It is for us to decide to fly with them, to open to the great love and peace they bring, and to remember that the love and peace they bring is the love and peace of the Christ, the Lord of Love.

Methods of discriminating true messages

How can you recognise a true angel? How do you know the messages you receive are of Light? If you are unaware about whether a message you have received is of Light, there are a number of things you can do to test it out. Ask yourself,

"Does this make sense?"
"Is it helpful?"
"Is it kind?"
"Is it harmless?"

Use your imagination to consider what might happen if you implement the directions in your message. What are the gains? What are the losses? If you find the message given is helpful, you may wish to implement it. If you find it is decidedly unhelpful, you may discover that it is not, after all, of the Light. You may wish to meditate upon the message and see what that brings, or take it to a healing and contemplate it further before acting. If it is true, it will stand the test of time and will continue to reveal itself to you in a multitude of ways. It is important that you do not worry about it, for as you worry you stir up the clouds of astral matter and make it impossible for you to discriminate and discern what is true or not.

You must always remember to guard yourself against your own personality which has a tendency to conjure up a magic which is according to its own wishes. This does not mean that if an angel gives you a message and you are happy about it, you cannot trust it; it simply means you should proceed with caution and try to decide what is of your personality's making and what is the true message from the higher forces of Light. You cannot expect to be able to know immediately, for the process of discernment takes time and a concentrated method of analysis, with a view to being receptive of the truth.

We live in a world where we are accustomed to instant gratification and we must learn that things that last and are of value take time to build in energy. We need to train ourselves to be at peace in our process, regardless of outcome. In this way we learn the lesson of non-attachment, and we allow our lives to be guided by the higher forces of love and Light.

When people try to find inner contact, it is possible that they may make contact with their own astral body or their own mental body and feel that they have made contact with something higher, especially if the message from their astral body suits their personality wishes. Many who think they are in contact with higher beings are not, and many who do not presume to be, are.

Further signs of true angels

If you really wish to discover the truth of whether you are in contact with angels or not, there are a few things you really need to understand. If you sincerely wish from your heart to contact an angel and you do not get a response straight away, you can rest assured that the angel will hear you. It doesn't matter whether you think you are in contact or not, you can talk to the angels. It is through the angel that God hears you. When you are in contact, it is likely that you will feel happy and uplifted and have a warm glow. Sometimes the hairs will stand up on end or there is a sudden rush of energy through the body, a tingling at the back of the neck or a funny feeling in the heart. Trust plays an important part in contacting the angels. A person healing with the help of the angels has to trust that the person has been healed. You must trust that you have been heard. The effects may not be immediate and may come later. You cannot let your expectations and demands interfere with the trust and knowing. You can't expect great clairvoyant phenomena; you must simply know that the angels do hear and act according to the Will of God. Your karma must also be considered. It may be that even several years later your answers will come, as God in His-Her infinite wisdom may need you to learn certain lessons first. You need to be ready to receive God's gifts. It may be also that you need to prove this to yourself. It is when you come to live as the angels do, to give without counting the cost, to give in return for the love and Light you receive that you can truly open to God's gift of Spirit.

If you are touched by the angels, you are touched by God and you will change your life. It is at such times as near-death experiences, when the angels come in close contact, that you see evidence of this. People report the blessing of the great Light and communication with angels at such times of crisis. When people have these experiences, their whole life changes and they need to put these changes into action. It is after the near-death experience that people seem suddenly to want to give and find themselves moving into fields of humanitarian work. Many books are appearing now which have researched and accounted for these changes in people resulting from near-death experiences.

The touch of the angels makes people believe in the existence of God. In near-death experiences and also when there is a trauma in life and the help of the angels is felt, a raising of consciousness occurs. It is as if the veil has been lifted. Seeing the glory of the inner worlds gives hope and faith before unknown. Such experiences are not something you forget; they can stay with you in this and many lives to come.

Powerful experiences such as these may be likened to the experience of those who have seen the eyes of Jesus: they will never forget this experience and the memory will assist them to work for the Christ, in this life and in those to come. When people go through the near-death experience, they usually lose the fear of death because they realise how active they can become when the physical garment is cast away and they are free to move in the Light. In the inner worlds they can help so much, as they are free to move so quickly and assist those in need.

How can the angels help us?

Some angels know our karma and they are linked with the Grace of God. Sometimes the Grace is given and the karma released, sometimes the karma must be played out; but when we ask for the help of the angels, the help is given. Perhaps it will come in an understanding of our situation and our part in creating it; perhaps we will be spared going through something we feel we cannot face. The karma and the Grace can unfold in our lives in a multitude of ways, but when we pray to the angels we come to know that we are not alone during the unfolding. We can endure anything that is given to us to endure, for we come to understand its role in helping us to grow and helping us to come to accept God's plan. In so accepting we can become closer to God through the angels, and feel the blessing that this gives. No longer separate and alone, we are unified with the Divine even in our vulnerability, for it is our vulnerability that takes us to Him-Her. We must always remember that the angels are the Messengers of God and that they bring the Love, the Light and the Care of God with them, along with the great Wisdom and Heart of enormous intelligence and compassion.

In our little worlds it is difficult for us to comprehend the greatness of this Universe, yet we are a microcosm of it and can experience within ourselves the battle of Light and dark. By calling on the angels we strengthen the Light in us. We come to know the Christ-self and experience the birth of Christ within our hearts. The Lord Archangel Michael Who is the Defender of the Faith, the Protector of the Earth, is the Archangel Who brings forth God's Plan and gives us the blue-print of what is to come. He serves the Lord of Love, Who is the Unifier, the Teacher of angels and humanity. The Lord of Love, the Lord Maitreya, reveals to us the Plan for His coming in the next five hundred years. The angels work ceaselessly to assist in the unfoldment of the Plan through their understanding of the Hierarchy that exists within the angelic kingdom, where every being within that kingdom seeks to serve the Light, dedicated to its task. We are given a vision of how we could choose to cooperate and help the Earth reach its destiny as a Star of Light. To do this we must call upon the help of the angels. We must believe in them, for they can set us free and bring the liberation of Spirit that we need to release ourselves from the shackles of our unredeemed past. Then we can work and cooperate for the Light.

What is the intent and purpose of the angels?

The angels of the Christed One live their lives with the intent and purpose of serving the Christ. They trust whatever is asked of them and they act upon it with their whole existence, never questioning, never doubting their Master. Because of this deep loyalty, the Christ can rely upon them to carry out the tasks that are needed to restore the planet to a state of Light.

The angelic kingdom and the Hierarchy

At this time many of the angels, especially those of Raphael's group, are busy helping to bring forth the Light of Christ and the Spirit of Resurrection in a special blend of energy that will bring forth the new humanity. This will help us on Earth to begin to merge our consciousness with that of the angels, helping us to function simultaneously in the physical plane as well as in the inner worlds. This is a needed Light which will help to change our consciousness and help to transform the planet Earth. The Masters, in particular the Lord Count of Saint Germain (the Master governing the violet Ray or Light) and certain female Masters, are working to assist in this process. We can call on

Them to help us make the necessary shifts and transitions which we in our life on Earth must make.

The Lady Portia and the Count of Saint Germain can help us to redeem and transmute our shadow selves, the darker side of our nature. They can help us learn to discriminate and recognise what is shadow and what is Light. They are Masters of alchemy and can help us to separate the darker substance within us, recognise it, acknowledge its source and transmute and release it in the Light, allowing us to change our constitution and turn from darkness to Light.

The Lady Yasodhara can help us find the joy of working and living in the Light. She helps us find compassion for ourselves and others as we walk the Path, giving great wisdom and understanding previously unknown. She is known for Her perseverance; through Her link with the Lord of Love She can help take us home to His Heart. In so doing we find our own hearts and can learn to walk the Way of the Heart. We can call upon Her and Her many angels of golden Light to help us when we need to find the joy, the compassion, the wisdom and the never-ceasing love.

We can call on the Lady Nada and Her host of angels in the pink Light when we wish to help heal those who are sick in body and mind or to help heal the suffering deep within. When we know someone is suffering, we can ask Lady Nada to send a healing angel to be with the person until the healing, in whatever form, is complete. We can call on the Archangel Raphael to send His healing angels to help heal those who are suffering on Earth and to help them find comfort and relief.

There are so many beings we can call upon when we or others around us are in need. The Masters and the Archangels, the angels, and the angels assisting them dedicate themselves to the work of Light. It may be that when we call upon these great beings to assist us that the Masters and Archangels may not come; however, Their assisting angels will do so and will give us the help we need no matter how insignificant we may see ourselves as being, no matter how tiny may be our needs in comparison to the needs of many. The help will be given.

The fallen angels

Some angels have taken the dark path, they are often referred to as the fallen angels. They are the ones who have rebelled against God's Laws. Many religions do not like to even call these dark beings angels. They represent the negative forces whose qualities are vices such as pride, greed, gluttony, lust, jealousy and envy. Some of these forces work to trick and tease human beings in a mischievous and negative manner. These beings are known to be able to change shape and form and exist at varying levels of ability. When we make a choice for darkness instead of Light, there are associated lessons which we only need look into history to learn. Let us look, for example, at Noah's Ark when the great prophet Noah was alerted through God's messages of the dangers if humanity did not change its way. No one would listen and the great floods came. Perhaps now, many centuries later, when the prophets are again warning us, we might listen and make the choice to lift into the realms of the celestial beings rather than follow the downward path of the fallen ones.

We are all prone to being tripped up by our own negative natures. However, we can learn from this how the darkness works, and with practice and determination learn to overcome it, to keep our shadows in check and to strengthen the Light within with the help of the angels of Light. Our choice of working for darkness or for Light is an important one and it is one which we must make regularly in all our interactions and life choices, for the veils of deceit can be strong. We must pray for the help of the angels to help us lift, so that we are not caught in the glamours and illusions which make it so easy for us to fall. When we fall, we must learn to recognise this and acknowledge the truth of this falling. We must stand again and never give up our search for the Light. By our falls we find humility again, which has usually been lost in the glamour. We find truth again which is lost in the illusion, and we are reminded of our place in this mighty universe. We are like grains of sand on the floor of the mighty ocean - nothing; yet when God is within us we are One, we are Everything. We often fall, sometimes through conscious intent and often due to our lack of discrimination. So let us think, "do we wish to continue to fall victim to glamour and illusion, to the lords of deceit, or do we wish to rise with the angels to a world of great Light, love and compassion?" The choice is ours, we can decide. All we need to do is remember to ask the angels to lift us, and they will lift us to the Heart of their Teacher and ours, the Lord of Love. If we really wish to become like them, we can pray to be like them one day, to become one of the shining ones. We will be given help in learning to discriminate and God will hear our prayer and act accordingly.

So how do we discern a true angel when other voices, such as desires of our personality, may interfere? When we decide to live a life based on truth, we open to the spiritual forces. When we open the heart and decide to live a life based on love and truth, we begin to receive attention from greater beings who can utilise us for Light work. It is not until we are cleansed and purified sufficiently that higher powers support us in the work. When the higher forces know that we will use the Light given for good purpose without thought of return, it is then that we can begin to be trusted. If we wish to send Light for certain purposes, we must be open to the Will of God. The work then becomes a suggestion designed to benefit the good of all. Our motivation must be to serve; an impersonal yet heartfelt approach is needed. We ask the

Christ-self to overshadow our personality so that we may work impersonally with the Divine.

Psychic phenomena can disrupt good group work. Through it people get caught in glamours and illusions and lose sight of the spiritual purpose and intent. They may talk about these inner experiences in a way that belittles the purity of the experiences and makes them like a grand picture show. When people do this, the work loses its power. This is not to say that such beautiful experiences cannot be shared. It simply means that if it is done in a manner that is self-aggrandising instead of in love and wisdom, it will destroy the beauty and grace of the energies and experience given. In silence and purity of heart much can be done. Where the motive is simply to be a vehicle for the higher Light, the Light can work through us. If we would like to have the help of the angels, we must keep this in mind.

If there is a specific work we wish to achieve, it is good to know that regular activities, for example, at a certain time each day or week, will attract the angels, and an energy of cooperation can build. In all this we must remain forever mindful and be realistic about what can be achieved. We must work with the sense of pride that may come as we work with the angels and guard against self-deceit. If we are to obtain cooperation, we must have clarity of thought and focussed concentration to use the energy given in an efficient and well-directed way. When we understand right use of colour or words we can fine-tune our cooperative efforts. There is a certain greatness of energy and oneness of the human vehicles when we work together in cooperation for the Light.

Certain angels are linked with Divine consciousness. In *The Kingdom of the Gods* Hodson (1987) speaks of the Rose Angel, a great angel radiating a beautiful luminous pink Light, which can be thought of as an incarnation of Divine Wisdom and Love.

When we get the help of such angels to cooperate in service, it is indeed an honour.

When we work ceremonially, and when we heal, we should do so with the right motive and purity of heart, invoking the Light and Love of the Holy Spirit and the Christ Light, leaving, in full faith, the healing to the higher powers in accordance with the karma of the person being healed. We must put our personal will aside and have no attachment to the outcome. When the healing angels are involved, they will direct their streams of purified energy into and through the aura of the person being healed to disperse congestion and drive out harmful substances.

Guardian angels

Guardian angels have the job of protecting and guarding people and places, giving protection from negativity and keeping a holy space around whatever it is they are guarding. They use their Light body with its forces of Light to create Light around the object in their keeping.

We all have a guardian angel. Our guardian angel may stay with us over many lifetimes, and it strives to cooperate with the will of the soul or the solar angel. Together the solar angel and the guardian angel work to guide us in our evolution. We can come to know our guardian angel as an energy we can trust. Some may feel it, some may communicate through inner symbol. It will speak to us through colour, Light and sound as the angels do.

Our guardian angel works at helping us to strengthen the goodness in our nature. It can warn us when there are dangers, whether they come from the outside or from parts of our own personalities. When we call on it, we can ask it to protect us from the darkness or the fallen angels we spoke of earlier. When we develop a strong communication with our guardian angel, along with the inner trust that brings, we discover that we are not alone and help is at hand.

Our guardian angel has other angels who assist it in its tasks, who may run messages for it, and therefore, for us. As long as we strive to live by the spiritual Law, these angels can help. Our guardian angels are often aware of our karma and may work to help us understand what needs to be understood. They may tell us the next step on our path and can even alert us to negative people or environments we may enter, hinting that we move with caution. They communicate with us at a level we can comprehend. In spiritual circles today many people speak of "the Higher Self," when they are referring to inner guidance they receive. What they are probably really communicating with is the guardian angel whose task it is to guard and guide us on our path. The Higher Self is another term for the soul or solar angel which cannot be contacted readily by us because it is at a level of consciousness that we cannot comprehend - thus, we have the guardian angel to help us. The solar angel can freely contact the guardian angel who finds ways of passing on the message, so to speak.

The relationship you have with your guardian angel is an important one. Like all relationships, if you abuse it in one life, it may be difficult to have a good relationship in the next. There is often a strong karmic link between you and your guardian angel - perhaps you have walked the Earth together at some point. Much karma can be released and learning gained by being a guardian angel to a human being or even to a place such as a waterfall, a mountain, or a tree. Guardian angels are ever ready to shield us from harm. They bring harmony and love and work to keep away all influences of danger, or darkness and disease.

Solar angels

The solar angel is a term used for the soul. The solar angels are angels of Light. It is the solar angel who does Light work and through meditation, aspiration and control is able to influence the lower forces and make them its servants. When we wish to achieve positive Light work, we can work with our solar angels to achieve our positive ends. When we heal and call upon the soul, the solar angel becomes active and sends the Light needed to assist in the healing work.

There are solar angels of the planetary scheme and of the solar system, but here we are focussing on the solar angel of individuals. The solar angel, or the soul, transforms the Light from the highest levels of consciousness to a vibration that we can bear. If we are healing and do not wish to bring too much energy down, we know we can rely on the solar angel, as well as the guardian angel, to keep the healing at a vibration with which the client can cope. This ensures that the healing takes place according to the karma of the individual and the Will of God. Solar angels work as the great builders putting life force into form. Guardian angels hold this Light given by the solar angels and act as way-showers, shining the Light for us as we walk our path. The solar angels and their great work is here very simply described. If you wish to pursue a deeper understanding of them, you may refer to Alice Bailey's book *A Treatise of Cosmic Fire*.

Hodson (1987) in *Kingdom of the Gods* tells us that studying the angels on an individual basis sometimes brings confusion. They so often work in groups and are a conscious part of the one pulsating universe. When we try to understand their work, we do so lacking their consciousness and so can easily misinterpret their work by comparing it too much with individual human life patterns. The angels are able to show us, through their example, the possibilities of how our lives can one day be. When we cooperate with each other, we can help each other to evolve. The solar angels are aware of the higher scheme. The guardian angels work to convey to us what we need to know in order to work and cooperate with that higher scheme.

The angels' purpose is to serve the Christ. They know how to serve and display the virtues of faith, trust and loyalty which we so need to learn. There are hundreds of virtues which the angels embody, and if we need help to develop just one of them, we can call upon the angel of that virtue. In this chapter we have looked at the angels in the grand scheme of the universe and have seen how they also help in the process of our daily life with what may seem like small things, which nonetheless assist us in creating a smooth and harmonious flow to our lives. Let us remember to call on them for the help they can give. Let us open our hearts to them and let them teach us what it is to relax and trust. Listen for their message, whether it comes through Light, colour or symbol, or as a beautiful feeling in our heart, and learn to fly with them so we can experience the freedom and liberation of Spirit which they bring.

The devas on the Seven Rays

On the Seven Rays there are angels who bring the colour of that Ray and work with it. These angels are often referred to as devas. The Seven Rays are Great Beings sending streams of Great Holy Light that contain particular qualities. When a Ray energy is needed to do particular work, for example, the violet Ray to transmute, we can call upon the devas of the violet Light to help with the process of transmutation; or if purification is required, the devas of the blue and white Light may be called to help with cleansing and purification.

The violet devas are associated with the building of the etheric doubles (see the chapter: *The Human Structure*); the green devas preside over the magnetic spots of the Earth, guarding the forests and defending them from interference. It is from these groups at a certain stage in their evolution that some guardian angels are chosen. The violet devas educate human beings in the perfecting of the physical body.

The white devas can be called upon to help us purify. Alice A. Bailey (1982), in *A Treatise on Cosmic Fire*, tells that there are white devas of the air and water who preside over the atmosphere and work with certain aspects of electrical phenomena, controlling the seas, the rivers and the streams. Alice Bailey (1982) also tells us that the path of service for the green devas is in their work of magnetisation and protection of the vegetable kingdom and of sacred places of Earth, and that the path of service for the white devas lies in the guarding of individuals within the human kingdom and the control of air and water elementals. Through this work these devas can themselves evolve, just as we can, through our service for the Christ.

Forgiveness

Many of us feel unworthy of receiving help, and we find it difficult to forgive ourselves of real and imagined errors. Perhaps we have realised our own negativity. It is difficult then in the shadow to open to the Light of the angels and to feel deserving of it. Our lack of self-worth acts as a barrier to our letting in the Light; however, it is in these darker moments that we need the help of the angels the most. We need to remind ourselves to call upon them in our times of inner crisis. We can call upon the Angel of Forgiveness to forgive ourselves and to forgive others. The Angel of Forgiveness can appear as a white, light violet or pink angel. It has magnificent Forces of Light that pour from its heart, through its wings which gently work on and transmute our grievance and replaces it with love.

When you call upon the Angel of Forgiveness, you can visualise the light violet Light coming down from its heart, through the Angels' wings into your heart centre; allow the violet Light to gently release the grievance you are holding onto about a situation or a person or yourself. In *The Living Word of the Hierarchy*, Ananda Tara Shan (1993, p. 59) writes about the Law of Forgiveness:

> The Law of Forgiveness must be understood and then invoked in every situation where the shadow self has made chaos and destruction. It is through that Law that you learn to laugh, to be gentle, to be just, and to act with wisdom learned from making numerous mistakes. Invoke the Law and become Master of your own destiny.
>
> Do it this way:
>
> Law of Forgiveness, Mercy of God, I have erred. I have learned my lesson. Descend into . . . . (the problem), and neutralise the negative substance created by my action/s, replacing it with the loving Light of Tara the White.

The White Tara, the Mother Christ, shines Her great Light upon us as an Avatar of Light and helps us to face ourselves. She accepts us and will take our shadow and lift it when we call upon Her, taking it in as a mother would take in a tiny child. She gives us the nourishment we need and the courage to see ourselves in truth. In Her Light and the Light of the Lady Portia, Lady Nada and Lady Yasodhara, we can find forgiveness.

When we visualise the Light of Forgiveness, we can see it as light violet Light entering into our heart. We can see the hearts of those we forgive radiating with pink Light, allowing the white

Light to purify the link between us. We can see how this Light helps all of our relationships move into Light.

Conclusion

The angels are increasingly working to make themselves known to us. Why? Because they can help us lift our consciousness and so help the Earth to lift and become a planet of Light in a Lighted Universe. When we heal, the angels are at hand, ever ready to help us and to lift the burdens and sorrow from our stilted paths. The angels help us to raise our awareness to the Lighted Path which we can find within us. If we dare to follow it and fly with them into the Light, we can begin to live in Love.

Messages from Light

I found it difficult to find a clear enough space in my life to get guidance. I was aware that there were certain steps I could take to get closer to God. One was to go out into nature. I became aware of the power of certain spots on the Earth, particularly at waterfalls and rocks of great moment along ley lines; places where there was mineral water coming from the Earth. I would go to these places to get free from the maya, the thickness, denseness and heaviness of my own aura, and to allow the richness of the prana and the natural healing energies at certain spots upon the Earth to help me. When I take time and space and make room in my life to listen to the higher energies, to the messengers of God, the angels and the devas, the guidance is always forthcoming. I sometimes use the excuse of being too busy to listen. I may have many questions and be confused for days ... but unless I actually stop to listen to the silence it is very difficult to get the help that I need. I've eventually learned to incorporate into my life some time alone and some with nature, tuning in to the messages given from the Light beings that are there to help.

There are many waterfalls around where I live. When people visit waterfalls there's a space, place and time made for each person. The guidance can be given if the people choose to go into the stillness.

One particular day I went to the Carisbrook Falls in southern Victoria. They aren't far from the sea, along the Great Ocean Road. I love climbing the rocks and ambling up towards the falls, allowing the sounds of the white water flowing down the falls to act as white light, coming in physical form, to cleanse and purify my being. This particular day I'd had difficulty being content with things in my life. I didn't really have anything specific to ask. When I went to the waterfall I tuned in to the deva where it gave forth the message.

"Open to the will of God in your life. It is there to be found."

It seemed an important message and all I could do was pray that I stay in the Light long enough to know and hear the guidance as it came. To be able to discriminate regarding the quality of guidance given on the inner levels I said a prayer to the Lord of Love that I remain open to the Love and that I be given guidance whenever I'm most in need. I could see that it was a matter of choosing where you put your focus, for when your thoughts are heavy and the mind dull it is not so easy to find answers. But guidance is available, even at those times. If you use your will to not be overshadowed and clouded by the darker thoughts and feelings and you take positive steps to move beyond that darkness and tune into the Light, you can tune into the messengers of God that are here to help us: they live around us. Whether we know it or not, we are never alone.

Sometimes my mood and thoughts became quite heavy and were not only dull but sabotaging and negative. If I looked for guidance or an image to help with an issue I would be shown something that embodied my negative nature and that image would play havoc with my senses. One particular image which remained for a long time, because I felt inferior to an archetypal image of a witch with a long nose, a black cap *and a wart on her chin. When I would try to find answers and direction she would appear huge and omnipresent in my consciousness and there seemed to be no way I could make any sense within. It developed that the image started to frighten me and instead of enjoying the process of meditating and healing that I'd come to know and love, I avoided it. There was no pleasure in it - it was simply a battle. I had to confront it in order to move through it. One day I did.*

I went to a man who gave regression healings and worked with a lie detector, which was useful to him, to let him know when I was experiencing fear. I told him the problems I was having. I felt I could not do this on my own and the added support of someone I trusted helped a great deal in giving me the strength I needed to face this creature. I went within, the image loomed large and it assumed its usual sabotaging disposition. With the help of the healer I found appropriate questions to ask it. I became very scared and could feel the fear expanding in my inner bodies. It gave me a feeling of being overwhelmed. I would open my eyes every few minutes to help bring me back to Earth.
"Is there an image or a symbol that you trust?" Pater asked. A red rose came immediately to mind. I told Pater.

"We'll work with that first and ask it how we can deal with this other image," he said.

It felt so good to be getting some help. It was easy to visualise the rose and I felt safe to ask it questions.

"Why is this image haunting me?" I asked.

"Because you have given it the power to do so," it replied immediately. "Your spirituality is unfolding just as my petals do when I open. It frightens you to be open - to be. There is something called the shadow which sits at the threshold of darkness, at the point where Light and dark meet. Sometimes to find Light you must pass by what sits at that

threshold. In this instance, for you, the darkness takes the form of the witch."

"How can I get by her?" I asked.

"You created her. You can uncreate her just as easily."

"How?"

"Let me ask you that," the rose replied. "How?"

I searched my knowledge. The only place I had seen witches being dispelled was in the story of the Wizard of Oz, from my memory of it, where the wicked Witch of the West had disappeared and dissolved by having water thrown upon her.

"I could throw water on her," I replied.

"Go ahead, do it now."

I felt a little ridiculous at this point, but I was desperate. I could see the huge overwhelming figure of the witch entering.

"Here, use this bucket of water and throw it all."
I picked up the bucket of water and threw it all over the witch. She became smaller, the more water I threw.

"Speak to her," the rose said, "tell her what you need to tell her."

I looked at the witch.

"You are not as powerful as I thought you were. I've been frightened of you and I can see now, in looking at you, that you don't deserve to have that sort of power over me. You are really nothing."

The witch turned into an empty hat and the hat crumpled into a piece of black material.

"Send it Light," the rose suggested. "Purple Light, to help it change form."

I imagined the black material filled with violet Light until the black material was no longer. In its place there came a white rose.

"Let your spirituality unfold. Be like a bud ready to bloom. Be not afraid to face the darkness within you, for in facing it you will eventually find peace and purity. The forces of Light always help those who truly seek love with a pure heart. Knowing this is your strength and protection."

As I came back to consciousness, I thanked Pater for his help.

"I didn't know it would be so easy," I said, "as to throw water on her," and I laughed, aware again of the child within me. As I spoke to Pater I could still hear the voice of the rose in my heart.

"Come ye, as little children, to the kingdom of heaven."

The Kingdom of Angels

I am free
as a bird with wings,
I love to love
and to sing -
sing until my heart's content,
sing until there is descent
of the angels.

Far and wide,
close and near,
the angels they are so dear

Giving of their light to all,
making us stand ten feet tall -
see them come,
see them go,
be open to what they show.

Subtle glimpses of the past,
future possibilities,
their magic on us they cast,
an ocean of eternity.

We are the ships that sail their seas -
they are the forest
we are the trees

They lift us to the height of love,
they reveal the wings of the dove.

We fly with them into the Heart
of Love, to Maitreya.

The Human Structure

The human structure is threefold: it consists of the Spirit, the soul, and the personality. In a great deal of spiritual literature there is a lot of confusion with the terms "soul" and "Spirit," and even "mind." Similar confusion about these concepts is evident in other fields such as psychology and Buddhism, and much misunderstanding about human nature and the human structure or constitution results. This chapter will make clear the distinction between these terms and what they mean, and bring forth the theosophical viewpoint.

Put simply, the Spirit, soul and personality are all bodies of consciousness. Spirit is a pure, formless body of consciousness that is the essence of God. So that the Kingdom of God may manifest on Earth, Spirit reaches into matter by creating a vehicle through which it can work. It needs the vehicle to incarnate as it cannot do so without it. The vehicle it creates is the soul. The soul exists on lower levels of consciousness than the Spirit. Similarly, to express itself on lower levels of matter and thus satisfy its desire for sentient experience, the soul creates a vehicle through which it can function. The vehicle which the soul creates for its expression is what we know as the personality. The personality is made up of the physical, etheric, astral and mental bodies. The personality functions on lower levels of consciousness than the soul. Let us examine this in more detail.

The human constitution

Many people are becoming aware that we are much more than our physical body, or the gross material existence. We are multi-dimensional beings existing in the spiritual, mental, emotional and physical planes. As we come to know ourselves, we begin to comprehend the reality of who or what we are. Paradoxically, we cannot begin to fathom the full depth and vision of who we really are. For example, in the outer life we may come to know ourselves by aspects of our personality. Perhaps we are intelligent and moody, have a job in retail of computers, and are a mother. Does that make us a smart person, a temperamental one, a shop assistant, a computer person and a mother? Well, perhaps in one sense it does. But is that what we really are? No, we are not that: we are not our mood, our character, our role or our job. We are not our physical body; we are not our emotions; we are not our mind, although the latter three bodies are forms through which we manifest ourselves.

We are soul and Spirit. What does that mean? In *The Secret Doctrine*, Volume 1, H.P. Blavatsky (1963, pp. 79-80) suggests something of the difference between the Spirit, the soul and the body. In the text below Blavatsky refers to body as "Matter." She says:

> Life we look upon as One Form of Existence, manifestation in what is called Matter; or what incorrectly separating them, we name Spirit, soul and Matter in man. Matter is the vehicle for the manifestation of soul on this plane of existence, and soul is the vehicle on a higher plane for the manifestation of Spirit, and these three are a trinity synthesised by Life, which pervades them all.

These words from Blavatsky help us see how together the three bodies are all one and are the basis of life as we know it. Her use of the word "incorrectly," where she is referring to our separation of these three aspects in order to understand them, reminds us that they are all part of one whole, making up the human constitution, and in truth are inseparable. Geoffrey Hodson (1981, p. 124) in his book *Basic Theosophy: The Living Wisdom*, helps us to see that our Spirit and soul are not separate from us, they are inseparable and are part of us:

> The deity then, is in no sense external to, different or separate from man. God and man are one and indivisible throughout all eternity. This is the one supreme truth taught in all Mystery Schools and in all religions.

To understand further the distinctions and differences between the Spirit, the soul and the personality (which incorporates "Matter"), we will look at them as separate entities. I would like to remind the reader to remember that although we are looking at them as separate entities, they make up the Oneness of our existence and together they provide the essence of the human constitution.

The Spirit

What is Spirit?

Spirit is the principle of life. It is a spark of God: a pure, formless body of consciousness that is the essence of God. Blavatsky (1990, p. 306) in *The Theosophical Glossary* defines Spirit as "that which belongs directly to Universal consciousness, and which is its homogenous and unadulterated emanation." She continues by saying that "Spirit, in short, is no entity in the sense of having form." Spirit then, is pure universal consciousness that is formless. Bailey (1987) sees Spirit as a term synonymous with the Monad, life and energy. She says, "The word Spirit is applied to that undefinable, elusive, essential impulse of life which is the cause of all manifestation." Spirit is also called the Divine Self and the Point, and is referred to also as Monad. Spirit resides permanently on the second plane of nature which is called the monadic plane. (There are seven planes of nature within our solar system: the

Adi; the Monadic; the Atmic; the Buddhic; the Mental; the Astral; and the Physical. These are levels of existence or planes of consciousness that correspond to vibrations of matter on the seven levels. Each plane has seven sub-planes, where the vibration within the plane varies.) Spirit corresponds to the very highly vibrating matter. Spirit is immortal. Spirit is found in what we call "Active Intelligence" or the Holy Spirit. Bailey (1990) points out that the Spirit is primarily the expression of Will, with love and intelligence as secondary principles.

What is the nature of Spirit?

When we refer to the source of Spirit, in all its greatness, where "Spirit" is a body of consciousness that is of God, it is often capitalised. The term "spirit" can be used in a variety of ways, for example, when we are in high spirits, when we do something in a particular spirit or energy, or to refer to a spirit such as an elf, fairy or angel. Usually when spirit is referred to in this way it is not capitalised. When Spirit (capitalised) takes form and manifests through the lower planes of nature, it becomes known as spirit (not capitalised). It is found in all living beings. It is evident about us, especially in nature, for example, in forests, mountains and even in our gardens. The human spirit is a direct manifestation of universal consciousness which we often refer to as "the One." In us the nature of spirit, or the life principle, is such that it manifests through the mental body and the brain as the will to live, to be and to act. Spirit (not capitalised) is a dynamic energy in which we find our purpose and most basic incentive for life. According to Alice A. Bailey (1987), in her book *A Treatise on White Magic*, the energy of Spirit corresponds with our spirit nature through the nervous system, the brain and the eyes. Through the eyes we can see the spirit of another. We become aware of the enthusiasm for life which spirit gives. Spirit is as close to us as our breath. When we are present at a birth or a death we may witness how Spirit enters and how Spirit leaves the physical being. We know then that it is not simply the physical body we are connecting with when we experience being at-one with our soul-mates or close friends. At such poignant times we may connect with the soul and Spirit. Please note here that such moments are rare; I am not referring to closeness that may be experienced on the astral or emotional levels.

The soul

What is the soul?

The soul is known also as the spiritual triad, the Ego, the higher self, the causal body, the higher triad, the Christ-self, the Angel of the Presence, the Self and the solar angel. It is a body of consciousness that exists on the atmic and buddhic levels of the planes of nature. The soul extends its body of consciousness to the first three subplanes of the higher mental plane. This part of the soul is often referred to as the causal body. The soul is a vortex of energy that is on the path of evolution. It puts an expression of itself into the lower planes, which is what we call "the personality." Alice A. Bailey (1990), in her book *The Soul, the Quality of Life*, defines the soul as another name for the Christ Principle; neither Spirit nor matter but the relation between them, the mediator between God and His-Her form. The soul manifests with different characteristics and different forms in the three kingdoms of nature.

The soul is the basis of and source of awareness or consciousness, which is produced through the union of Spirit and matter. It possesses the quality of group consciousness, mediatorship, attraction and unification. The soul manifests as a conscious response of the Spirit to matter. The soul is not limited to human beings. Planets and stars, for example, have souls. Other living beings, such as those of the animal and vegetable kingdoms, also have souls. However, these are group souls and are not individuated as in the case of human beings.

Amongst many people the soul is often seen as some sort of mystical attribute that is vaguely connected to us and as something that, although we don't really know what it is, we should endeavour to save from the evil one or cultivate through living a life of good moral fibre. Others see the soul mistakenly as our emotional part or where we hold our feelings and sentiments. Unfortunately, lack of knowledge has meant that the soul has been quite grossly misrepresented and therefore the teachings about it have also been wrongly conceived. What many see as the soul is the astral body.

Theosophy teaches us that the soul is nearly immortal. It is nearly immortal in that when we reach Adeptship or Mastership (a very developed point of our evolution which occurs after many thousands of lives on the path of Light) the causal body (the soul) explodes. The causal body remains from incarnation to incarnation throughout all of our lifetimes on Earth. Our physical, etheric, astral and mental bodies are given anew in each incarnation.

The soul is our healer and our teacher. When we meditate or invoke healing energies the soul may pour down the Light of the Holy Spirit. It is the vehicle through which Spirit comes to us. The soul is our guide and through its healing power we heal and evolve. The causal body holds within it a record of our past. When we incarnate, the soul works with the knowledge of the Law of Karma, and in some cases assisted by the Lords of Karma (great inner Beings who work in the office of Divine Justice) in the process of the building of our mental and astral bodies. The soul knows our karma, what we have learned and what we have not learned. It sends forth the karmic seeds that are built into the etheric double in each life and it keeps them safe between incarnations. The soul is unceasingly in deep meditation. Through its outer expression, the personality, the soul is able to gain certain experiences through which it can acquire certain attributes. It is also able to work out certain needed effects which may have been initiated through previous expressions of itself. In so doing the soul can work to co-operate in the Plan (the unfoldment of the universe according to the Will of God) according to its karma.

What is the soul's nature?

In *The Soul, the Quality of Life*, Alice A. Bailey (1990) describes the soul's nature as one that understands the creative purpose and Plan of God. It is free from the concerns of the personality as it is absorbed in consciousness of the whole. It is serene, calm, responsible, wise and the opposite of self-centred. Its nature is love and the will-to-good. Its love is inclusive, gentle and unchanging, with detachment and indifference in the best sense. In the soul's realm, Light is the major characteristic. It is through the Light that the soul intuitively understands and knows. (When I speak of the soul's intuitive faculties I am referring to intuition as a flash of Light on a level far beyond what we know as intuition in our personality consciousness.) The consciousness of the soul is one of unity, in eternal Light. It has a great stillness and undisturbable peace. It knows the purpose, meaning and method of life. It is power, wisdom, and knowledge, with a perpetual consciousness that is not limited by time or space. Perhaps the most notable qualities of the soul are spiritual will and spiritual love. The soul provides us with the blueprint through which love may manifest. Love is its dominating principle, with will and knowledge acting as secondary principles (Bailey, 1990). As the soul develops and evolves, its wisdom and loving influence also develop and evolve. The soul evolves in order to manifest more Spirit.

The soul possesses certain qualities and attributes which we in our personality consciousness are trying to cultivate, develop and learn. The soul brings forth the Light that illuminates the nature of the personality. The soul Light may emanate through the personality. The soul is responsible for transmitting the Light to the personality. For example, when we call on the healing Light in meditation and healing work it is our soul which directs the Light.

What method does the soul use to incarnate?

The method of reincarnation can be seen as the descent of Spirit into matter. Annie Besant (1985, p. 38), in her book *Reincarnation* states:

> The Lords of Karma, aware of the karma to be worked out, provide the mould suited to express the karma to be worked out.... The brain is built into the etheric double. This determines the mental habits and qualities of the human being to be incarnated.

Our incarnations follow the process of evolution. If we develop our good qualities and persevere, we slowly learn. Our character as expressed in each life becomes moulded through our actions in each incarnation. The manifestation of the expression of the soul, that is, the personality, or the physical, etheric, astral and mental bodies, is determined by past actions. Thus, it is important that we develop virtues in each life so that they may become innate. The qualities we develop in any one life persist across lifetimes. We return incarnation after incarnation to continue the perfecting process on Earth. Our perfection comes not with desire to be perfect but through willingness to give service and sacrifice for the Plan. The soul knows the higher plan and the personality must learn to align to the soul. It is a necessary cycle, that of incarnation and reincarnation. It is one of the fundamental Laws of the Universe. More discussion of reincarnation is found in chapter: *Reincarnation*.

Why does the soul incarnate?

The soul sends forth a vehicle of expression onto the lower planes of existence - the physical, astral and mental levels. Through the cycles of reincarnation over the long process of evolution, the potentialities of the soul's divinity can be realised. Karma can be worked out and qualities can be developed which help the soul to evolve. The soul incarnates because of its desire to have sentient experience, and by will and knowledge of the Plan. It does not have desire to be perfect; it has a willingness to give service and sacrifice itself for the Plan. Hodson (1981, p. 127) in *Basic Theosophy: The Living Wisdom* describes the purpose of our existence as being for "spiritual, intellectual, cultural and physical evolution."

What do we mean by the terms - soul group, soul mate, twin soul and old soul?

Terms such as soul group, soul mate, twin soul and old soul are used to describe relationships among souls. As the terms are not well understood explanations are offered here.

The soul mate

The love of the soul acts as an enormous force of attraction. Because of this force throughout lifetimes we attract the same souls to us again and again. Of course we also have karmic ties that bind us which also serve as a force of attraction. Through these ties we have the opportunity to learn and to bring our relationships into love. The souls who we keep attracting, through love and karma, are called our soul mates.

The soul group

We have a number of soul mates, perhaps thirty or forty, who belong to a particular soul group. The soul group which we belong to is called our dual group, some of whom will incarnate on Earth and others of whom are spread out in the universe having a different training. When we come into contact with people who are our duals, there is usually a strong relation because we have had many strong interactions in the past. The strength of these interactions may cause us to react to these people when we meet again in our current life. We may feel challenged by them. This challenge motivates us to grow. Often the feelings for these people will be of strong dislike or great love. Often people from our dual group come as our parents, close friends, children or partners. We often recognise them when we meet and can often tell each other through the eyes. The attraction between souls which causes us to embody with the same souls throughout time is well described by Ananda Tara Shan (1993, p. 99), in her book *The Living Word of the Hierarchy*:

> We must appreciate the good and loving things in life. For example, in a world that has not much love in it, it has become nearly a miracle to have loving parents, who, on behalf of Spirit, are raising and educating their children with a true purpose and true love. We must learn to appreciate every day of health with joy and laughter, and we must be prepared and ready for the grief and sadness it is to "lose" a loving parent, a loving partner, a loving friend. For such is life that we must learn to take both joy and pain with a smile on our lips. We must believe in Theosophy that has taught us that there is no death, only life to the ones who live with God. And so we as a matter of fact, as a reality, never lose love; but love is a magnet that shall attract us to embody with the same souls throughout time.

The twin soul or twin ray

In the beginning of the creation of Spirits or Monads, God, the Solar Logos, sends forth a stream of life or a spark of God. Within that one spark or stream, there are many life streams which are divided and which develop into a twofold structure manifesting as a masculine life-stream and a feminine life-stream. This is the concept of the twin soul or twin ray: we have on the soul level a perfect partner who is the "other-half" of the spark of God we share. This twofold nature of our ultimate body gives rise to the desire for wholeness, the desire to be completed by our twin ray. Many people however, misconstrue this teaching and spend their life searching for the perfect soul mate or their twin soul. A soul mate is not a twin soul or a twin ray. It is rare that one has the karma to be partnered with one's twin ray on Earth for often the twin ray is not embodied during the same incarnation. If twin rays are embodied at the same time, there are many sorts of relationships which are possible. Unfortunately, much misinformation exists about twin rays or twin souls and people get caught in the glamour and illusion associated with this misinformation. We can meditate to attract our twin ray, but we must realise that it will bring forth an energy that essentially helps us to become whole - it will not necessarily bring us a partner. There is a great deal of media hype that feeds on the glamours and illusions of the soul mate and the twin soul and unfortunately, it creates in many people a lot of confusion. Life's purpose is not just to find one's twin ray; at this stage in human development, life's purpose is more about learning to live according to the will of one's soul.

The old soul

Souls are considered to be old or young depending on the number of lives they have been in incarnation and the finer qualities they have developed in that time. When a soul has been in incarnation for thousands upon thousands of lives, it is considered to be an old soul. An old soul may be recognised by its personality's wisdom and love.

The personality

What is the personality?

The personality is the outer expression of the soul and Spirit. It is the personal nature of the individual who has incarnated. Unlike the soul and Spirit, the personality is mortal, that is, it is subject to death and disintegration. The personality is made up of four bodies of matter, namely:

1. the physical
2. the etheric
3. the astral
4. the mental

These four bodies reside on the three lower planes of nature - the physical, astral and mental planes. The four bodies interpenetrate each other.

The physical body

The physical body is the soul's "vehicle of action and self-expression in the physical world" (Hodson, 1981, p. 126). It is the densest, heaviest part of a person's consciousness. It is made up of solid, liquid and gaseous material. It is the vehicle through which we act and move in space. It enables us to function on the physical plane. We need to look after our physical body so that we may live a long and healthy life; we should treat it as a temple for the Spirit within.

The etheric body

The etheric body, sometimes referred to as the vital body, is composed of matter finer than the gaseous state, and exists on the four higher subplanes of the physical plane - the etheric, super-etheric, subatomic and atomic subplanes of the physical plane. The etheric body has a magnetic energy and has seven focal points where Light and energy merge and are intensified. These focal points are the etheric chakras. The etheric body gives us our health and vitality. It is the vehicle through which subtle forces that emanate from the sun, such as prana (vitality), Fohat (electricity) and kundalini (pure spirit) flow into the endocrine glands and the nervous system which control the dense physical body. Bailey (1987), in A Treatise on White Magic, suggests that the etheric body is seen as the symbol of the soul in the individual. The etheric body carries the life energy or spirit through the body, enabling the soul to be "en rapport" with the environment all the way through to the nervous system and the brain. Because of this capacity the etheric body makes it possible for us to be used as vehicles for the distribution of Light. It links the dense physical body with the subtle astral body. The state and functioning of the etheric body affects our health. To assist its functioning we should get plenty of rest, retire to bed in the earlier hours of the evening, eat properly, exercise regularly and spend an adequate amount of time in nature. Our health and vitality also improve if we avoid stress and worry.

The astral body

The astral body is the soul's vehicle of emotion and desire. It is the body through which we feel and have sensation. It is made of astral matter from the astral plane. Annie Besant (1990, pp. 34-35), in her book *Man and His Bodies*, refers to the astral plane as the astral world. She describes it as follows:

> The astral world is a definite region of the universe, surrounding and interpenetrating the physical, but imperceptible to our ordinary observation because it is composed of a different order of matter.

The astral body is made up of matter from the seven subplanes of the astral plane, and has fine and coarse matter that is drawn from these sub-planes. Through it we feel lower and higher feelings. An example of higher feelings would be devotion, love, compassion; of lower feelings, grief, jealousy, anguish. The astral body permeates and extends around the physical body like a cloud, radiating a variety of colours in varying degrees of brightness, hue and luminosity. Like the etheric body, the astral body has seven major focal points or vortices of energy which we call chakras. The development and action of the astral chakras affects the astral body. The astral body depends upon the chakras to function and to develop.

The level of vibration and type of astral matter we have are determined both by our level of development on the path of evolution and the particular karma and life lessons our soul and the Karmic Board have chosen for us to work through in this lifetime. The lower the nature of a person, the grosser is the matter of the astral body. Fortunately, the matter in our astral body can be purified if we choose to live clean and more holy lives. When we sleep the astral body separates from the physical body and floats in the air above us. It is through the astral body that we are able to travel through time and space.

The astral body is influenced by beings such as elementals and devas or angels that live on the astral plane. Elementals are beings which are on the downward path of involution, moving more into dense matter, whilst we, as evolving beings, are moving out of dense matter into Light. When we persist in the negative habits of uncleanliness or turning to alcohol, for example, the elementals are happy. The devas are higher in vibration than the elementals and are on an evolutionary path as we are; they can assist us in the astral realm.

The mental body

The mental body is made of mental material. It is the soul's vehicle of intellect or concrete thought. The mental plane is divided into two planes - the higher mental plane, which consists of the four upper sub-planes and is formless, and the lower mental plane, which consists of the three lower sub-planes, and has form. The mental body, or the mind as we experience it in the personality, is made of matter from the three lower sub-planes of the mental plane. The four higher sub-planes form part of the causal body. The mental body is the finest of the bodies of the personality. It is ovoid in shape and interpenetrates the physical, etheric and astral bodies. Its size and radiance increases as a person evolves and as the intellect grows. Annie Besant (1990, p. 68), in *Man and His Bodies*, tells us that the mental body grows by thought - through the "exercise of the mental faculties, by the development of our artistic powers, our higher emotions, we are literally building the mind body day by day, each month and year of our lives." If we do not exercise the mind, we do not develop:

> For it is only by the exercise of the mind itself, using its faculties creatively, exercising them, working with them,

constantly exerting them - it is only by these means that the mind body can develop, and that the truly human evolution can proceed (p.69).

Our evolutionary progress is also influenced by the vibrational level of the thoughts that we are thinking. If we continually think negative and harmful thoughts of others or the world generally, the mind strengthens in a negative way. If we think vague or "nothing" thoughts, we do not strengthen its capacities either. As we cultivate a higher vibration of content in our thoughts, perhaps thinking of the goodness in others and thinking loving kindness towards others, we do strengthen the mind's capacities in a positive way and assist our evolution. Memory and imagination are developed through the mental body. We can assist the growth of the mental body through concentration and meditation.

The mental body, at the end of our incarnation, gathers the virtues, the good qualities which we have cultivated throughout our life, and passes on their essence to the causal body in the higher subplanes of the mental level. The causal body stores permanently the characteristics and faculties which are carried on to the next incarnation. The virtues have a positive effect upon the causal body. The vices do not enter into the matter of the causal body, but are recorded through the action of karma. When we re-embody, the vices become part of the karmic seeds that are built into the etheric double in lifetimes to come.

What is the nature of the personality?

The personality is a complex organism, especially when we consider that it consists of all the bodies outlined above - the physical, etheric, astral and mental - and their interrelations. We know that the bodies of the personality do not function in isolation. Rather, they interact and affect each other. When we try to purify ourselves and lift our vibratory matter we must work in all the bodies. As we effect change in one body, we will effect change in the others, like a domino effect.

Unlike the soul, the personality knows what it is to be separate. It has a shadow side with which we must deal. The shadow is a part of the personality that, like the elementals described above, chooses stagnation and involution; it does not want to change or transform. It also has a feminine side and a masculine one. To understand the personality it is useful to study psychology, which looks at the astral and mental levels of personality by studying our emotions and our thoughts. According to Geoffrey Hodson (1981, p. 30-31), in his book *Basic Theosophy: The Living Wisdom*, the personality can be: lonely; subject to the delusion of separation, parting and bereavement; unhappy; in darkness; fatigued; anxious; worried; doubtful; can know want of power, wisdom, understanding and knowledge - mental, emotional and physical. The personality is also limited by time and space.

But what would we do without it? In spite of its problems, the personality is the vehicle through which we experience life. We experience emotion, and can have thoughts and take action. We use it to communicate, and to feel pleasure and joy as well as emotions that are less pleasant to experience. Through the personality we can experience union, happiness, Light, energy, fearlessness, power, wisdom, understanding and knowledge. We can communicate and express love to each other through it.

The personality struggles with the duality of its existence. It is of God, yet feels separated from God and yearns to be in unity again. This is the paradox in which we must live and which motivates us to grow and evolve as the soul would have us evolve.

Evolution

What is evolution?

In God the power of Spirit is fully manifest. The degree to which the power of God is made manifest in us varies according to our evolutionary stage. The expression increases as our evolution increases. Geoffrey A. Barborka (1992, p. 533), in *The Divine Plan*, describes evolution as "the progressive development of everything - worlds as well as atoms." In human life, evolution is the unfolding of the spiritual potencies within us. The Spirit, soul and personality together make up our individuality. Evolution is the unfoldment and development of these three aspects of our being. It takes place when the personality reaches upward to the higher realms and the Spirit assists the upward urge, perfecting "the vehicle through which it demonstrates, and thus shines more radiantly" (Bailey, 1987c, p. 29). For a human being evolution is the process of becoming spiritualised. As we bring Spirit into the matter within us, we evolve. Our soul evolves. As it evolves, the soul becomes capable of working for Light in greater ways, and the capacity of its loving influence grows. Our personality also goes through a process of evolution as it purifies. We may find that this purification reflects in the way we talk or behave towards others. The transformation of the personality to function in higher realms of consciousness is necessary in order that we may evolve. Through the evolutionary process we increase in consciousness and rise to higher levels of vibration. Our evolution is a process that we as personalities are responsible for. We cannot simply leave it up to the soul and Spirit. We must also put in the effort and aspire towards alignment with the soul.

What is the evolutionary path?

The infusion of Spirit into matter through the soul and personality is what leads us to evolve. The path our soul must take in that process of evolution is referred to as the evolutionary path. The evolutionary path is divided into stages. These represent stages of consciousness that we go through on the path on our way to Mastership. It is a path that takes thousands and thousands of lives to walk. It is beyond the realms of this book to go into a full description of these stages; however, I will briefly mention them here as you may have already heard of these terms. If you are interested, you may wish to research further by looking into Alice Bailey's book, *Initiation, Human and Solar* (1959). The stages, in order of evolution or development of consciousness are: average humanity; the aspirant; the probationary disciple; the disciple; the initiate; the Arhat; and the Adept or Master. Our soul must pass through each of these stages to evolve. As we pass through each stage, our level of consciousness increases. We must work to bring the consciousness that is bestowed upon the soul at each stage down to the personality level. This requires much hard work and dedication to a path of selfless service and co-operation with the soul.

Purification, transmutation and redemption

Purification, transmutation and redemption are processes we can use to help us infuse Spirit into matter and so continue along the path of evolution.

Purification

When we work with Light or the Holy Spirit in our healings and meditation, we start to purify our inner bodies. This process of purification or cleansing frees us from the heavy and dense matter

- the "rubbish," the results of negative and lower experiences - that keeps us from rising to higher levels of consciousness.

Transmutation

Transmutation may also take place when we work with the Holy Spirit Light in healing. Transmutation is an alchemical process whereby the nature of the dense matter within us is changed to matter of a higher vibration or form. By the process of transmutation our dense matter is transformed to a higher consciousness and Light.

Redemption

We redeem ourselves as we pay back our karmic debts and make changes for the better. Through the process of redemption we are able to make amends for our past actions and character and find forgiveness for ourselves and others. Redemption enables us to throw out the old, negative ways of being and make a fresh start. Redemption brings us salvation.

How can we become more aware of and aligned with the soul?

William Blake was a great artist who has depicted the synthesis of soul and personality very well in one of his engravings entitled *The Reunion of the Soul and the Body*. In the painting the soul is depicted as a mighty angel reaching down to the personality, who is represented by a figure that is obviously yearning for union with the soul. The figure is kneeling with arms outstretched in surrender and ecstasy, its whole focus upon the soul. In his painting, Blake has captured the necessary ingredients for the reunion. These ingredients are the yearning heart and the total surrender and openness to the soul. When one looks upon this engraving the One-ness of this union is felt within the heart. Through it we see just how much the soul works to assist us, and the total love it has for us as personalities.

In *A Treatise on White Magic*, Alice A. Bailey (1987) gives a number of practical suggestions of how to better develop our soul contact and soul manifestation. These are through:

1. Meditation.
2. Control of desire.
3. Organising and control of the mind.
4. Purification of our physical, etheric, astral and mental bodies.
5. Selfless service, self-sacrifice and devotion.

To become more connected to and conscious of the soul, meditation is a key tool. The soul communicates with us through the process of meditation. "The Solar Angel collects himself, scatters not his force but, in meditation deep, communicates with his reflection" (p. 51). The Solar Angel is the soul; the reflection is the personality. Communication takes place in "meditation deep." Meditation is effective when the mind is stilled, the emotions calmed and the lower bodies are transcended. The I-Am-Presence is a body of consciousness that contains Spirit and soul. By calling on the I-Am-Presence, we call upon our Spirit and soul. The I-Am-Presence sends to us Spirit of the purest source. For example, in the Basic Exercise meditation when we send Light from our heart centre through the crown centre to the I-Am-Presence, which can be seen as a star of Light above our heads, we are sending love to our soul and Spirit. The I-Am-Presence is the vehicle through which the soul can communicate to the personality.

In *A Treatise on White Magic*, Alice A. Bailey (1987) tells us that to achieve the kind of meditation required, the mind needs to be controlled and organised, and the desire nature needs to be controlled. These are ideals which need to be worked towards with intent, effort and persistence. To achieve these ends we need to constantly observe and watch over our mind and emotions and try to cultivate thoughts and emotions that are of a higher order.

As we purify our lower bodies, we increase the potential for soul contact. We must purify in order that we may discriminate and evolve as our souls would have us evolve. We work to purify ourselves so that we may become worthy vehicles for the Light of soul. The purification process helps refine the matter of our inner bodies and helps us ascend in vibration, releasing resistance and inner congestion that make contact more difficult. This purification can take place through regular meditation and healings and through living a life of right effort and balanced meditation. To purify ourselves we must also put our ideals into practice in our daily lives, striving towards all that is holy and living according to the principles of right human relations.

Right human relations is the practical application of the Divine Principles through which we live life in true spirituality instead of a life of materialism, with its emphasis on, and abuse of, money, power and sex. Right human relations involves both choice and will. When we choose to live according to good and exercise our ability to truly love, seeking truth, harmlessness, justice and liberation of Spirit, we are choosing to live according to the principles of right human relations. We are beginning to embody the seeds of right living when we:

1. think of the consequences before we act;
2. give to others in need without counting the cost;
3. speak our truth in the energy of love;

4. bring forth the energy of forgiveness to our lives and relationships with ourselves and others;
5. work towards the purification of all our inner bodies;
6. work practically to better our thoughts, feelings and actions;
7. give our energy, time and effort for the benefit of Christ's work;
8. do our best to live our dharma; and,
9. manifest our God-given talents, skills and abilities for the betterment of all around us.

When we bring these qualities to group life and effort, we begin to grow the needed roots that will make a solid foundation for humanity's future. Right human relations involves selflessness, sacrifice, understanding, compromise, the comprehension of many and diverse points of view, and surrender to and acceptance of Divine Law. As we move our focus away from a selfish one and cultivate in ourselves an attitude and approach that is selfless, self-sacrificing and geared towards the good of the whole rather than the good of the individual, we align ourselves towards our soul.

It helps to want to consciously align to our soul. We can set the intention through prayer. In doing so we become receptive to the soul's plan and purpose for us, and become more capable of adjusting our nature and lives to suit the Higher Plan. It is through our aspiration to align with soul that we can learn to overcome our lower nature. It is the aspiration which gives the motivation to do the needed work.

> Only intense love of the soul and of all that knowledge of the soul entails will carry the aspirant with sufficient steadiness toward his goal (Bailey, 1987, p. 28).

Finding our purpose

The universe is a mighty and complex system. Understanding our place in it, considering where we have come from, and where we are headed, gives life a new meaning. We have a purpose. To evolve, we need to align to our soul's purpose. The soul's purpose is sometimes referred to as our dharma. Dharma is the performing of tasks or living of the life according to the wishes of the soul. Everyone has a dharma to perform. We also have qualities which we need to develop as part of our evolutionary process and karmic patterns that we need to redeem. Some people are very aware of their life purpose, and many struggle to find it. Sometimes people worry about finding their dharma. It is not always easy to know what our dharma is. The extent to which we know or don't know our dharma can be a karmic condition. It may be that as we try to align to the soul and involve ourselves in the needed spiritual discipline required to live a spiritual life, the understanding of our dharma will be gradually revealed.

Sometimes people are already living their dharma without knowing it. Sometimes, though, a re-adjustment of career and values leads to helping a person to find the right dharma in the physical life. When we live our dharma and come to accept our karmic condition, life becomes a lot more meaningful and an inner joy is radiated. The joy is a higher joy which comes from the soul. It is possible that our personality may not like the dharma in store for it and may express its resistance. This is part of our learning process and, gradually, when the dharma is accepted, the personality will learn just how much the soul is aware of what the personality in fact needs. This understanding may take time to come to, but when it is reached a great degree of liberation of Spirit is felt and we can then just get on with doing it.

If you are trying to find your dharma, try to focus first on living a spiritual life in right human relations. As you do this, your life will turn around and you will slowly attract your dharma to you. You can find hints through meditation and healing and by asking your guardian angel for help. Do not forget to pray. When we ask for that help, help is given. Sometimes we forget to ask. When we ask, we must remember to ask from the purity of our heart and not be asking from the glamours and illusions of what we would like to do or be. Try to ascertain what gifts, skills and abilities you have been given in this life and see how you can put them to use for the benefit of the whole. Try to figure out what skills and abilities you would like to develop, or that you think are needed for you to fulfill your dharma, and allow yourself to have the further education that may be needed.

Try not to worry about finding your dharma. Often that simply distresses you and makes you feel that you are not worthwhile. This alone can be enough to cloud you from what your dharma is. For example, I can remember myself trying to find my dharma - I was concerned as there are only so many hours in a day. Was it painting, acting, teaching, healing, singing, writing songs, being in a partnership, being alone, working for the spiritual cause, working with the public, or being a psychologist? So much choice. When I prayed and meditated and looked in healings, nothing seemed to come and I became confused. Then one day when I was just driving along in my car, heading towards Melbourne to run a class, an angel gave me a message, "Bring Spirit into matter." As I pondered on this I realised how great and expansive those few words were. They included all the things I have written above, provided I was working in those processes to bring Spirit into matter. There were so many things I could do that with, even the cooking and the washing. Suddenly I realised that so many things are a part of the dharma and that there are larger dharmas and smaller ones and that all work together to create the bigger picture. The angel told me more - "Don't be attached to any particular way of bringing Spirit into matter, and be ready to change what you are doing at any moment when the Hierarchy wants it." As I contemplated this I could see the key to not getting caught in glamour or illusion about the dharma: Not to think, "I'll be a great artist or playwright," rather, to realise that I am not here to satisfy myself through my identity, but to serve God and help manifest the Plan in whatever way I can. I felt here I was being asked to trust in that higher Plan and that if I remained open to it, what was expected of me would be revealed as I live my life. If I was simply to follow basic guidelines about living a good life, such as being loving, truthful, honest, harmless, living in right human relations and applying what I know and am learning to living my life, then my life, because of the good principle behind it and the spirit in which it is lived, would, like a tree carefully planted in a garden and nurtured in the right way, sprout seeds for new growth in lives to come. One of the great beauties of reincarnation is that the skills you acquire and the effort put in to build a solid and pure foundation in your life are never wasted. They will stand you in good stead for lifetimes to come.

The Chakras

When reading all of the information available on chakras and all the different healing books that are coming onto the market these days, you might find some contradictory information. I know when I began working with Light and energy I started to get worried when a book would tell me the chakra was a different colour or a different name even. I would think, how can that be, this can't be true then, and get bogged down in the specifics of it. Now I would suggest a different approach. In this chapter I will outline the varying characteristics of each chakra. The basis of the knowledge I will present is the Theosophical view. If this conflicts with something you feel, then just let it sit and see what you prefer to go with. It is like spiritual development itself: when we come to understand some of this knowledge, an unfoldment takes place. We can build on the foundation that we have already. That foundation can then grow. Slowly, we get to know more. As we raise our consciousness, we can start to discriminate about what information feels most correct. The best approach is to try to develop the ability to listen with your heart.

The fullness of the chakras

The chakras are living organisms. Often in healing texts they are presented only in a simple two-dimensional or perhaps three-dimensional way. The chakras are a vortex of energy, vibrating according to the frequency of our Light bodies. They are not something we see in the physical world. Instead they exist at the physical - etheric level and at corresponding inner levels of the astral and mental planes. They are the doorway to the spiritual world. Through them we can gain contact with the inner world and come to know a great deal about ourselves. Through certain chakras such as the sacral, solar plexus and third eye we can gain access to past life memory. Through our heart we can find all our past and gain access to the Hierarchical energies. The world of the chakras seems limitless. As healers, working with spiritual Light and activating the chakras with it, we need to gain knowledge about the chakras so that we can adequately assist the client when things start to happen as a result of this activation. Ananda Tara Shan (1991, p. 2), in *The Last Chakra*, outlines the importance of the chakras:

> The chakras are the keys to the inner worlds, to the knowledge, the Divine knowledge, to your clairvoyant abilities, to the talents you bring into this life. The chakras show the truth; the development of the chakras show exactly how long you have been on Earth, they show your level of understanding, your level of consciousness, your level of initiation. The texture of your chakras, how much your chakras are open, all this shows the truth.

What is a chakra?

Chakra is a Sanskrit word that means wheel. It is the word used to name the force centres, which are points of connection where energies flow from one inner body to another, for example, from the etheric body to the physical, the etheric to the astral, and so forth. There are chakras in each of our inner bodies. The force centres are called chakras because they rotate like wheels. We have many chakras and smaller centres called nadis which play a similar role throughout the body. Here we will deal primarily with the seven main chakras according to the Theosophical system.

Chakras in the etheric and astral bodies correspond closely to one another with a protective web or sheath in-between the levels to ensure that there is not a premature opening up of communication from one plane to another. Although the astral and etheric chakras correspond, they have different functions. In both the astral and etheric bodies the main chakras that correspond closely to one another are given the same names, which are the root, the sacral, the solar plexus, the heart, the throat, the third eye and the crown.

See Table 1 (pp. 108-109) for descriptions of powers that are awakened in each chakra.

Chakras in the etheric double

We will look first at the etheric chakras. In an adult the chakras range from 2-6 inches (5-15 cm) in diameter. Their function is to transmit the fires of energy. They absorb and distribute Prana, the life force, to the etheric and physical body. They also bring the qualities of the corresponding astral centres into physical consciousness.

Chakras in the astral body

Chakras in the astral body are vortices of four dimensions. These chakras extend in different directions from the etheric chakras. The function of the chakra is to awaken a certain response in the particles of the astral body that pass through it, for example, the power of clairvoyant sight or hearing.

Chakras in the mental and causal body

Chakras also exist in the mental and causal bodies, as points of connection at which force flows from one body to another. Apart from this fact, very little is known about the chakras in these bodies.

What are the forces that move through the chakras?

Many forces move through the chakras. Three distinct forces acknowledged by students and researchers in Theosophy are Fohat, prana and kundalini. Fohat is electricity; it comes in the form of physical forces such as light, heat, magnetism, sound and motion. It is a primary force. Prana is a vital force which we need for our health. Kundalini is a force which can spiritualise our inner bodies.

The seven major chakras in the etheric body

In the following descriptions please note that the number of petals given for each chakra represents the petals in a chakra that is fully open. Our level of development determines how many petals can be seen in our chakras. The colours given here are the colours from the etheric chakras. When we look at the chakras on other planes, for example, the astral and mental planes, the colours appear differently. Also people with clairvoyant ability, who see the chakras often, see differently, which accounts for the variation in the literature about the colours.

The root chakra

The first chakra is the root chakra, the Muladhara, located at the base of the spine. The root chakra is generally a "fiery orange red" (Powell, 1987, p. 54) and is associated with the planet Mars. It is connected with the adrenal glands and has four petals. The root chakra is related to instinct, and is the point where Spirit and matter meet. It is our connection to the Earth where we have the will of self-preservation. It also connects with the blood and the skeleton. This chakra is the seat of the money complex, gives us the desire for food, exercise and sleep, and is the seat of the kundalini.

The sacral chakra

The second chakra is located in the sacral centre, which is half way between the root chakra and the navel. It is the Svadhisthana chakra, generally orange and is associated with the planet Mercury. It is linked to the reproductive organs, the glands of the gonads, and has six petals. Through it we get the inspiration to create. This centre is very much responsible for our health and vitality. The sacral chakra contains the desire for sex and the desire for relationship with family and friends, and is also the seat of the sex complex.

The solar plexus

The solar plexus centre is the Manipura chakra. The colour "is a curious blending of several shades of red, though there is also a great deal of green in it" (Leadbeater, 1980, p. 12). It is associated with the Sun. Usually situated about four inches above the navel, the solar plexus chakra is where we digest things that happen to us in life. It is linked with the intestines, and has ten petals. It impels us to develop our ego and identity. The solar plexus chakra is associated with our feelings and the astral energies of desire and touch. It is the seat of the power complex, where the need for power and control over others is evident. It can be developed through selfless service. When purified, the solar plexus chakra energises the whole body.

The heart chakra

The heart chakra is also called the Anahata chakra and is "glowing golden" (Powell, 1987, p. 54). It is usually located around the middle of the chest. The heart chakra is associated with the planet Venus and the thymus gland. It has twelve petals and substantially assists the lungs and the heart. The heart chakra is the seat of balance in the body between the lower and the higher chakras, the three above and three below. It is the chakra used to distribute the Hierarchical energies. Even though it has twelve petals, inside it has a lotus, eight-petalled, called the Ananda Kanda. That is the esoteric heart within the heart, which develops through suffering and unconditional love. Bhakti Yoga or faith is the motivating force. Through the heart we become aware of karma and life actions. It brings that awareness when the desire nature is controlled by the soul, for then the heart comes into action. The only way to open the heart is through devotion, suffering and selfless service. The heart contains all our negative past and present. For this reason it must open slowly, through total commitment and fearlessness. The heart chakra and its development play an important role in the spiritual development of those souls who choose to walk the Way of the Heart, especially as such souls are to become the Children of the Heart in the Age of Maitreya. The main task is to help pave the way for the Lord of Love. As He is the Lord of Love and Compassion, the Master of Hope, the hearts of His children must be prepared for His Great Love and Hope to enter. The hearts of those souls must be cleansed, purified and made ready so that He can come.

The throat chakra

The throat chakra is also called the Vishuddha chakra. It is "violet-blue" (Powell, 1987, p. 54) and is associated with the planet Jupiter and the thyroid gland. Located at the throat at the base of the neck, it has sixteen petals, and is the seat of the higher Creative Intelligence. It is through this chakra that we express ourselves; here communication, written and oral, comes forth. Psychic energies are associated with this chakra as well as clairaudience. It is through this chakra that the lower ones are refined and brought into "akasa," which according to Blavatsky (1990) is "the subtle supersensuous spiritual essence which pervades all space" (p. 13). When this chakra starts to awaken, we get a thirst for knowledge, for truth. It often governs us between the ages of 28 and 35. It is the door to the lower mental world.

The third eye

The third eye, the Ajna centre, is violet or "purplish-blue" (Leadbeater, 1980, p. 13). According to C. W. Leadbeater (1980), in his book *The Chakras*, part of the third eye is also rose-coloured with a good deal of yellow about it. It is located a little below the middle of the forehead, and is ruled by Saturn. Associated with the pituitary gland and with ninety-six petals in the third eye chakra are the male and the female, and the site of our higher clairvoyance and intuition. It is the seat of our wisdom. The third eye is also the point where the Ida, the Pingala, and the Sushumna (three aspects of kundalini) meet when the kundalini rises. It links us to the higher astral and lower mental levels.

The crown chakra

On the top of the head, the crown chakra is our connection to the Divine Plan. It is the thousand-petalled lotus associated with the pineal gland, ruled by the planet Ketu. Its colour is "predominantly violet" and has "a central whirlpool of gleaming white flushed with gold in its heart" (Leadbeater, 1980, p. 15). Its sanskrit term is the Sahasrara chakra. The crown chakra is where we align our will, the personal will, to the Divine Will, where we start to connect with the Divine Self. It links us to our soul and Spirit.

A chart of the chakras

The two charts provide details about the chakras which have been gathered together from a number of sources; these are cited at the top of the Table 1. Table 1 gives a summary of characteristics about the chakras while Figure 1 shows the glands that are affected by the particular chakras.

Table 1 : Summary of characteristics of the chakras

Sources: Ananda Tara Shan, 1991; Bailey, 1984; Johari, 1987; Landsdowne, 1993; Leadbeater, 1980; Powel, 1987, 1992
See References for specific listing of reference source.

Name	Sanskrit term	Ruled by (planet)	Gland	No. of petals	Further descriptions
Crown	Sahasrara	Ketu	Pineal	1,000 petalled lotus (972)	Is the seat of the Guru within. Represents illumination. Radiates Aum or Om. Point of and connection to the Will of God.
Third eye	Ajna	Saturn	Pituitary	96	Knowing, feeling truth, beauty and goodness. Where we experience the state of realisation. Point where Ida, Pingala and Sushumna meet. Soma chakra within Ajna centre, Kahu, 12 petals. Victory over disease, death. Seat of wisdom. Higher clairvoyance and intuition.
Throat	Vishuddha	Jupiter	Thyroid	16	Seat of higher creative intelligence. Expression. Communication. Psychic energy, clairaudience. Lower chakras are refined and brought into akasa (anti-matter). Follow knowledge. Truth, speech. Governs age 28-35.

Heart	Anahata	Venus	Thymus	12	Aids lungs and heart. Seat of balance. Brought into desire action when nature brought into control by Soul. Chakra used to distribute Hierarchical energies. Eight petalled lotus, within it is the Ananda Kanda or the esoteric heart. Develops through suffering. Unconditional love. Bhakti or faith become motivating force.
Solar plexus	Manipura	Sun	Pancreas	10	Impels to develop ego, identity. Asttrakl force, emotion. Desire for touch. Seat of power complex. Can be purified through selfless service.
Sacral	Svadhist	Mercury	Gonads	6	Inspiration to create. Vitality, health. Desire for sex, and relationships with family and friends. Seat of sex complex.
Root	Muladhara	Mars	Adrenals	16	Instinct. Point where spirit and matter meet. Connection to the Earth. Will of self-preservation. Seat of money complex. Food. Exercise. Sleep. Seat of kundalini.

Figure 1. The chakras and the associated glands

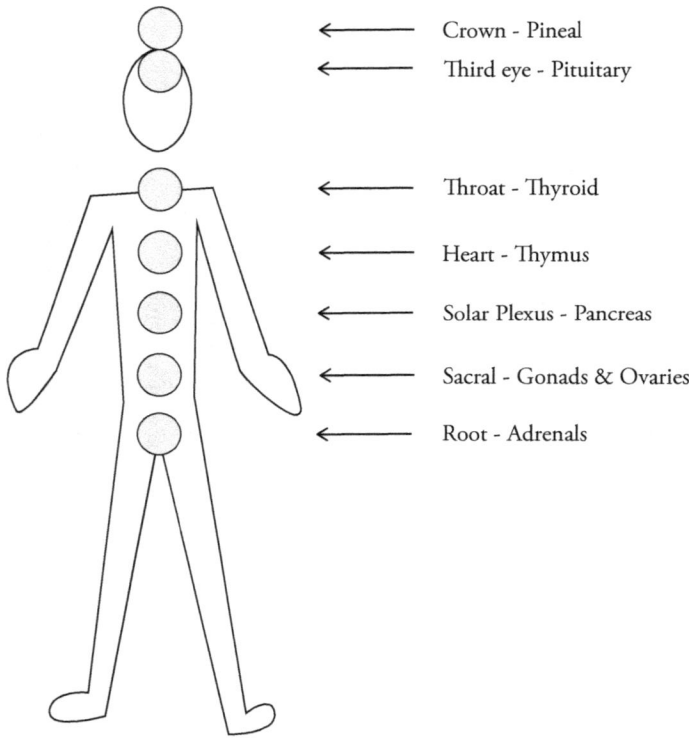

The lower and higher chakras and their condition

The root, sacral and solar plexus chakras are often referred to as the lower chakras and the heart, throat, third eye and crown as the higher chakras. Sometimes when people talk about the lower chakras and the higher chakras, there is a tendency to think that the lower chakras are no good, and to define them as bad. All the chakras are necessary parts of our being that we need to be aware of and work with. Without them we couldn't function, we couldn't be here. The root chakra, for example, is one that links us to our existence on Earth, it links us to our instinct, our survival nature. It is important to be aware of our lower nature, the lower chakras, and what it is in them that we would strive to move away from when we are working towards enlightenment. If we choose spiritual development we need to lift the energies of the lower chakras into a higher frequency, and work with the higher chakras as well.

The lower chakras have a definite purpose. Most of humanity functions through them. Part of what we are here for is to spiritualise our own matter. The chakras have a lot of different energies within them and they need to be spiritualised. A functioning chakra is often open a long time before it becomes spiritualised through the effort of the aspirant or disciple.

Chakras may be described in a number of ways: a *spiritualised* chakra is one where the denser, more negative matter is transmuted, making the chakra more light and positive. An *open* chakra is one where the petals have started to open; the degree of openness is dependant upon the amount of petals that have opened. A *stimulated* or *activated* chakra is one in which the energies within the chakra are stirred into motion, or brought to life, by the Light. This has nothing to do with openness of the chakra. The activated energies can be positive or negative and the person's response to the activation determines the direction in which the energies will continue to move, on the upward spiral or the downward. A *vivified* chakra is one that is enlivened or brightened, usually in a positive way.

Does sensation in the chakras mean they are open?

The chakras constantly transfer energy from the lower to the higher chakras and across the planes. It takes lives to open and awaken the chakras. When awakening happens fully to the heart chakra you become Christed.

> To awaken your heart chakra you must really work for hundreds of lives, unselfish in actions, working from a pure heart and living with spiritual discipline (Ananda Tara Shan, 1991, p.1).

People often think their chakras are awakened and open when they are not. For example, the solar plexus is often confused with the heart as they are very close, and when emotions are stirred for the love of humanity, it is often the large solar plexus which stimulates the heart chakra rather than a developed or awakened heart.

The kundalini

The kundalini is the 'serpent fire' or the creative power which the alchemists use. The word 'kundal' is the Sanskrit word for coil, and it relates to the kundalini as a coiled serpent or a snake that sits in the root chakra. The kundalini sits at the base of the spine and moves upward through the chakras at a time when the progress of spiritual development calls for it to rise. When the kundalini rises in its natural course, it contributes to the further development of the chakras, in particular, their vivification. The kundalini is an energy which may become activated when we start to meditate and purify ourselves and as we begin to heal with the Light and Love of the Holy Spirit. The rising of kundalini usually starts to occur when a person begins to develop the quality of non-attachment to the physical form, and wants to aspire to the higher world. The kundalini can also be activated when people begin to purify themselves and their lifestyles; to think in a more positive way; begin to embody the Theosophical principles of goodwill, justice, and harmlessness; and to live according to the principles of love and truth.

The kundalini can be activated in many ways. Some people will use practices of fasting or cleansing through the throat to activate the kundalini. In the opinion of experts, it is better not to engage in such practices, as damage may occur to the protective webs within the chakras. A better way to faster development that fits more readily with western life is to concentrate on and bring in a particular spiritual discipline to purify our life, through balanced living and regular meditation. There is also the need to bring discipline into our emotional life and bring forth the development of spiritual will. This approach does not focus directly on the chakras. Rather, it is a way of trying to re-educate ourself to look at the whole being in a new way. In that way, when imbalances come up, which they can do, they can be dealt with in the wholeness of the life itself.

Many people start upon the spiritual path very much unaware of changes that will occur in them as spiritual development progresses. When the kundalini rises up, a lot of energies are stirred up in its path. When it starts to rise through the spinning vibration of the chakras, the serpent fire starts to come up through them, stirring all that sits in the chakra and is lying dormant. When the chakras are vivified by the kundalini, the kundalini can create physical illness, spiritual vision, heat, cold, hallucinations, memory of the past, and awareness that is not our normal consciousness. The energies which are awakened can be both negative and positive. The kundalini is often called the creative fire, and it is a fire energy. Because of that, it can burn and destroy or it can burn and create. When it moves, the kundalini activates each chakra and brings to consciousness everything in the chakra. This creative energy rises when the energy turns inward and upward to higher levels. It moves from sexual energy to creative energy, from emotional response to love and from the energy of the mind to the energy of the Spirit. The energy is transmuted as it rises. Rather than repressing desires and passions, one can lift and transmute these energies to become aligned with the Divinity. The Divine fire of creation gradually burns all earthly dross out of our nature until the effect of the great transmutation is felt and nothing but pure Spirit remains.

When a person goes through the rising of the kundalini, the sexual energy may be stimulated. If a person wants to benefit from the kundalini energy, it is important not to let that energy just stay in the sexual realm but rather to transform it to creative energy. When we choose to live in a balanced way and begin to follow a balanced spiritual discipline, the energy of kundalini can be used to help purify the emotions and the mind and also link us with the spiritual realms. This process will happen naturally, with regular healings and a spiritual lifestyle. If we play with the kundalini however, for example, by trying to speed up its development, it is like playing with fire. Etheric webs exist between the chakras. As the kundalini rises up, it pierces the webs and activates the chakras, causing them to open. Those webs are there to stop the chakras from producing or transferring more energies than we have wisdom to deal with. If the web is pierced prematurely or burns too much in the fire, we become imbalanced and unable to control the influx of denser matter and negative input from the shadow. The shadow then is activated. Instead of being vivified in a positive way, leading to the spiritualisation of the chakras and the strengthening of our virtues, the chakras come to life in a negative way and our negative qualities are strengthened. In contrast, when the kundalini rises in its natural way, we are able to cope with the imbalances that occur as a consequence through healing, meditation and/or counselling.

The psychological processes connected to the rising of the kundalini

When we start to develop spiritually, we start to be aware that some of the negative aspects of ourselves, before hidden, become more obvious - parts we would rather not see. The Light stimulates our growth, which is stimulated from the soul. The Light reveals to us things that we would rather not know about ourselves, and we have to deal with them. For example, it may reveal the anger we have towards other people and ourselves, the fears, the jealousy, the envy, the greed, the guilt and the resentment. We might then think, "I don't really like this spiritual path, I'm going to stop meditating, I'm going to go away, and maybe have another go in a few years." This can happen to people who feel unable to deal with what comes up from within them. Often what comes up is projected onto whatever it was that stimulated them. It could be a healing we have had, or a weekend course we did, and we think, "that wasn't a good workshop" or "that wasn't a good healing system." It is often our inability to realise that we have to face this darkness in ourselves that makes us project onto others.

We all have darkness. When we find the negative energies, when we meet the jealousy, the fear and the envy, the ambition and the greed, we realise that those negative aspects are there and we can do something to purify them. Usually we see them because the kundalini fire is rising up and brings them to our attention. As we deal with them, the kundalini can keep moving through the chakras, and we can come to a form of enlightenment, truly embodying the principles of truth, goodwill, love and honesty. It is very easy for us, instead, to prefer not to deal with what is stirred up, to try to deceive ourselves about it and to push it down because we feel it is a bit too much to look at.

Staying in balance

It is very difficult to remain balanced when the kundalini is rising up. The degree of the imbalance is what becomes important. If we are educated enough and aware, then we can say, "OK, I'm going to go through some things on this path." When they happen, we then do not get the fright of our lives and run. We become aware and we think, "Oh, I'm feeling fear." We talk to someone about it, work with it in healing or counselling, or maybe talk to a good friend and begin to understand that these things are quite normal. Sometimes we can work through one energy, such as fear, and find another one arises very suddenly, such as guilt. We may also connect to such energies that are within us from other lifetimes. If we start to talk about our experiences and patterns and acknowledge them, we will often find that other people have the same processes and feelings going on, too, in their own way. We can relax with it, and then we can keep going. If we endeavour to lead a pure life with pure thoughts and feelings, we manage the opening of the chakras. If not, disruption occurs in the life and we become disordered.

Misuse of the Holy Spirit

When the kundalini is activated, perhaps through the healing Light of the Holy Spirit, as mentioned, the sexual energies may be activated. Because of humanity's attachment to the desire nature, the sexual energies have often been abused. The misconception has been to see sex as a gratification of the lust of the moment and thus to turn the creative energy outward and downward instead of inward and upward. The outward and downward motion of the kundalini energies serves only to strengthen our shadow nature and heighten the negative energies stored within the chakras. The inward and upward path links us to Spirit.

The myth of nirvana

Some New Age magazines have advertisements about creating happiness and nirvana (bliss). If people are expecting that from the spiritual path and they do not find it, they often become disappointed and disillusioned. It may take a lot to become motivated again. It is important to be aware that the path of spiritual development is not always a rosy one, although it can be. The kinds of energies that we might meet along the way include rebellion, resentment, guilt, fear and anger. The kundalini will, on its path, awaken those things for us to work with in life. The work may not be pleasant. The process of spiritual development is not a matter of perfection at this stage, even though that may be what we strive towards. More accurately it is a process involving the awareness of wholeness, of accepting the negative self that is there as well as acknowledging the Light within us.

Finding a loving approach

When we find aspects in ourselves that we do not like, it is not a matter of claiming that these aspects are purely a negative entity and saying, "I have to get rid of them, I have to send in the violet Light! Good, they're gone!" The energy of love and compassion is missing in such an approach. That may be an old way in which we have worked as healers in the past. Now we need to embody the understanding and compassion that gives love and higher knowing, through the Ancient Wisdom, to the little entity that we are working with. We bring it into the Light, hear its story, and understand what it is. Sometimes it has some good solutions or advice for us. Other times we see its qualities of ridiculousness or ignorance. As we give it love, compassion, and acceptance, we find that we don't need to let ourselves be controlled by it. We send it Light. We do it in a way that we would do with other people, or with ourselves. The idea of self-love becomes very important as well. We start to give compassion to ourselves and to other people, and develop the way of wholeness in all things. Then when the shadow aspect rises, as we start spiritual development, it can be dealt with and managed, through love and understanding, enabling the negative to be controlled in such a way that we can keep on walking forward.

Spiritual and psychological development go hand in hand

What I have seen happen often on the spiritual path is that the shadow aspect rises up, and if a person is of the belief that this could not happen if the path were a spiritual one, the shock is sometimes great enough to make the person leave the path altogether. Hopefully, this abandonment of the path will happen only for a time and the person will soon wake up to the truth. If we are aware that this shadow aspect is part of what will come on the path, we can take a different approach. We cannot just meditate and then fail to take care of our emotional body and all of the psychological problems we have in life as well. Meditation and dealing with emotional and other challenges go hand in hand. We have to deal with our issues as we are going along, so we can walk along as a whole person. If we try to go along without doing this, eventually the pull between the parts becomes too great and the shadow usually wins out. One part is aspiring to Light and one part is resisting and rebelling. Eventually this resisting part says "No!" and up it comes and a big explosion and crisis in life occurs. The person has to stop, has to take stock. We can prevent that kind of battle and the need for a big break if we allow our spiritual development to happen in a balanced way.

How does the state of the chakras affect our health?

Negative thoughts and emotions can influence our state of harmony and affect the flow of energy through the chakras. Negative environments where sound or energies are jarring can also diminish our harmonic state. If we ignore this negative effect upon the chakras or allow it to accumulate, our life flow becomes affected and we then become more susceptible to illness. The negative energy lodges itself in the etheric body and within the chakras. If we do not clear away the build-up of energy, it can move through to and affect the physical body. In Figure 2 we see how the life force energies affect the inner bodies, the chakras, and then move into the system of the physical body.

Figure 2: The energy flow

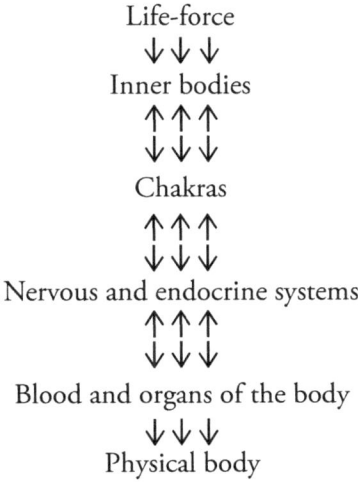

In Figure 3 we see how negative energies from the mental or emotional planes pass through the inner bodies and interfere with the flow of energy into the physical. The imbalance that occurs as a result leads to a build-up of negative energy in the physical which manifests as illness or disease.

Figure 3: Blockage to the energy flow

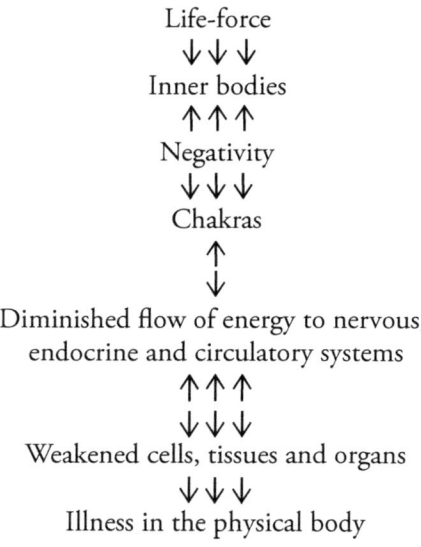

Healing and the chakras

Through the process of our daily life, we accumulate an energy debris in the chakras which is called 'congestion.' There are methods of cleansing and healing which can help us to rid our auric fields of this congestion and strengthen our physical, emotional, mental and spiritual states of harmony. Many techniques are available to assist us in cleansing, balancing and strengthening our energies. A number of these work through directed use of Light, sound, music and voice. For example, chanting the sound of 'Om' into each chakra allows the vibration of the sound to cleanse the chakra.

As we develop the ability to discriminate between energies, recognising what will raise and what will lower our vibration, we can also learn to use specific techniques to keep our energies vibrant and strong. Such healing is carried out through the chakras. Healing the chakras can help to liberate the creative energy in our nature from its entanglement with our lower nature and the world of senses, and rise to the world of spirit. Through the knowledge of the chakras it is possible to come to know where particular energies are stored that need release. For example, if a person comes to you with a great degree of fear that stems from childhood and past-life traumatic experiences, it is likely that the solar plexus will need healing (it is in the solar plexus that fear is often stored). A healer, through concentration and intent, can direct the healing energies to a particular chakra to alleviate the source of the distress. Healing can be sent to specific areas, and it can also be sent more generally into the aura of a person to assist the healing of that person's overall well-being and disposition.

The chakras have connections to each other, and knowledge of these connections can help the healer determine the appropriate pathways for healing. Root chakra energy is transmuted by moving the energy to the crown centre. Sacral chakra energy is transmuted when it moves to the throat. Solar plexus energy is transmuted when it moves to the third eye. When we are healing, it is possible to bring the energies up, if we are aware of the links among the chakras. We can know where to place our hands to bring the energy from one chakra to another. In order for the higher chakras to be cleansed, the lower chakras must first be cleansed. For example, if the solar plexus is not cleansed, the third eye will not be cleansed; to cleanse the throat, the sacral chakra must first be cleansed. This lifts the vibration of the client and helps transmute, for example, grief to joy, anger to compassion, fear to love, guilt to innocence, egoistic attitudes to humility, low self-esteem to balanced pride, rebellion to obedience and true authority. The client can then learn and implement as an active process the principles of good living, and begin to live a life of balance according to the Theosophical principles. Through healing and meditation, the chakras are stimulated. They start to cleanse, purify and open. As they open, they admit us to the inner worlds.

A meditation to help balance the chakras

The following is a meditation which you could do daily to help balance the chakras or simply when you feel the need. You may wish to play some soft, gentle music that is conducive to relaxation in the background and find a comfortable position where you will not be disturbed.

Go within yourself. Place your hands relaxed on your lap. Be aware of your spinal column, full of white Light, like a beam of white Light. Feel the vibration of Light as the Light moves up and down the spine. Be aware that you can move your awareness up and down the spinal column and stop at any chakra you choose. Take your awareness now down to the root chakra at the base of the spine. Place your hands at that centre. Visualise now that centre being filled with red Light. (If you have trouble visualising, imagine something of that colour.) Send the red colour into the root chakra. Visualise a beautiful red rose sitting in it. Allow that rose to slowly close its petals until it forms a bud. Chant the word Om into the chakra. Om. See that chakra now filled with white Light, it is protected in that white Light.

Move your awareness to the sacral centre by moving your hands also to that centre. See this centre being filled with orange Light. It is the centre for health and vitality. Visualise an orange flower, perhaps a rose or whatever other flower you like. You see the rose or the flower, sitting in it and gently closing into a bud. Chant Om into the chakra now. See the chakra filled with white Light, increasing the line of protection from the root chakra to the sacral centre.

Now move your hands to the solar plexus centre and see the solar plexus filled with yellow Light. Visualise a golden flower. See that flower wide open, then gradually closing itself into a bud. Feel how your emotions are calmed and soothed in that process, in the waves of golden Light. Let them move. And as the flower closes to a bud, see the white Light enter into the chakra, increasing the link between the root, the sacral and the solar plexus, creating a protection of the lower three chakras. With awareness, first chant Om into the solar plexus. Om.

Bring your hands to the heart centre, see the colours pink and green enter into the heart. Visualise the flower, perhaps a pink rose, very open, gradually closing into a bud. See the green of the stem and the leaves, entering into the energy of the heart, feeling the love, the pink Light, the Light of unconditional love. As the flower closes to a bud, see the white Light enter, and chant Om into that centre. Om.

Moving to the throat, see the throat filled with blue Light, see the throat filled with a blue flower in its centre. Bring in the blue Light, sending healing Light of truth into the throat. As the blue flower closes into a bud, the white Light enters and sound the word Om. Om.

Your awareness lifts once again to the third eye centre. Place your hands on the third eye centre, seeing it filled with violet Light, violet flowers, the violet Light transmuting negativity of thought, creating positivity. Visualise the violet flowers closing into buds. Chant the word Om into the chakra. Om. The white Light pours in now, connecting all the chakras.

Move your awareness to the crown centre where we visualise a white twelve pointed lotus. This white lotus is your connection to God. Allow the petals to fold over but not completely, keeping still your connection with the Divine, aligning your personal will with the Will of the Divine. Chant this last Om. Allow it to come in fullness, a celebration to the connection to the Divine Light. Let it come from your heart, connect with the Star of Light above your head. Om. Open up your hands as if you are a lotus now sitting in the chair, ready for Divine inspiration in your life. The white Light is all around you, pure, clean, brilliant white Light. Place your hands now in front of your heart in gratitude for the healing and cleansing received. Slowly and gently let yourself return to daily consciousness.

Alchemy seen through the chakras

The story 'Ahimsa' on the following page is an example of the healing process of alchemy, or transmutation through symbolism. The healing takes place through the chakras. In the story, a negative quality within needs to be transmuted and released. When that happens to us generally the darkness begins to come up and we become aware of it. We then need to identify what actually needs to be transmuted and call on the Light for help. As the Light does its work we see the changing of the symbols. As we decide to make change and bring in the energy of will, the Light can better work to help us. The symbols given bring messages of Light. In the Ahimsa story there are a lot of symbols - blue butterflies, black snakes and blue snakes with a golden eye, the phoenix, the man in the purple cape and Mother Mary. These symbols are on the inner planes. We may see them in meditation; they can be symbols to guide us to understanding where we are and understanding our inner nature.

The symbols, what they are and their placement in the chakras, give an indication of what healing has occurred and to what degree the transmutation has taken place. In this story the experience is both visual and on a feeling level. Sometimes it is only one of these senses in action that assists us, sometimes more. The revelations and changes in consciousness that come from such a healing do a great deal to help us change, and to understand the change that has taken place in a way that affects us, not only intellectually, as a concept, but integrally, all through our being. The knowledge given becomes a wisdom, a knowing that simply is. When we are prepared to confront these not so pleasant aspects of ourselves that are stirred up, sometimes by the rising of the kundalini, many gifts of wisdom are bestowed and we move further toward enlightenment.

Through practice and spiritual discipline we can develop our senses of seeing, feeling, sensing and knowing. If we take the time and effort to do that, the rewards are an inner life that we come to know and love, that can help guide us with love and compassion as we tread the Path to Perfection.

Ahimsa (harmlessness)

"What does motivate you?" she asked.

The question in itself was quite confronting. I never seem to stop, always busy, always having no time. I was aware of the voices in my own consciousness constantly telling me to keep going. Why don't you take a look? I looked within. On the one hand, I could see that there was a drive within me to help others that was pure of heart and motive, in an effort to give to others without counting the cost for the pure Love of humanity. On the other, there was something not right, something seething, and I knew there would be no peace until I could identify and make tangible the uneasiness I felt.

I went within and became aware of a fat, juicy gold-and-black snake. I really didn't want to know about it, but there it was and I was writhing underneath it. It seemed there was no escape.

"What are you?" *I asked.*

"I am ambition seething, you have to acknowledge that I am here."

It seemed awesome - it was so big, so fat, and so long.

"I don't think I can deal with you on my own; I need help," *and I felt myself pray to God.*

A man appeared in a purple cape.

"I am a snake charmer," *he said.* "I can help."

I could see that he was playing the flute and had what seemed like hundreds of snakes under his control. I knew if anyone could help me, he could. I looked at the gold-and-black snake once more. It didn't seem quite as fat and it had stretched out to one long shape.

"I have been built up over a long time," *the snake said,* "from Egypt, Atlantis, Lemuria and Sirius."

I asked the man in the purple cape, "What can I do with it?"

He said, "Be with it awhile, acknowledge it and when you truly feel you wish to change it, call on me again."

I sat with it and I prayed within for help, and within minutes I could feel it moving within me and coming up through my throat and I could feel the pressure it was putting on my chest.

"You put a pressure on yourself to perform and don't give yourself time to simply be."

I could feel myself beginning to choke with the ambition in my throat centre. I knew the man in the cape was helping me, and he was using an alchemical process to transmute this quality within me. Within seconds, the snake came out of my neck, and wrapped itself around my throat. It turned blue and had a golden eye. It felt cold, clammy and I wasn't sure that I liked it sitting there. I told it so.

"Some people don't like me," it said, "but I am truth and I need expression. People experience me as cold when they don't want to know about me, others live in fear that I will bite; but if you just sit with me awhile, you will get used to me and you will find that I am harmless." "All right," I said, "just for a little while."

A vision came of a time in India when I had been visiting the Taj Mahal. Outside the hotel was a snake charmer who had snakes from which the poisons had been extracted that were used as a tourist attraction. For five rupees you could sit the snake around your neck. It had taken all my courage but I did it.

"Remember," the snake said, "how the fear left you once you were prepared to let it embrace you. The more you are prepared now to speak your truth, the more you will live your truth and not be so influenced by your ambitions and fears. Watch, I have something to show you."

The man in the cape re-appeared and held up a light and shone it upon an aspect of my past which brought tears to my eyes. It was Avalon and I could see my training as a priestess. I could see Morgaine. There were many blue snakes, and the way I felt about them was beginning to change, for I was touching upon the memory of their usefulness and purpose. They were like an army of protection bringing truth of Spirit to the Earth, and they were used when ambition, greed, power and pride got out of hand, bringing balance, and a reminder of what is good. They were not snakes but serpents of wisdom, and their golden eyes, alert and prepared, were the gateway to the understanding of the soul.

"There is a part of you that is being re-awakened; it is the wisdom, the mastery of lower energies. Come with me and I will show you more."

Mother Mary came forward and lifted me up in her arms. I knew She was protecting me. I could see clouds around me. We were in heaven. She lifted one arm and I could see there were many blue serpents in the clouds, alert and prepared.

"Why do you show me this?" I asked.
"Because I want you to see that you are more protected than you know and that the higher forces of Light and Love are always ready to protect one who is prepared to live in truth. Trust them, trust us."

The serpents were the Mother's army and their job was to protect her. The quality of devotion and loyalty was paramount in them.
Any sense of fear or ambition that I had was being burned away in this Light, and a deep inner trust in the forces of Light was present. I became aware again of the blue snake wrapped around my throat. It began to feel like a very comfortable blue silk scarf. Hundreds of blue butterflies flew from my throat centre. I began to sense that Truth is harmless and simply adds beauty to the world.

I could see the ground again, the Earth. There was a fire and beside it was the shell of the snake skin that had been my ambition. It was clear that a ceremony had been performed. The ground was prepared and the ashes were ready for the Phoenix to fly.

The Aura and Its Colours

Let us consider the human aura. What is it? How does it manifest? How does it appear? What is its purpose? How can we learn to see and feel the aura? How can we recognise the meaning of the colours in their different combinations and hues? What does our aura tell us about ourselves, our moods, qualities and development? What does the aura reveal about personality types? What are the effects of drugs upon the aura? What happens to the aura during the process of healing? How do knowledge of and insights into the aura assist us in our healing work? How can we read the aura? How can we cleanse it? How can we create a healthy aura? What are the effects of different colours in our environment?

What is the aura?

In today's age many people are becoming aware that human beings have an aura that is like a cloud around them, that some people who are clairvoyant can see or that kirlian photography cameras can photograph. What is this cloud we speak of? What is the aura and what is its purpose?

According to the Macquarie dictionary an aura is "a subtle emanation proceeding from a body and surrounding it as an atmosphere; the motion of the air at an electrified point" (p. 151).

H.P. Blavatsky was a great writer and theosophist who began the Theosophical Society in the late nineteenth century. In *The Theosophical Glossary* Blavatsky (1990, p. 44) defines an aura as a subtle invisible essence or fluid that emanates from human and animal bodies and even things. It is a psychic effluvium (a slight or invisible exhalation or vapour) partaking of both the mind and the body, as it is the electro-vital, and at the same time an electro-mental aura.

In H.P. Blavatsky's definition we see that the aura is a "subtle invisible essence or fluid" made up of charged particles that emanate from both the mind and the body.

Gottfried De Purucker was a theosophist who wrote a number of books clarifying many of the basic theosophical principles. In *Fundamentals of the Esoteric Philosophy* (1979), De Purucker suggests that the higher forces of Light and consciousness are poured forth into human beings to give us life. The splendour that we see as a result of this process is the aura.

We can see and feel the aura as radiations of energy that we may hear as music or see as light and colour. Human beings, animals, plants and objects have auras. Leadbeater was a theosophist who was a prolific writer known and respected for his clairvoyant abilities and research. In *The Inner Life*, Leadbeater (1996, p. 309) points out that

> The Earth has an aura; what we see of the Sun is its aura; plants have an aura; and even inanimate objects such as books have an aura.

We are a spark of God, of Divine life. Our aura is that which we pour out from within; it is the emanations we send outwards from within us. We clothe ourselves in these emanations (sheaths of vitality). It is the process of 'sending out from within' that is responsible for the creation of our individuality. The emanations which are sent out from within us are evident to those who can see with the inner eye as radiations of colour. The human soul is a being of Light. As the light shines through us, the qualities and characteristics which we have that make us the individuals we are take on particular colours. These colours shine forth for all to see. Each power and quality shines out in its colour. Each of these colours is expressive of a quality of character, a power and an attribute. The aura radiates and shines as we develop higher qualities, such as loyalty and compassion. As we manifest lower qualities, such as resentment and annoyance, it is more dull and the colours become heavy and murky. Our auras change as do the expressions of our faces. We produce these changes by thought. Harmonious thoughts and feelings harmonise, heal, help, and expand our consciousness. We affect our aura by such thoughts in a positive way. Colours become brighter and clearer. Harmful or negative thoughts make the aura murky and dark, the colours disappear. The aura is the means by which we record impressions of the world. It provides us with the sensitivity to monitor all that is going on around us.

The aura is generally seen as being composed of three auras. These are the health aura (physical-etheric), the astral aura (emotional) and the mental aura. However, the soul also has an aura. It is just that very few people on this Earth are soul-clairvoyant and it is generally therefore not mentioned. Each of the auras radiate and emanate colour, light and vibration in all directions.

Annie Besant (1990, p. 85), in *Man and His Bodies*, describes the human aura, in its fullest sense:

> It is the man himself, manifest at once on the four planes of consciousness, and according to its development is his power of functioning on each; it is the aggregate of his bodies, of his vehicles of consciousness; in a phrase it is the form aspect of man. It is thus that we should regard it and not as a mere ring or cloud surrounding him.

The four planes of consciousness to which Besant is referring are the planes of matter where our physical, astral, mental and spiritual bodies exist. In her definition she suggests we see the aura as the form aspect of a person which reveals the development of the physical, astral, mental and spiritual bodies and not merely as a ring or cloud surrounding that person. We clothe our consciousness with matter from the planes of nature. Our consciousness becomes clothed with matter from the mental, astral and physical planes to form vehicles of awareness and action in which the soul dwells. It is through our mental, astral and physical-etheric bodies that we experience life. To understand about the inner bodies more fully refer to the chapter: *The Human Structure*.

How does the aura appear?

In *The Inner Life* C. W. Leadbeater (1996, p. 334) points out that "ninety-nine per cent of the matter of a human aura is within the periphery of the physical body." He also tells us that "the aura of an ordinary man is capable of a certain amount of temporary expansion," and "extends about eighteen inches on each side of the body" (p. 332). When we look at the aura, the physical body appears as a dense form in the centre of the other bodies as the smallest of the bodies. The other bodies permeate it and extend beyond the outline of the physical body. The physical-etheric aura surrounds the outline of the physical body approximately two to five centimetres from the surface of the physical body. When a person's health is vital, this aura looks elastic and radiant. It is generally white, sometimes with a hint of blue or violet. When the health is low the physical-etheric aura looks limp, sometimes it takes on a grey-like colour. If you imagine how a flower looks when it has had no water for a while you get a sense of the limpness to which I am referring. When the water is given, the flower picks up again. This parallels the physical-etheric aura returning to health.

The astral body represents the desire nature and emotions of a person. It differs in fineness and colour according to the grossness or refinement of our emotions. The astral aura is the part of the astral body that extends like a cloud beyond the physical body (the astral body also permeates the physical). In most human beings the astral aura is by far the largest and most dominant.

The mental aura is usually quite small. In *Man Visible and Invisible*, C. W. Leadbeater (1987) suggests that the mental aura only begins to alter in a disciple (one who has committed him or herself to Christ's work) when the disciple consciously works at his or her development or begins to become more mentally polarised. According to Annie Besant (1990, p. 86) the mental aura differs in colouring "according to the mental and moral type."

In an average person we cannot see the soul aura very clearly. The colours of the soul aura are generally not as clear as the colours we may find on the astral levels. However, in the case of an initiate or adept (the more advanced souls on the Path), the colours of the soul aura are bright, luminous and radiant, beyond the colours that we are capable of imagining.

Seeing and feeling the aura

We can develop the capacity to see and to feel the auras. We can also become aware of the auras without seeing them. It is the physical-etheric and astral auras that we are able to become aware of in this way. The varieties of colours that we see in the aura are within the astral aura. As was noted earlier, the physical-etheric aura is white although it can be blue or violet. The vast majority of people who can see auras (clairvoyants) have astral clairvoyance and often do not see on other levels. It is very rare to find a soul clairvoyant. Clairvoyants need to recognise this limitation in their readings, as do healers in their healing work. We must learn also to let the colours speak, rather than impose our framework on the aura of the client. If we can do this, relax, and come from the heart, we can be helpful. The colours to be concentrated on are the more permanent ones, not the ones associated with mood. It helps if the client and the clairvoyant or the healer are relaxed and in a receptive state. In the case of a clairvoyant, this makes for a more accurate impression of the true character and abilities of the individual. Clients are not necessarily conscious of the character and abilities evident in their aura. As they come to know themselves these qualities can become more conscious. It is therefore possible for the aura reading to give a different picture of the person than the way the person sees him or herself. In the case of the healer, a more accurate diagnosis can be made if the healer relaxes, as the healer can then remain sensitive to the issues at play within the client.

When we are healing we may not see colour, however, we may still feel the aura with the palms of our hands when we move them over the top of the person's head. Gaining a sense of the aura by feel or inner sight is of enormous assistance to the healer to be able to correctly diagnose the kind of help a client needs. Understanding of the aura is as essential to the healer as paint and canvas are to the artist. When there is harmony the aura can be as beautiful as a rainbow. We see the aura most readily around the head, or other extremities of the body such as the hands and feet. To see the aura we have to "un-focus" our eyes from the physical world, as if we are looking beyond or through the person. We sense the aura best when we relax, and have a pure motive and open heart. Gradually, confidence comes with practice and slowly the colours become brighter to the beholder.

To feel the aura we can use our palms and sense through the chakras there. When we develop this sensitivity through feeling, we are developing "clairsentience," which is the ability to feel what is happening at deep levels in another. This sensitivity is developed in healers and clairvoyants alike to help bring empathy with others. It is also a way of receiving information needed to assist the healing process. We can sense the aura through our chakras as we develop and practice. It is easiest to begin by stroking the etheric aura that sits out from the physical body. We can tune into the aura by passing our hands over about four to eight inches from the person's head and body, with our palms down and hands held relaxed. Often in healing work this subtle and gentle approach is of great benefit. If a healer places his or hands on the physical body to sense the aura it can be disturbing to the client, and can even feel like an invasion. If the healer tunes in to the aura by sensing on the perimeter of the aura itself, the client experiences a gentle and soothing inner touch. This gives the person a gentle and loving reminder that he or she is more than the physical body, and that in the inner worlds there is the knowing that he or she is not alone. Sherwood (1994), in *The Art of Spiritual Healing*, suggests that by staying alert to sensations in our palms and skimming the surface of the aura, not entering into it at this point, we can discern more accurate impressions. Over time we learn to discern subtle distinctions and learn what they mean.

Sometimes when we feel the aura we may sense a concentrated energy or congestion of energy that may indicate the need for smoothing out or release. Other times we may notice a vacuum of energy which may indicate that healing Light is needed here, as is balancing between the chakras. There may also be a sense of heat, or an electric feeling or a coolness. When trying to ascertain what these may mean the healer needs to tune in to the individual concerned. We may receive more accurate impressions through discussion with the client before and after tuning in to the inner bodies. We may need to transmute congested energy. Transmutation is the process of transforming a low vibrating energy or matter to a more highly vibrating energy or matter, for example, resentment into forgiveness, anger into acceptance and love. This takes place through the chakras in healing. Through healing and meditation, we can enter into the aura to facilitate healing. We stimulate the chakras. They start to cleanse, purify and open. As they open, they admit us to the inner worlds. For a more detailed understanding of the chakras and their functions see chapter: *The Chakras*.

What is the purpose of the aura?

It is through our auras that the Masters (great Beings of Light who are well ahead of us on the Lighted Path) are able to know our success or failure. It is not so much through our daily actions, but through our auras that we reveal our true nature. To assess our development the Masters may not be looking at our actual actions, but rather at the aura and the effects in the aura of those actions.

It is the Light of the soul and the condition of the aura that determine where we are on the evolutionary path. As we develop along the evolutionary path, the aura and the qualifications within it, which are the traits, character and qualities that it exudes, increase in size, number and quality. If we wish to advance on the Path, we find that:

> the increased size of the aura is a pre-requisite for initiation, and the qualifications should be visible in it. The aura of a Buddha is said in the books to be three miles in radius....It naturally increases with each initiation (Leadbeater, 1996, p. 335).

In this quote from *The Inner Life* Leadbeater is telling us that as a person advances on the spiritual path the person will develop a larger aura with the needed qualifications in it. However, the sphere of radiation of the aura alone does not indicate a more developed soul. An aura can become large because of intense emotion and that is not a sign of spiritual development. For example, a highly emotional person working through an uncontrolled, over-developed solar plexus may have a larger sphere of radiation than another person who is not emotional.

The colours and their meaning

Table 2 (pp. 140-145) shows the colours of the auras and their meaning. If we consider the number of colours, their shades and mixtures of those shades, we begin to see how many different auras there are on Earth. By seeing the collective colours, for example, the groups of red and blue, with their many variations, we begin to see what spiritual development is, how it can be achieved and how beautiful the effect in the aura when it is achieved. We can move from the murkiness of greys and browns, connected with fear and selfishness, to the beautiful hues of violet and pink, by developing good qualities and virtues and by living a holy and sanctified life.

We have mixed emotions. Colours are also mixed. In reading the full meaning of colour we need to consider:

1. The many combinations and modifications of the colours.
2. The general brilliance of the astral body.
3. The definiteness of its outline.
4. The brightness of the chakras.
5. The luminosity of the bodies.
6. The size of the bodies.

The motive for looking into auras or reading another's aura needs to be checked. We must remember that we look through our own aura. It is not for us to judge people.

The position of the colours depends upon the density of the respective grades of matter. That is why the blues and violets - spiritual aspiration and devotion - tend toward the head area and above, the lower matter of qualities such as selfishness and jealousy sit in the lower areas. Each quality, expressed as a colour, has its own special type of astral matter. Selfish qualities, for example, express themselves in coarser matter, while unselfish qualities come through finer matter.

> The yellow of intellect, the rose of affection, and the blue of devotion are always found in the upper part of the astral body; the colours of selfishness, avarice, deceit and hatred are in the lower part; the mass of sensual feeling floats usually between the two (Hodson, 1981, p. 61).

Even when we know the general meaning of the colours we cannot judge a person by what we see. To read the colours we need to let the colours speak to us. There can be many reasons for the varying hues, combinations of colours and virtues.

> The British Colour Council has found 1,400 shades of blue, 1,000 shades of red, over 1,400 browns, over 880 greens, 550 oranges, 360 shades of violet, and more than 12 shades of white (Sherwood, 1994, p. 104).

Generally, more colours in the aura suggest more advancement of the person. Initiates, for example, have several colours, an average person two or three depending on their level of spiritual development. Some may have one or two and be dull and heavy with predisposition toward anxiety or depression. As we develop, the distinctions between the colours are more clear and the colours become brighter.

The composition of the colours varies with each individual through texture, shade, size, shape, vitality and brilliance of the aura. Through the aura we can tell about a person's disposition, health, character and emotional condition. The colours and their meaning that appear in Table 2 are selected from well-known authors and clairvoyants in this field. For each colour the source of the information about the meaning of the colour is referenced. Charles Leadbeater was a theosophist noted for the reliability of his clairvoyance on the astral and lower mental levels. Geoffrey Hodson was a well-known theosophist and Sherwood is a spiritual healer and teacher. Some of the information is from my observations.

Table 2 gives a clear indication of the general agreement among clairvoyants, healers and theosophists as to the meaning of the colours in the aura. An aura reader needs to pay particular attention to the shade and characteristics of a colour and to let the colour speak for itself. Though these generalities do exist, it is important that the truth of the colour be able to come forward with its own individual flavour, as it is truly representative of the person concerned. This can only be done by surrendering of the knowledge and allowing the colour to reveal its true meaning through the intuitive or sensory faculties. The knowledge gives something that can be gone back to for assistance once this process has taken place.

Table 2. The colours and their meanings

Colour	Meaning
Black	Black nearly always indicates darkness. "Hatred, malice, passionate anger" (Leadbeater, 1987, p. 66). According to Sherwood (1994), the only exception to its meaning is when the black appears in a narrow band often seen between the physical body and the etheric aura (what we call the physical aura). "When streaks of black are seen within an otherwise normal aura, the effect of the streaks is unfortunate, since they neutralise the good aspects in the aura" (Sherwood, 1994, p. 108). Strong red and black in the aura show the work of darkness. Black is not always negative, however. There can be two blacks in the aura. Pluto is a violet black which is a spiritual shade. The other black, which is purely black, is the left hand path black. Traces always remain in the aura if someone has worked for the left hand path. These remain until the fifth initiation when the soul becomes an adept (this is a very advanced stage of development).
Red	Red in its positive form indicates a groundedness. It can give a physical strength and is energising. Red in its negative form indicates anger, rebelliousness, malice, destructiveness and hate. I have noticed that when a person has a mental disorder such as schizophrenia, it can be evident in the aura by the presence of red. The darker the red, the more selfish the person, and the selfishness increases as it is muddied by brown. Red can also indicate passion, which can become lust as it is filled with the selfishness of brown.

	"Red which has brown in it indicates fear, and when the brown darkens and becomes black, it indicates malice. When red has a tint of yellow, we see uncontrolled emotions and desires. When we see a red light, it indicates a nervous temperament and a bright, clear red shows vitality, generosity and material health. A rosy brightness shows filial affection and the love of home, while red which moves into pink shows happiness and tenderness" (Sherwood, 1994, p. 106).
Deep red on black Brilliant scarlet Sanguine, lurid red	Anger. It also can be strong health or irritability, it depends on the hue "Noble indignation Sensuality" (Leadbeater, 1987, p. 66).
Ultra Red	"Lower psychic faculties of one who dabbles in evil and selfish forms of magic" (Hodson, 1981, p. 58).
Brown	Brown in the aura can, like grey, represents physical disease, or an emotional program leaving. I have generally found it to be a somewhat negative colour, sometimes representing self-obsessiveness and selfish interests. I have noticed it to be common in long-standing drug addicts, who have a kind of dislocated brown aura.
	"Most healers associate brown with negative human characteristics. In its various forms, it indicates stinginess, greed and the lower material instincts. Only when it becomes a golden brown does its vibration rise, showing an industrious, organised character and a methodical temperament." (Sherwood, 1994, p. 108).

Brown red almost rust	"Avarice, usually arranged in parallel bars across the body (The miser is self-imprisoned)
Dull hard brown grey	Selfishness.
Green brown with red or scarlet	Jealousy." (Leadbeater, 1987, p.66)
Grey	Grey is a negative colour and can represent fear and depression, also a dull or shady character, lacking in vitality. Sometimes, for example, when our physical organs are in distress and unhealthy they may appear clairvoyantly as grey. The grey indicates disease. Arranged in parallel lines, conveys the impression of a cage" (Leadbeater, 1987, p. 66). "Heavy, deep greys indicate fear, confusion and often a dull, heavy, leaden personality often bordering on morbidity. Grey in the aura often indicates an unreliable, deceptive character" (Sherwood, 1994, p. 108).
Livid grey	Fear (Leadbeater, 1987, p. 67).
Crimson	"Love

Crimson - tinged with brown	Selfishness
Crimson - tinged with violet	Love of humanity, more spiritual
Crimson - Rose only	Unselfishness love" (Leadbeater, 1987, p.67)
Orange	"Pride or ambition....with irritability" (Leadbeater, 1987, p.67). "Orange in its clearest form indicates forcefulness and vitality. When it becomes reddish, it tends to indicate self-centredness" (Sherwood, 1994).
Yellow	Yellow usually indicates intellect. Sometimes it is seen in the aura when someone is making a point that he or she has thought about, appearing often around the head as he or she speaks. "When it is dull, it indicates intellect, but of a mundane nature. When it becomes brighter, moving into gold, there is an elevation of the intellect and it becomes purified through spirit. Muddy or dirty yellow indicates cunning, greed and self-centred egotism" (Sherwood, 1994, p. 106). Intellect, lower intellect deeper and duller (Leadbeater, 1987, p. 68).
Dull yellow ochre Clear gamboge Primrose yellow	"Implies direction of faculty to selfish purposes. Indicates a distinctly higher type. Intellect devoted to spiritual ends.

Gold	Pure intellect applied to philosophy or mathematics" (Hodson, 1981, p. 59).
Green	Emerald green is the colour of the Holy Spirit. When green is in the aura it often represents healing or healing abilities. Deeper greens can represent truth. Green can indicate harmony with nature. "In its negative form, green indicates extreme selfishness. When it is muddy and dirty, it shows deceitfulness and greed. When it becomes brownish, it indicates jealousy" (Sherwood, 1994, p. 107).
Grey green	"Slimy in appearance. Deceit and cunning.
Emerald green	Versatility, ingenuity, resourcefulness applied unselfishly
Luminous blue green	Sympathy and compassion, perfect adaptability.
Bright apple green	Vitality" (Hodson, 1981, p. 59); (Leadbeater, 1987, p. 69).
Blue	This represents religious feeling and the mother energies. It is often associated with Mother Mary. It can also represent the beauty of truth and feminine mystical qualities. "It is associated with inspiration and the higher forms of intellect, spiritual aspirations and the feminine aspect of nature, the subjective intuitive mind. When blue deepens into indigo, we find a person with a devotional character and a deeply religious spirit" (Sherwood, 1994, p. 107).

Dark clear blue	Denotes a religiously oriented person.
Indigo	"Pure religious feeling
Muddy grey blue	Fetish worship
Light blue	Devotion
Luminous liliac blue	Higher spirituality" (Leadbeater, 1987, p. 69).
Violet	Denotes spirituality. Generally found in spiritual people.
	"Those who have violet in their aura have advanced in their spiritual evolution. It is the colour of royalty and indicates nobility of character. Violet in the aura acts as an insulator and purifier. It is not a common colour in the average aura. It is a colour that comes from the higher realms.... When it shades into lavender, it denotes high spirituality as well as vitality. When it shades into lilac, it shows a compassionate and altruistic character."
	"Violet first appears above the head and looks like an ovoid atop the crown chakra. As the adept advances, the violet radiates from there, filling the entire aura with its light" (Sherwood, 1994, p. 107).
Ultra Violet	"Higher and purer developments of psychic faculties" (Hodson, 1981, p. 60).

The effect of mood and the emotions

The colours of mood come and go, giving a clear indication of what the person is going through at any given moment. When we look in the aura we may perceive fear, joy or anger at a particular time. It may quickly pass. The aura can be quite affected by intense emotions such as an anger fit, or sudden shocks such as a car accident. These can jolt the aura and can create a hole in the aura, or a gap, until the aura is realigned, perhaps by a healer, or by the person creating a sense of calmness again through meditation or quiet, peaceful contemplation.

> Joy shows itself in a general brightening and radiance of both mental and astral bodies, and in a peculiar rippling of the surface of the body. Cheerfulness shows itself in a modified bubbling form of this, and also in a steady serenity.
>
> Surprise is shown by a sharp constriction of the mental body, usually communicated to both the astral and physical bodies, accompanied by an increased glow of the band of affection if the surprise is a pleasant one, and by an increase of brown and grey if the surprise is an unpleasant one (Hodson, 1981, p. 60).

The astral body's particles are always in rapid motion: colours melt into one another, appearing and disappearing. There is, however, a normal position to which they tend to return. According to C. W. Leadbeater (1987, pp. 85-91), a sudden rush of passion or feeling moves and mixes the colours enormously. A sudden shock of terror will cause vibration of such violence as make the aura hardly recognisable. It turns completely grey and all light fades.

The soul puts itself in the lower planes out of desire to feel alive and for the sake of the experience gained and of the qualities developed; it takes the fruits of this experience back into itself. The risk of this process is that in incarnating it may become tangled in the matter of the lower planes. The effects of energies in our aura, when we become conscious of them, can be used to direct us in such a way as to not become caught in the lower planes. A sensitive being, for example, cannot listen to heavy jarring music for too long without feeling and seeing the effects in the aura. A fit of anger gives a horrific effect. Leadbeater (1987) illustrates this well with diagrams of the appearance of the aura after a fit of anger. The diagram is characterised by black spirals and red jagged strokes. The desire elemental is so strong that the person loses control of his or her vehicle. Likewise, Leadbeater shows the effect of fear dramatically with zig-zag grey overtaking the aura; all the colours fade, and with them, the talents and abilities of the person involved. The aura quivers and the effects of violence are experienced.

In *Man Visible and Invisible*, C. W. Leadbeater (1987) also speaks of the effect that "falling in love" has in the aura. While it brings beautiful crimson colours to the higher parts of the aura, which has lasting effects, it brings also murky green brown colours of jealousy to the lower part of the aura. Fortunately, the good qualities linger longer. If affected in this way and working to live a holy life from the heart, the initial jealousy will disappear leaving the person more able to lift the energy of love.

Specific types of people

Specific types of people are depicted by C. W. Leadbeater (1987) in *Man Visible and Invisible*. These are the irritable person, the miser, the scientist, the deeply depressed person and the devotional type. All are radically different in form as well as colour. The most striking features are:

1. The miser has deep brown parallel horizontal bars which appear to lock him in like a cage.
2. The deeply depressed person has a similar effect in grey.
3. The irritable man has floating specks of scarlet.
4. The scientific type is blocked to the higher levels by the presence of orange pride on top of the head.
5. The devotional type has substantial blue, but may have the religious blue being muddy and mixed with desire for personal gain.

The sharp contrasts in these auras alone make us aware of the enormous variety possible. Some features are longer lasting and some are a function of sudden emotions.

Reading the aura - clairvoyance and clairaudience

By looking at the aura of a person and the stages of development of the person's inner bodies we see the stage of development of the person. We begin to see this as our higher vision develops. We know this capacity to see on the inner as clairvoyance. It is through our chakras that we open up to clairvoyant abilities. Most clairvoyants see on the physical, etheric or astral levels; some, on the mental levels; however, very few are clairvoyant when it comes to seeing the soul. There are many different levels and kinds of clairvoyance. It is possible, for example, to see the past lives of a person in the aura of that person. This skill is astral clairvoyance, which we need to employ with caution. Ananda Tara Shan (1994, p. 5) tells us about astral clairvoyance from a healer's perspective, in her booklet *Spiritual Healing*:

Astral clairvoyance is the ability to see, to look into the patient's astral life to discover the emotional problems that may be hidden and suppressed even to the patient him- or herself. The healer may discover the reason or reasons for the afflicted body or mind and may talk things over carefully with the patient.

With astral clairvoyance some healers see certain past lives of the patients. This skill helps in determining the causes of diseases which are seen in patients. A professional healer will only disclose what he or she sees if this is absolutely needed.

Astral clairaudience is the ability to hear communication from the inner planes. We may glean the same information as that given by astral clairvoyance except that it comes through the sense of hearing instead of sight.

Clairvoyance and clairaudience are topics here just touched upon, but they are as vast as the topic of the aura itself. The healer will often use clairvoyance or clairaudience as a way of reading the aura of a client. These abilities will enable him or her to find information that will help him or her assist the client as best he or she can. Clairvoyant abilities are a very great gift from God, providing extremely valuable help in the work of spiritual healing. The healer needs to cultivate a pure motive. The healer needs education in the Divine Wisdom to make good use of such abilities. If the healer should exercise the clairvoyant abilities within the boundaries of the spiritual Laws, good results will come of them. If the motive is selfish, and the clairvoyant is not of good character, only negative and destructive results will occur.

Sometimes clairvoyant abilities come to us and when we are ready to go to a higher level we might lose them for a time - while they are being purified and we are going through a state of learning, or an initiation to higher levels. When we get to higher levels the abilities may come back as a gift that we are more able to use in another way. As we ask for development and purification, that gift is taken to be purified, and others come forward. It is a matter of trusting our abilities, and knowing that we have them for a reason. It is also a matter of using such gifts wisely and ensuring that we remain within our common sense and the spiritual Laws as we employ them. Perhaps the approach best taken is that summed up by Ananda Tara Shan (1994, p. 7), "Ask not for clairvoyance, but for the ability to see truth, and then learn to impart truth with wisdom."

In order to see the truth we need to be aware that we see the world and people around us through our own aura. We also perceive others according to our character. Whenever we see the world, others and our environment, we look through our aura. We have to deal therefore with all our glamours and illusions before we can begin to see and live in truth. Glamours, in short, are ideas that colour our emotional desires which are not in alignment with the soul. Illusions are our cemented thought forms that prevent or distort higher inspiration. Illusions appear in the mental body because they are the cemented thought forms. Glamours appear in the astral body; they represent our attachment to our desires. In life on Earth we are usually caught in some glamour or another, or some illusion or another. When reading the aura of another, therefore, we need to be extremely careful and seriously look at our motives for doing so. We must let the colours speak to us and pray that we are simply a vehicle for the true Light. We must also seriously consider the effect the information we receive may have on the client. Is it for his or her benefit that we impart our findings? Or is it simply making us gain a sense of grandeur and importance? We must consider carefully, because the wrong information given, or even the right information given at the wrong time, will incur karma.

Healing and the aura

What happens to the aura during healing? When healing takes place, the aura of the healer merges with the aura of the client. The soul of the healer sends down Light to help raise the vibration of the healer and the client. When a healer is doing a healing, the Holy Spirit raises the healer to a higher vibration of consciousness. This lasts for the duration of the healing. The Holy Spirit lifts both healer and client. It brings forth a protective mechanism for the client; and if a healer is healing from the heart, with pure motive, he or she can very quickly establish this connected and protected state of being. The healing stimulates the healer's love for humanity, and everything else in life pales away into insignificance.

The healer is there for the client one hundred percent. It is helpful to cultivate the idea of being there for the client one hundred percent, for that hour, for those forty minutes, whatever time the healer is with them. The faster vibration of the healer influences the vibration of the client to lift. The aura of the healer expands to encompass the aura of the client. When the healer has the intention to heal with purity of motive and heart, the Holy Spirit is able to stimulate the goodness in the client and transmute the negative qualities. It transmutes the negative qualities with the higher frequency of Light. It is more than the merging of souls that makes this possible. It is also the calling on higher forces of Light through the Christ Light.

This method of healing has been around for a very long time. In the Atlantean temples people came to healers so that they could rise in consciousness. They did this because healing helped them to see what they needed to see about themselves, change what they needed to change and go back out into the world with the new awareness of what they had found in that healing. Healing works in the same way today, although the process of healing has been refined over the years and has become more purified as we have developed.

Protection and the aura

It is through our aura that we can protect ourselves when needed. The way to do this is to visualise Light in it. When we visualise ourselves surrounded with a spherical shield of white Light, our auric matter obeys and moves to create that energy shield for us. If we call on the Christ Light it comes to help us in that process. Doing this as a common practise gives us protection from negative influences, negative thought and draining people.

> The aura responds very readily to the impulse of thought, and if by an effort of the imagination we picture its outer edge as densified into a shell, we readily make a protective wall around us (Besant, 1990, p. 87).

Drugs and the etheric body

By looking at the condition of the etheric body in the aura we can get an indication of the health of a person. Sometimes we can find disease, the beginnings of it, before it manifests itself in the physical. Drugs have an effect in the aura. Strong drugs taken for long periods can destroy the etheric body; this damage can take ten to twelve years to heal, or lifetimes depending on the choice of lifestyle of the person affected. The effect differs in different people. In severe cases the aura can be perforated. The etheric web is either ossified (hardened) or becomes full of holes. That is why severe alcoholics have deliriums and hallucinations. The astral levels open up, and they lose the ability to control their entry into the other worlds. In users of speed or heroin, over a period of several years the aura can dislocate itself. It loses colour, and appears brown, and the energy of selfishness extends throughout it.

The aura's effect on our disposition

H. Edwards (1974), in his book *A Guide to the Understanding and Practice of Spiritual Healing*, reminds us that the aura is a reflection of our spiritual and mental health. He suggests, therefore, that it is not the aura we heal. Instead, we heal the mental tension and/or the release of fears and insecurities from within the client. Once we release them the aura will reflect a more peaceful condition. The healer can help the client to release built-up energies of stress through healing. Most often the client needs good counselling to help him or her understand what has created the condition. The healer does not give advice, rather he or she assists the client through a gentle exploration of the factors that have led to the imbalances evident in the aura. Counselling and healing are useful partners. It also helps to work with the client to see how the client can best cooperate with the healing effort.

A healer needs to develop compassion and love for the people he or she is working with, a higher love of humanity. When the client comes into the aura of the healer those energies touch the client and touch the fears and insecurities, sometimes moving the client into tears for some time. The beautiful energies of love and compassion that healers develop are passed on to their clients, even if it only happens momentarily. When the Light touches the clients they want to begin to develop those higher qualities. They want the love and the compassion. This starts them trying to develop better qualities in themselves. They are inspired by the love and the compassion and may strive to give it to others because they can see and feel the effects it has had on themselves.

Aura cleansing

Aura cleansing is an art used in healing often prior to healing work, after healing work as a brush-down after the healing, or as a method of healing to help centre a person when a full healing is not required. An aura cleansing generally takes between two and four minutes. The aura cleanser cleanses with the use of a crystal or crystal rod or simply with his or her hands. The aura cleanser can use peaceful music, either New Age or classical, to help create an uplifting and peaceful environment. Generally the healer invokes the Holy Spirit, and cleanses the person's aura with the Holy Spirit. The healer cleanses the aura by raising and lowering his or her arm or arms, moving up and down the aura with angelic motion, in rhythmic strokes or brushing, whilst visualising the aura being cleansed. In this process the healer stays alert, sensing where there is congestion in the chakras and directing the Light in such a way as to help smooth out the aura. This helps to release any unneeded energies and bring the aura to a state of harmony.

Aura cleansing is very useful if someone has had a shock, or has been angry or subject to another's anger. Many churches utilise aura cleansing and healing as part of their service to humanity. Aura cleansing is a process that has been a part of the healing process for many centuries.

Indigenous tribes such as the Native Americans also have this as part of the healing practice, done with crystals or other healing tools such as the drum, the rattle or bells. It is a practice also employed by the Tibetans, who use meditation, the singing bowl, the cymbals, or the bell and dorje for that purpose. It helps us to balance our masculine and feminine polarities, maintain health and well-being, and clear away any unwanted stress or tension.

The congestion in the aura is evident in the energy or dross present. Dross is negative matter that gathers in the aura. It can be seen in the aura as a dark film or be as thick as a black, tar-like substance. Dross in the aura and the inner bodies has the effect of dulling our senses and our openness to the Light. Having an aura cleansing in the Light of Christ enables the Christ to bring us the Grace of God. Sometimes through aura cleansing we are healed of ailments before they manifest in our physical bodies, or saved from emotional traumas or mental anguish by release and insights given.

As with spiritual healing, we must remember always that the cleansing does not take place through our power. It is the power of the Holy Spirit that heals. To be able to invoke and radiate that Light in the aura cleansing, the aura cleanser must tune into the Divine Presence through the indwelling Christ. In so doing the cleanser becomes centred in the Light and a vehicle for the Divine healing. The cleanser becomes a vehicle through which the Holy Spirit may flow. Spirit guides and directs the movements that the cleanser makes, thus allowing the flow of energy to be full of healing Light. The aura cleanser is able to become a pure vehicle by tuning in to the Father-Mother God, the Christ and/or the Holy Spirit. The healer affirms that he or she is pure of intent, willing only that which is the Will of God to take place in the cleansing given.

How to make the aura healthy

If we wish to have a healthy aura we can do so through right living, balanced meditation and the cultivation of virtues and higher qualities through service. We do so through living a holy life and not by meditation or focused concentration on the centres (Bailey, 1987). The aura reflects that which is within us. If we wish to make our aura light and holy we must seek to live in a manner that is light and holy. We can do this by living according to right human relations; by cultivating positive thoughts and having a balanced expression and control of our emotions. We can also seek to assist the health aura by getting enough rest and exercise, and giving ourselves a well thought-out and balanced diet that suits our needs. People cannot expect to have a healthy and balanced aura if they do not will themselves to live a healthy and balanced life. No amount of healing, for example, will help a drug addict who after every healing utilises the good effect of the healing to go home and get high. Such a case is a waste of the healer's energy and time. The client must have the will to become balanced, to change habits where needed and to create a more harmonious life. Healing may initially assist the client to find the impetus to give up the drugs. The healer is wise to consider seriously whether treatment should continue if the client makes no effort to move out of his or her problem.

Colours on the outer and inner

It can be helpful to become aware of the effects of colour in our lives, especially in relation to our clothing and the colours of our environment. Pastel shades, for example, have a calming effect, while strong shades, such as deep blue or bright yellow may stimulate us in certain ways. Imagine if we were to paint all the rooms in our houses black and red. What effect might it have on our moods? The colours we choose affect us. It is worthwhile to look at the colours we have around us and to consider the effect they are having on us. Are we content with them or do they need to be changed? What effect would we like to achieve? How can we go about changing that? Are the clothes we wear too dark? Are we making ourselves unduly negative and depressed through our apparel? These are questions we can ask ourselves if we wish to beautify our environment in such a way as to bring harmony to our lives.

When we meditate on the colours of the rainbow we can enhance both our inner and outer lives and bring balance into our aura. By such meditation the path to the Higher Self is opened, it is with our guardian angel that we communicate while this pathway is being cleared. By meditating on the colours we can help our personality develop through giving it the needed energy to do so. Meditating on the colours helps us to become healthy and whole.

Conclusion

When we look at a human being through our inner eye we see not only the flesh that is so evident in the physical, but also the higher vision. We see the Divine potential, and sometimes within that the possible future of that person. Such are the gifts of the clairvoyant who can see on such levels, to see the possibilities inherent in humanity. Such are the gifts we receive as we come to know ourselves. As we come to study the human aura, we can see where we are destructive to ourselves through our choice of thoughts and emotions. We can also help ourselves evolve, through the cultivation of finer qualities, close observance and control of our thoughts and emotions, and the decision and action taken towards living a moral and holy life.

> Our aura shows just what we are; we add to it as we grow in the true life; we purify it as we live noble and cleanly lives; we weave it into higher and higher qualities (Besant, 1990, p. 88).

The Healer

> Healing is therefore not only a laying on of hands. It is a toning of an instrument who over many years of training becomes a powerful and hopefully refined instrument for Spirit to descend into and stream forth from. (Ananda Tara Shan, 1995, p. 2).

How does a healer work?

The spiritual healer is the instrument to whom Ananda Tara Shan is referring. The healer is an instrument for the Holy Spirit. The healer uses his or her inner bodies and chakras in order to heal. The etheric body is usually developed throughout lifetimes for this work. Depending upon the type of healing and the vibration with which the healer is working, the healer uses certain chakras and inner bodies in order to create an energy flow, using himself or herself as a vehicle for the Light of the Holy Spirit.

When a healer prepares to heal, he or she first opens the self as a vehicle for the higher Light. The soul sends down the Light through the mighty I-Am-Presence into the heart centre of the healer. The healer can then use his or her arms and hands as channels to transmit that Light, often utilising the chakras in the palm of the hand. Some may choose to heal through will power, in which case the third eye chakra can also be used. When a healer becomes more proficient and sensitive to the work, he or she can heal from the higher chakras at will. It is important that the heart is involved in the healing work, for this creates a healing performed with the Love of Christ, where the intention and motive is pure and the will is left to the Lord Christ - "not mine but Thine Will be done."

A healer can choose to send the Light from his or her heart chakra into the person being healed without touching that person. Some people choose to work in this way using the chakras in a more radiatory sense, where the Light is radiated through the chakras. Others prefer a more hands-on approach. This is magnetic healing. The radiatory and magnetic methods can also be used in combination.

The method a healer chooses is usually determined by his or her life purpose and karma, as is the healing Light to which they will be attracted to work. It takes many lives of development to come to a point of working with healing as one's dharma. Quite a degree of purification is needed. There are many levels of healing Light, some of which are coarser or less fine than others. The degree of development of the healer will determine the "fineness" of the vibration of the Light that he or she can transmit.

How can one become an esoteric healer?

For a healer to heal esoterically a great deal of purification is needed, and the healer must strive to live a holy life, living according to the Principles of Right Human Relations, with a balanced diet accompanying this. The art of spiritual healing, like any art, requires both dedication and practice in order to develop and refine skills. Practice makes perfect. In the case of spiritual healing, practice also helps to purify the healer and prepare the healer for greater work. When a healer is prepared to work regularly, this shows the Christ that the healer has made a commitment to the work, and the Christ will help that person in the development of healing skills. This has great impact on the life of the healer.

What effect does healing have on the healer?

Healing brings forth qualities such as compassion, empathy and love and develops an understanding of the universe and how it works. Reincarnation and karma which once may have been a theory in the mind of the healer become a living reality within which we are all functioning. The healer bears witness to many of God's great works that come through the Grace of God; not to mention the closeness that develops with the angelic kingdom who is ever present and working unceasingly to bring Christ's Light to humanity. Being exposed to these gifts of God's creation changes the healer, instilling in the healer the qualities of faith, hope and trust in the higher life. To work with healing is to open one's heart and mind to the greatness of God and to allow the universal flow of love and healing to pour into our lives. It is a constant process of choice, surrender, renunciation and purification, which eventually leads to our healing and transformation. Through this process we begin to comprehend our own part in the creation of our lives on Earth and begin to see the need for taking responsibility for our actions. Healing gives us a way of dealing with the shadow side of our nature as we acknowledge it and bring it forward to be purified. Healing also helps us to move out of the glamours and illusions in which we live and find a life based on truth, love and the higher principles.

Skills and ethics

When people come for healing, they often reveal their innermost fears and secrets. The healer must always remember the great honour it is to be privy to this and respect the confidentiality of what is revealed. What transpires in the healing is the client's private concern and should not be discussed with others. The healer's role is to provide a safe place for the person to discuss situations and issues, discover what is needing to be healed and talk about and discuss the effects of the spiritual healing. The qualities of compassion and empathy need to be cultivated in a healer as do basic listening skills, which enable such a safe place to be manifested. The healer does not sit in judgement of his or her client for what transpires, but seeks at all times to create an atmosphere of love and Light where understanding, insight and revelation become possible.

During the transmission of Light and energy, the healer must become impersonal, that is, allowing the higher Will and the Light and Love of the Holy Spirit to flow through. In essence, the healer cultivates the ability to get his or her personality out of the way so that the Christ Light can flow through unimpeded. Such skills can be learned and developed with practice and sometimes simply come naturally, depending upon whether or not the healer has healed in past lifetimes. Some feel they are born with the gift of healing; in others it awakens as the life progresses and as certain lessons are learned and purification achieved. Anyone can learn it. All the Christ needs is one who strives to be pure of heart and who wishes to help other people, the animal kingdom, or the Earth.

When a spiritual healing takes place, many things are possible. For example, it is possible for the client to have memories or visions of unresolved situations from the past, perhaps in this or other lifetimes. It is possible that these memories and visions will set in motion varying responses from the person's astral body or thoughts and that emotions will be stimulated, sometimes in an overwhelming manner. Understanding of the process of redemption is needed, with space given to the client to re-experience what needs to be experienced, to see what needs to be seen, to feel what needs to be felt, and to understand what needs to be understood. Clients respond in many ways to the healing energies, and with time and practice the healer develops a sensitivity that allows for this variation in response and therefore gives the client the space to heal. It is of vital importance when the vulnerabilities and the deeper inner nature of the client are being revealed that the healer remembers the nature of his or her relationship with the client and respects the boundaries of the professional healer/client relationship, whilst radiating human love and caring. The intense personal nature of the healer/client interaction must be handled with some care. The healer, for example, should make sure that his or her needs for intimacy are met elsewhere, and care needs to be taken to ensure that the client does not become emotionally dependant on the healer. To allow this to happen can destroy the benefits that the healing work is giving and the sense of wholeness that the healing is trying to achieve. The basic message here is to keep the contract clear. Clearly define the boundaries of the relationship before you, and wherever they are uncertain through the process of the relationship, redefine them again. I recommend that anyone who heals professionally obtains training in counselling skills and ethics.

The lifestyle needed to heal with the Holy Spirit

We have seen that the spiritual healing Light that is the Holy Spirit, known as the Fire of Creation, is the secret fire of alchemy that transmutes the negative matter into Light. In order to work with this Light the healer needs to have reached a point in his or her development where he or she is purified enough to work with It. This does not mean that we have to be perfected beings who never have anger or fear or guilt; it simply means that the healer must be striving to live a holy life based on right principles and values. The motives for the work need to be pure, coming from a good heart, and the healer needs to have thoughts that are harmless and of good intent. If a person is not at this stage, there is a danger of misuse of the energies for selfish gains and purposes. By law, healers attract those clients whom they are able to assist, and as the healer purifies him/herself, so the clientele changes accordingly. To have a holy life takes effort and the development of conscious awareness in every thought, word and deed. The principles of goodwill, justice and harmlessness must be followed through the practical application of living in love and truth. A general balance in lifestyle needs to be maintained. Because of the amount of etheric energy used in healing, a good diet, exercise and balance in sleep and sex life are needed so that there is plenty of healthy etheric energy available for the work. If this is not the case, the healer very quickly experiences 'etheric drain' and the clients may not be able to receive the full benefit of the healing energies which should have been available to them.

When healing, one's senses need to be alert, alive and ready to be utilised by the Christ for the work. The intuitive faculties need to be operating and an inner focus needs to be maintained throughout the healing. A good diet for a healer is most often a vegetarian one or at least one with no red meat. It is also good to stay away from refined sugar and alcohol. The use of excessive alcohol and drugs can seriously affect the etheric web. Either the web ossifies, which means it hardens and loses the elasticity needed in the healing work, or it perforates, allowing unscreened astral energies to come through. The same applies to the use of tobacco which also severely affects the etheric web. This does not mean that you will be unable to heal if you have an occasional drink or even a cigarette; however, prolonged use of tobacco, alcohol or drugs will affect the capacity to heal as it will affect the degree to which the healer can be purified and therefore the degree to which he or she can be utilised for Christ's work. It is sometimes through the renunciation of these addictions that we show the Christ our level of commitment to the work. The sincere student of healing who truly wishes to serve the Christ will make every effort to purify him or herself accordingly on all levels of existence; that is, on the physical, etheric, astral, mental and spiritual levels. To live a holy life helps us to find balance in the psychological and physical worlds. We need a healthy body in order to do the work, and a healthy state of mind. We must always remember when looking at our potential for healing to consider our karma and dharma, and to question whether there are any limitations which could prevent us from working with healing that need to be considered? Is it a part of our life's purpose? As a healer heals and bears witness to the beauty and glory of a life lived and guided by the Holy Spirit, the desire to purify strengthens and aspiration takes over, bringing the higher part of the healer into operation. When people enter into the field of healing, life changes and the desire to serve the Christ and the yearning to live a life of service to Him grows in the heart centre, so changing the course of that life forever.

Of course, being healed by the Holy Spirit may also stimulate resistance and rebellion from our lower natures. However, the healer begins to sense the true meaning of freedom and liberation of Spirit that comes when the life is dedicated to the purpose of serving Him. In such cases it is only a matter of time before the life becomes transformed.

The use of clairvoyance

When we open our chakras, we open the doors to the inner worlds and open our clairvoyant abilities. To ensure that our clairvoyance develops along the right path, we must develop our sensitivity and intuition and strive to be selfless in our work, remembering always that we wish to be vehicles for the Light of the Christ. It is better not to give clairvoyant readings along with the healing Light that comes to us, for the wrong word at the wrong time can destroy the work. Rather, we can use the healing energies in such a way as to assist the clients to find their own answers and be stimulated within their own inner bodies to see what they need to see, feel what they need to feel, and come to know what they need to know.

Clairvoyant abilities are gifts from God and need to be used ethically in such a way as to help create the effect that the Christ would wish to have happen in the client. As we heal from our good hearts, pure intentions and with love for our fellow beings, our clairvoyant capacities will be purified. If we wish to truly help those around us, we should pray to the angels to help us learn wise use of our clairvoyant capacities as well as for the purification of them.

In the chapter *The Aura and its Colours* we saw that Ananda Tara Shan gives us some hints about astral clairvoyance, and she advises us to work with the knowledge that Christ observes our every action and our every thought. Ananda Tara Shan (1995, p. 5) also tells us in her booklet *Spiritual Healing* that:

> Here lies a danger, however, in that the healer may not have the full ability needed to see the greater details. Because of this, the healer must refrain from diagnosing the astral condition of the patient if he receives only a few, unclear understandings of the conditions. Many so-called clairvoyants pretend to do psychological work when they do not have the education or training to do this. Rather than do this without such training they should instead learn professional counselling skills to help the patients. Astral clairvoyance will then support these skills.

We can see by these hints the importance of questioning ourselves about the use and abuse of clairvoyant capacities. Healers need to ask themselves whether they should tell their clients what they see. If the answer to that question is yes, the healer must also ask, how will it benefit the client's soul? What are the healer's motives for wishing to disclose this information? Is disclosing this information indeed the correct thing to do? Clairvoyance can be used by the negative forces just as it can be used by the forces of Light. The healer needs to look seriously at the tendency or desire to rescue, save or fix another and look at how this plays a part in gratifying his or her personality, creating the glamour and illusion of being a saviour. It is easy for the personality to become too involved and to seek gratification from the reputation of being clairvoyant and possessing powers that the client does not have. Therefore, a situation arises where the client becomes disempowered rather than empowered through the process of the healing work. We must never forget that it is the Christ who heals, and if we are to be true vehicles of the Christ Light, we must work at remaining humble in that Light so that Its great benefits and effects can be realised.

Using discrimination and overcoming fear

A healer needs to realise the power of Light and never underestimate it. On the higher mental level the forces of Light have the advantage. It is up to us to try to lift ourselves to the protective forces that are given on those levels and to yearn from the heart to be connected to that love. The dark forces are at play in the astral and lower mental levels. We need to learn to discriminate and put effort into purifying ourselves and becoming Light. Unfortunately, because of ignorance and fear we may let the darkness win. We need education about the power of Light and need to learn not to live in victim consciousness. When we live in victim consciousness, we are at the mercy of fear, which is the entrance the dark forces use. We fall victim to our negative thoughts and can even assist in the process of strengthening them by not controlling our own lower nature and our negative emotions and thoughts. We must learn to control our thoughts, allow ourselves the needed emotional expression and help our astral bodies to become still, by utilising our mental capacities.

Attunement

The process of attunement in healing helps us to raise our consciousness and reminds us that we are vehicles for a greater Light. To lift ourselves to the place of being a receptive vehicle for the Light we need to put in some effort. We must put in the effort required to calm our thoughts and emotions and prepare ourselves for the beauty of such work. We may have unresolved emotional issues, or thoughts of low self-worth. Perhaps we feel we are 'mightier than Thou.' All this makes the process of being a pure vehicle difficult. The beauty of healing is that we are lifted out of our normal consciousness and given the grace to heal. Our inferiority and superiority complexes may get in the way. We can be filled with the glamours and illusions of seeing ourselves as great masters of Light, healing and wisdom, ready to fix and heal the problems of everyone who comes to us. The sub-personalities of the martyr, rescuer and perfectionist can come into operation when we work. How do we rise above all of this? The following process of attunement will help us to do that.

1. We relax.
2. We breathe.
3. We protect.
4. We attune.
5. We visualise.
6. We invoke.
7. We heal.
8. We give thanks.

This process of attunement serves to protect both the healer and the client. It helps us not to drain our energies and allows the Christ Light to overshadow our personality so that we can work impersonally for the Divine. We protect ourselves by calling on the

Archangel Michael. He has given us that help of protection from darkness, for many centuries. We can attune to the Christ Light, the Holy Spirit, the Lord Jesus, the White Tara, depending upon what form we are working with or how we feel most comfortable to work. This attunement enables us to still ourselves enough to be lifted by the Light and to be used as a vehicle for the Light without our lower nature getting in the way.

We also attune to the aura and chakras of the person we are going to be healing. Taking time for the attunement process is a necessary part of healing. If we are going to tune into a radio program, we need to turn the tuner and make sure we are on the station before we can settle in and listen to the program being transmitted. It is similar in healing: we need to spend time attuning ourselves, making sure we are in alignment with the Christ Light and asking to be used as vehicles for that Light, working impersonally from pure heart, pure motive, pure thoughts. For example, we are about to give a healing, and prior to giving the healing, we have had some personal stress. The attunement process helps us to rise above the energy of stress and work from a higher place, giving the clients the help they need. The attunement helps us to lift and be alert. The protection defends us from our lower nature, negative thought forms and the elemental forces. It gives us a space to work freely, provided we adhere to the higher Laws and do the healing work needed. It is important in healing to attune to the heart, as it is in the heart that we lift above the three lower chakras. By visualising the heart, seeing it filled with pink Light, for example, we can lift our energy and raise our consciousness to a place where the elementals, lower thought forms and lower rampant desire nature cannot touch us. We set the intent, and the soul sends the Light that helps raise our vibration to the point where we are ready for the work.

The soul or Higher Self is the true self. The goal towards which we strive is to merge our consciousness with that of the soul.

In healing work the healer seeks to build up beautiful healing energies and to link with the soul as well as the healing devas and angels. By calling upon Archangel Michael (who brings forth the Will of God - "Not mine but Thine Will be done"), and tuning in to the Christ, the Holy Spirit and the healing angels, we bring forth an energy that helps lift the burdens, pain and suffering of the client.

When we call upon the Light, visualisation helps us to attune. Visualisation is a skill that can be learned over time. For example, if during your visualisation you say mentally, "I visualise the blue Light," and you cannot see it, you should not worry, but simply know that it is there. The thought of it is enough to bring that energy down. You can ask to attune to your Christ-self and ask your soul to overshadow your personality so that you can work impersonally with the Divine.

In our daily life, we can call upon the White Tara and Her many angels to guide us and protect us. She is the Avatar of Light and is especially helpful when we are working with children or adults who are suffering or in pain. She protects and helps us lift beyond our own negative thoughts and feelings. In our daily life we can attune when we are about to study, write or do a particular task we need to do. We may attune as a group when we are about to set up for Earth healing work and ask for help from the angels and beings of Light so that we can work without interference in a smooth and orderly manner. If we are running a workshop, we can attune and protect that workshop. When we are in the garden we can attune to it and find what flowers or vegetables are ready to be picked, or we can attune to waterfalls and trees in nature. When we eat at night, we can attune and ask that our food be filled with vital Light and be blessed. The process of attunement will help us in our daily life to stay focused, alert and open to the help of the higher life. We need only remember to ask. We can even use quotations from books we like, which speak of the higher virtues. I like to use the following text given from the Christ, the Lord Maitreya, to help me to attune:

> Remember Me in everything you experience, in everything you see and feel, in everything delightful as well as difficult. Remember Me in all your thoughts, in all your desires, and you can never do wrong or take a wrong turn in life. For this I promise you, let Me always come first with you, and I shall give you paradise.
>
> So I speaketh, your Brother and your Deliverer. So I have spoken always. So I will speak always.
>
> My words are Law.
>
> My Body is Life.
>
> I Am Christ.
>
> (Ananda Tara Shan, 1993, p. 30)

When you have read this text, you may like to do the following:

Let yourself be in the Heart of the Christ now. Let His Love embrace you, lift you, let yourself go beyond your personality and link with your soul and Spirit. Transcend your thoughts and feelings. Go with your Spirit into the Light. Let the angels take you to the Christ. Affirm mentally, I am love, I am, I am, I am. I am peace, I am, I am, I am. Let the Christ's Love and Peace touch your heart and still your mind. Slowly and gently let yourself return to daily consciousness holding His Light in your heart.

Transmitting Light and energy

When transmitting Light and energy we visualise the Heart of Christ sending Light to the soul, and from the soul to our etheric heart and out of the palms of our hands, radiating the Light. In transmitting Light we are aware that we are not the source of the Light. The Light comes from the Christ to us, through the soul, to the brain and heart. We transmit that Light out through our hands. We invoke the Heart Light by our affirmations, and the attunement serves to lift us into that Heart. From within that Heart we heal. This process of attunement parallels the inner attunement taking place within us to the Light of Christ and helps us become familiar with the Christ energy. The Light pours forth from the Heart of Christ through the I-Am-Presence or the Star of Light above our head, into our heart and then out through our hands. You will find the visualisations that help you best.

Healing forms

Healing forms are the format and words a healer may use to help him or her to heal. Sometimes healers are given a specific form to follow by one further advanced along the spiritual path. When you work with a specific form, you should follow the guidelines that come with it. The form may contain an attunement; protection; invocation for calling forth Light and energy; a visualisation to transmit this Light and energy; and a prayer of thanksgiving for the Light and energy received. For example, you may call upon the Lord Jesus or the healing angels to help you attune and to protect you and the client. You can visualise your aura and the aura of your client surrounded by white or blue Light, and you can transmit Light and energy calling forth the Holy Spirit and ask to be used as an instrument of Its great power of healing. To complete the healing you may say a prayer of gratitude for the healing Light and energy received. This is one example of a form that could be followed.

When the healer is ready, the Light and the true techniques are given. Those further ahead on the path who have the dharma to disseminate these techniques give us the wondrous gift of healing forms which enables us to transform this Light to an energy level where we can receive it and heal through it. Alice Bailey (1979, p. 155), in *Letters on Occult Meditation*, speaks of the gradual imparting of forms to the earnest student by the Teacher. When this is done with "strict obedience to the Laws, and steady adherence to the rules laid down, with skill in action aimed at .... the effects then are sure, and carry no karma with them." When the student is a person of good heart who is given such forms for use and the form is followed as it should be, the form will do the work, even though the student may be unconscious of it. As the student advances and the subtler faculties are developed, consciousness of the work done comes.

Creating a sacred place

When you work in your own healing room, you will find you need to cleanse and protect that room regularly. On the etheric plane such rooms can collect a lot of dross (a build up of congested energy) because of the amount of cleansing taking place on all levels. You can use crystals to help lift the vibration but you should be careful not to have too many. Just one crystal programmed to that specific task is enough. Perhaps a clear quartz cluster or an amethyst will help. Physical cleaning is also needed. The elemental forces love physical dirt and attach themselves to it. Regular wet dusting, vacuuming and etheric cleansing ensures a light atmosphere where good healing can take place. Many clients come with dross and over the day this collects. You need simply to be alert to this and have discipline in your cleansing and cleaning practices so that you can provide your clients with the right conditions for their healing. To do etheric cleansing you simply take a glass of water and with two fingers (your index and your middle finger) make the sign of the cross on the top of the glass three times saying, "In the name of Christ I ask that this water be made ready to cleanse and magnetise." Then place your palm over the top of the glass and visualise Light entering the water from your palm chakra for about a minute. The water is then ready to be used. Place the tips of your fingers in the top of the water and gently flick the water around the room.

Living by the Laws

The spiritual Laws are our protection. We must live by them. The teachings themselves are our greatest teachers, that is, the teachings of Theosophy; of Right Human Relations; of the Noble Eightfold Path (the Middle Way, a path for balanced living, as described by the Lord Gautama Buddha); the principles of Love and Truth. When we strive to live by them we are given a practical understanding of attunement and protection. We must learn to rise above the lower nature, overcome our fears and ignorance and begin educating ourselves with the needed knowledge, that will, when linked with our yearning hearts, become the wisdom we need to advance on the spiritual path.

Reincarnation

What is reincarnation?

In the chapter: *The Human Structure* we explored the fundamental aspects of our being - the Spirit, the soul and the personality. We learned how the Spirit creates a soul to manifest itself on the lower planes of nature and the soul creates a personality to help Spirit to manifest on still lower planes of nature. By experiencing life in the mental, emotional and physical worlds the soul is able to learn its lessons and grow. In so doing the soul evolves. Each time the soul casts a personality through which it can function the soul creates an incarnation, which we refer to as the lifetime of an individual. Reincarnation is a cyclic process; the process of returning again and again from the inner worlds into incarnation:

> The Law of Reincarnation asserts the existence of a living individualised Principle which dwells in and informs the body of a man, and which, on the death of the body passes into another body after a longer or shorter interval (Besant, 1985b, p.10).

> As a man, casting off worn-out garments, taketh new ones, so the dweller in the body, casting off worn-out bodies, entereth into others that are new (Besant, 1985a, p.26).

Through reincarnation we become aware of the cycle of existence. We become aware of the ethereal, eternal, immortal matter of Spirit and soul that live on after the death of the physical encasement. Each life we are given a new personality through which to function. It is carefully designed according to our karma, and to the lessons we need to learn in the course of our lifetime. Our successive bodily lives link with the common thread of the soul. Though our personality life changes in each incarnation, the soul remains constant.

Reincarnation is one of the Divine Laws. We sometimes call it the Law of Rebirth. It exists under the Law of Evolution which is the process of progressive development towards spiritual perfection.

What is it that reincarnates?

It is the soul that reincarnates, expressing the Will of God. The soul chooses and builds a suitable vehicle on the levels of the physical, emotional and mental planes. Through this vehicle it learns the next lessons needed to further its evolution. We develop our mind and feelings from birth and our personality takes its shape. Eventually, when the soul considers the personality to be ready, it slowly reveals its nature to the personality.

The role of karma in reincarnation

Reincarnation can also be referred to as the Path of Return. It is the process of returning incarnation after incarnation to continue the perfecting process on Earth. If we develop our good qualities and persevere, we slowly learn. To understand the process of the Path of Return, an understanding of the Law of Karma (Cause and Effect) comes into play. If we do not achieve perfection, the soul must return and continue the perfecting process on Earth. C.W. Leadbeater (1987, pp. 44-46), in *An Outline of Theosophy*, likens each incarnation to a schoolroom in which we have to learn the needed lessons. If we do not learn them in this life, we come back to learn that lesson in the next. To explain this, Leadbeater tells a story written by Berry Benson in the Century Magazine, May 1894:

A boy went to school. He was very little. All that he knew he had drawn in with his mother's milk. His teacher (who was God) placed him in the lowest class and gave him these lessons to learn: Thou shalt not kill. Thou shalt not steal. So the man did not kill; but he was cruel, and he stole. At the end of the day (when his beard was gray - when the night was come) his teacher (who was God) said: Thou hast learned not to kill. Thou shalt do no hurt to any living thing. But the other lessons thou hast not learned. Come back tomorrow.

On the morrow he came back, a little boy. And his teacher (who was God) put him in a class a little higher and gave him these lessons to learn. Thou shalt do no hurt to any living thing. Thou shalt not steal. Thou shalt not cheat. So the man did no hurt to any living thing but he stole and he cheated. And at the end of the day (when his beard was gray - when the night was come) his teacher (who was God) said: Thou hast learned to be merciful. But the other lessons thou hast not learned. Come back tomorrow.

Again on the morrow, he came back, a little boy. And his teacher (who was God) put him in a class a little higher and gave him these lessons to learn: Thou shalt not steal. Thou shalt not cheat. Thou shalt not covet. So the man did not steal; but he cheated and he coveted. And at the end of the day (when his beard was gray - when the night was come) his teacher (who was God) said: Thou hast learned not to steal. But the other lessons thou hast not learned. Come back, my child, tomorrow.

This is what I have read in the faces of men and women, in the book of the world, and in the scroll of the heavens, which is writ with stars.

In this story we see that reincarnation gives us time and opportunity to learn the lessons that God and our soul would have us learn. It is by reincarnating that our soul is able to evolve.

Why do we incarnate?

In *An Abridgement of the Secret Doctrine*, H.P. Blavatsky (1969) refers to the cycle of incarnation as "the cycle of necessity." This takes place according to the Law of Periodicity, ebb and flow, day and night, life and death, sleeping and waking. Reincarnation therefore is one of the fundamental Laws of the universe. It is the playground through which we experience the eternity of the universe. Blavatsky refers to it as an obligatory pilgrimage. According to Annie Besant (1985b, p. 52), its fundamental cause is "the desire for active life - the thirst for sentient experience." In individual terms it is "a renewed longing for the taste of existence on the physical form." The soul returns to a human life to have experience that can be felt and perceived by the senses. Unlike our personality self, the soul does not have desire to be perfect, rather it moves toward perfection as a natural consequence of the evolutionary path upon which it walks. It has a willingness to give service and sacrifice itself for the Plan. Reincarnation also provides an opportunity for us to work with our true nature, overcome our negative tendencies and cultivate virtues.

We bring with us predispositions and innate tendencies from former lifetimes. Our personality is different in each lifetime, yet we are a summation of all that has gone before and must repay our debts:

> All souls incarnate and re-incarnate under the Law of Rebirth. Hence each life is not only a recapitulation of life experience, but an assuming of ancient obligations, a recovery of old relations, an opportunity for the paying

of old indebtedness, a chance to make restitution and progress, an awakening of deep-seated qualities, the recognition of old friends and enemies, the solution of revolting injustices, and the explanation of that which conditions the man, and makes him what he is. Such is the Law which is crying now for universal recognition (Bailey, 1987, p. 338).

We can consciously cause our liberation from the cycle of rebirth by striving to cooperate with the soul. A disciple of the Hierarchy (a person initiated in soul, having experienced the birth of Christ within and who has decided to work for the unfoldment of Christ's Plan), for example, would incarnate with the desire to pay karma off rapidly and so be liberated for service. Then the disciple would work out what the service is that the Christ requires. This reveals the dharma, the life's work, of the disciple. The disciple incarnates to play his or her part in the greater Plan. For example, souls incarnate in groups. If a group is failing in its purpose, an initiate (a person who has received the third or fourth initiation in soul and who is guided by the Christ-self) may incarnate to balance that group. The initiate does so by expressing one perfected principle, for example, true compassion. Often this takes place not just in one life but in several successive lives. It is a sacrifice for the initiate who has nearly completed the cycle of reincarnation.

Reincarnation is not a punishment. Theosophy holds that God is both almighty and all-loving. Through reincarnation we can learn and are able to pay back our debts. We have all been both good and evil and can learn that from good comes goodness and from evil comes evil, sorrow and limitation. We are responsible for our limitations. The knowledge of karma and reincarnation gives us a framework within which to work, not a prescription. It is up to us to be aware of the Divine Laws; knowing them we can better live to create goodness and peace in our lives.

The method of reincarnation

Birth

We can see reincarnation as the descent of Spirit into matter. When the soul approaches incarnation, a new personality is formed, that is, a new mental, astral and physical-etheric body (the etheric double) is built. The Lords of Karma, aware of the karma to be worked out, provide the "mould suited to express the karma to be worked out and after this the etheric double is built" (Besant, 1985b, p. 38).

When the soul decides to incarnate, it needs to manifest the appropriate outer form on the physical level. This includes matter on the physical, etheric, astral and mental levels. The process is a complex one. Geoffrey Hodson (1985) describes it in *The Miracle of Birth*. The soul directs this process and is assisted by the angelic kingdom who form the inner bodies. The devas (angels) help on many levels, from nature spirits assisting in building of the etheric body to higher devas assisting in the formation of the mental body. Throughout conception, pregnancy and birth, the devas are at work in varying degrees at different stages. To grasp this idea it is helpful to think of the soul incarnating, not only into the physical body but also into the other bodies. The mind, the emotions and the physical body all become the vehicle for the soul. The soul itself still dwells in the higher regions, with will, wisdom and intelligence greater than is capable of being expressed on the lower levels. The foetus has a background of many previous lifetimes and has carried over into this life developed faculties. If you wish to find out more Hodson describes in detail the development of the mind, emotions and physical body of a foetus.

Death

We can look upon death as the rising of Spirit from matter. The more subtle bodies free themselves from the physical and etheric double that are disintegrating. At death most people go to the astral level and stay there between incarnations. The level people go to is determined according to their consciousness. The thought body goes through a process of consolidating and assimilating its experiences until these experiences are ready to be passed on to the soul for safe keeping and development (Besant, 1985b). We call this the devachanic period where we gain equilibrium. Eventually the thought body also disintegrates leaving the soul to stay on the inner levels, in a state of oneness, until the soul reincarnates and creates a new personality through which to function.

The place of reincarnation in evolution

The task of reincarnation is to bring Spirit into matter and to raise our consciousness to the Divine. In so doing we reunite the separated aspects to the One (Besant, 1985b). According to many theosophists, H.P. Blavatsky (1969), C.W. Leadbeater (1977, 1986) and Annie Besant (1985b, 1987) to name a few, our incarnations follow the process of evolution. Slowly we learn, if we develop our good qualities and persevere. We can turn our failures into correct actions and heal our wounds. Our character becomes moulded through our actions in each incarnation. Our soul keeps a record of our gains and our losses and this determines the next personality and physical manifestation expression of the soul. The virtues we develop become innate and are stored in the causal body. Our vices form seeds of karma which are built into the etheric double in lives to come.

Remembering our past

Reincarnation gives us time and opportunity for growth and life experience. The soul has within it the memory of all past incarnations and when it sees the vehicle is ready, it reveals that past. We cannot recollect previous incarnations from within the personality body, as this vehicle has not had any. It is as we come closer to the higher bodies and begin to wish to align with the soul that it reveals our previous incarnations. When we observe them we usually find a series of lifetimes geared to help us obtain particular qualities and learn particular lessons. We remember the lessons again and we have the opportunity in this current life to take note and choose accordingly. The understanding that comes from the lifetimes remembered helps to reveal the Law of Justice. The Law of Justice is Universal Justice. It contains the Law of Karma (see chapter: *The Law of Karma*). It takes into account all that we are and delivers to us our due. Through the understanding of a higher Justice and an acceptance that what we do to others shall be done unto us, we begin to see that a Higher Plan is in operation and become aware of the need to take responsibility for our actions.

Redemption

Redemption is the process through which we make amends for our misdeeds and failures. Our previous vices create negative character traits that live within us for us to redeem. When we work with the healing Light of Christ, redemption takes place. The high vibrating Light penetrates our grosser matter and redeems it. As the Light shines on us it reveals within us, the light and the shadow. In the Light of Redemption we see how we can draw upon our past for our strengths: we remember where our weaknesses led us, learning from each action and choosing the path we now decide to take. We also become aware of the need for forgiveness of ourselves and others for the vices and failures we experience.

Through the process of redemption we clear the way for the soul to gain more control of our personality. Redemption sees the Christ working in our lives and frees us from the negative feelings that we have gathered over lifetimes of experiences. Through redemption we retain the knowledge gained from the past and release negative energies like anger, rebellion, fear or guilt that are part of our experience. The redemptive processes that are possible through the reincarnation cycle, enable us to be liberated from the negative and unredeemed aspects of ourselves.

When we have felt suffering and pain we may become afraid of life and do all in our power to prevent pain and suffering again. This can happen during one incarnation or over a number of incarnations. The story below is an example of how fear can easily develop from one incident, and how it can continue to affect our lives until we become conscious of it and heal it. In this instance it is a story from my own childhood.

Beginning the search

Starting new schools was a common event for me. My father's job meant that we moved a lot. This particular school was red brick and the corridors were long and dark. I was just old enough to be trusted to walk to school. The school year had only just started this time and so even though I was a new girl, the friendship groups were not so strong that I could not enter. This particular day was sunny and warm, the usual Brisbane weather, I liked it here. I didn't have to wear shoes and I liked hiding under my big straw hat. The elastic under my chin gave me something to chew on when I got nervous which I always did when I began in a new school. It was Tuesday and the normal procedure was to begin with a general assembly. The bitumen was already getting hot and I could see that if I didn't ask the girl in front of me for one of her sandals to stand on my feet would blister from the heat, which made parts of the bitumen like melted tar. "God save the Queen" played over the P.A. system. It must have been an old record because it crackled quite a deal. We were having marching practice because the teachers hadn't been happy about the scraggly way we'd entered the rooms. Three times we went in and out. I hadn't eaten breakfast and was feeling a little faint. A knot began to grow in my stomach. I didn't know where I'd be sitting or who I could talk to yet. I didn't know anybody's name, except that my teacher would be Mrs. Donovan. I followed the lead of my group. We walked up the stairs and along the dark corridors. The doors to the classrooms were sliding ones. Mrs. Donovan wore her hair in a bun and had round glasses. She looked old. She asked me to wait while the others entered. I became more nervous now and she went in, leaving me outside. I could see her speaking to the class. She opened the door and beckoned me in. The class was deathly silent and she pointed to a seat - a double one- with no one else in it. I sat down. As she began the lesson, the knot in my stomach began to dissipate. I could see out the window. I became confident enough to look around the room at the other students. I began to get bored and started sliding from side to side across my seat.

I felt a mighty thud on my head, and saw Mrs. Donovan standing glaring beside me.

"Ow!" I said.

"Sit still!"

This was something I was not used to. I could see I would need to be very controlled here and so I began daydreaming immediately. That was far more peaceful.

The hours spent in the one room were long. I suffered varying states of physical illness in this particular class; ranging from nausea to diarrhoea and fainting. One day when I arrived the class was being divided up for religion education classes. They spoke to the whole group of classes in my year. We were to go to different rooms for these classes. There was a room for Methodists, a room for Catholics, one for Church of England children, one for Presbyterian and some other names I hadn't heard of. I began to be excited by this. Here was the chance to learn about all these different religions, I thought.

"What are you?" I was asked.

I looked blank. My mind raced. My mother had told me I was Church of England and I knew a bit about that. I'd like to know what Methodist is, I thought. "Can I be Methodist?" I said. "I would like to know what it is."

"What are you?"

"Well, I'm Church of England, or that's what my mother has told me I am."

With that Mr. Cain, who had been asking the questions, went red. He was the Vice Principal. He had a suit jacket on and he moved his arm rapidly and with a flick, a bamboo cane came out of his sleeve.

"Stand up and bend over," he said.

He was very angry. I didn't understand why and I was filled with terror.

"You'll go to room 22B and stay there for your religious classes," he said.

He caned me several times on the behind. I went numb.

"Move," he said. I went quickly.

As I went I wondered about Mr Cain's anger. I had been curious. I didn't know there were so many different religions. I only knew there were Protestants and Catholics. To hear of other ways of looking at God intrigued me. I wanted to know more. What did the Methodists think? Mum had told me the Catholics didn't eat meat on Fridays. The Church of England people didn't eat it during Lent and on Good Friday. How many similarities were there? How many differences? I had a thousand questions and I could see that for now they would remain unanswered. It was not until my early twenties that I dared to ask any of them.

I couldn't see why everyone didn't learn about all the different religions and then choose the one they wanted. I would've liked that.

In the story above my terror of the teacher who caned me went deep into my unconscious and remained there for many years, until I was ready and able to deal with the incident.

People can become aware of their past and sometimes previous incarnations in healing, meditation and regression. The soul reveals the memory when we are ready. When we become aware of our past we need to make sure that we perceive it with the love, compassion and understanding of our current level of consciousness. By going into our past, radiating Light, we can come to know our path and patterns. When we do this with the help of the Light we are looking from a higher perspective and can be more objective. We can know our past and not be influenced or enmeshed with the old emotions from it. By looking from a higher perspective on life - the past, the present and the future - we can become pure vehicles for the holy Light and free ourselves from unnecessary limitations. If we view our past incarnations without wisdom, understanding, love and Light, we can get false impressions about those lifetimes. The truth of those lifetimes can become distorted and we lose sight of the true lessons. The trick is to learn the lessons and not to lose perspective of the truth. In the story below this is made quite clear.

The stolen jewels

I had been planning my escape for some time. Each day I sat with the Queen and in my head, in the silence, as I brushed her hair the one hundred strokes, I would rehearse my plan. When I could steal a moment alone, I would raid her dressing-table - the jewels could provide me with the life I wanted, or so I thought. The opportunity came one evening when the Queen was called out to tend one of her children. The child's adversity was my opportunity, and I took it. I opened the dressing-table drawer and the jewels glistened. There were so many. I moved quickly, stuffing them down my corset, feeling the cold as they scratched my skin. Quickly I moved back to my former position so as to look as if I hadn't done anything but wait demurely. My heart was beating fast. It seemed that this was the final episode of a series of acts which had escalated in severity: a series of misdemeanours which had begun with small white lies and by their very nature had increased in magnitude in order to cover up for all the preceding untruths. I had lied and cheated and now I was stealing. It did not feel out of character for with every step on the road I had taken I opened a little more each time to the darkness within me.

In the days that followed I was wary of my movements. It was very soon discovered that the jewels were missing and I felt guilt for my actions; even worse, the fear of being caught began to overtake me. I felt the Queen suspected me but I could not be completely sure. A meeting of all the court was called. I sat in the back in the hope that I could hide. The Queen began to speak and it felt as though the Wrath of God had descended. Initially the accusations were general and I was pleading within with God, totally obsessed with the hope that I had managed to get away with my deed. No sooner had I convinced myself of my good fortune than her words came thundering towards me.

"Marion, you are to leave. I banish you from this court."

She knew, as she knew everything. My body felt as though it would crack. The energy within it was turned inward as if convulsing. Sharp excruciating pains filled my solar plexus and I stood, feeling lower than low: the scum of the Earth. I turned tail and ran, humiliated and ashamed, my mind was in chaos and I could feel myself going insane. There was no escape now from the guilt and the fear. Paranoia stepped in.

I had seen this scene before, but never so clearly and never with as much understanding and acceptance of my responsibility for my actions. Is it any wonder that I feel so low about myself at times, even now, centuries later.

"That is the problem - now you are not Marion and you must forgive yourself for the past, forgive yourself, the Queen, and all involved. When you see the past you must make sure that you go into it radiating Light. It is of extreme importance that you come to know your past so that you are not influenced by it. Only in this way can you become a pure vehicle of Holy Light, that is sanctified and free from the limitations of your past. If you enter into the past without today's understanding and Light and without love, false impressions can be made and the truth can become distorted. The truth is that you loved the Queen, but in that life, you let the shadow take over and the love couldn't get through. In this life, the love for your Teacher is very strong. In coming close to her life and aura, the shadow will have to fall away. It is squeezed out of the aura because it cannot stay there in that Light. If you are honest with yourself, you will recognise that this shadow is a past condition and not anything you need to be concerned about in this life. Justice is as it has always been. Your payment for your actions in that lifetime has been paid, and much of the karma due to that was paid in the same life. You know what it is to lose perspective of the truth and it is important not to lose perspective of it now. The issue here is not the karma, for balance has taken place. It is however necessary for you bring forth the *quality of forgiveness, send it deeply into that past within you, so that you can work now in trust of those around you: having faith that you will walk in truth, choosing Right Thought, Right Speech and Right Action, for you know the consequences of wrong thought, wrong speech and wrong action. You have used the memory of this life in a negative way. You have used it to punish yourself, to prove to yourself your lack of worth and as an excuse to not work for the Light as you are 'not good enough.' The memory was not given for this purpose. It was given so that you could see where you have come from; that you have learned and that you are moving into integrity, into Light. It was given, too, to balance you when you start thinking that you are so good, so full of Light and so perfect: to give you compassion for your fellow beings who grapple with the lessons you then learned in such tragic and unfortunate circumstances. The Light redeems and heals. Always look through Light, otherwise you may cast shadow upon yourself when it is not needed. You have been a liar, a cheat and a thief and you are still loved. With God you are forgiven. All are forgiven."*

I became aware that the world of matter and the world of Spirit were quite different. I felt myself to be in the world of Spirit looking into the world of matter.

"Remember to bring Spirit down into the world of matter. When you are in matter, look beyond to the world of Spirit. Remember what is real and what is unreal. Don't get caught in the aspect of form. When you look at past actions, remember you aren't the same person now. Get on with life, be enthusiastic, for life is a great gift. Use your freedom to express yourself, to be and to serve. Don't be afraid of suffering and pain as it helps you to grow."

I could see that I had to stop running and face this pain and suffering. For within it was enormous love and understanding and it held within it the key to releasing much of the negative patterning within me. In opening to it I could finally let it go.

As I did this, something very beautiful happened. An expansion began to take place within my heart centre and another positive lifetime was revealed.

"*You've been too busy casting shadow upon yourself for your mistakes. So much so that you have been unable to see any of the goodness within yourself. Finally now you are letting go some of that, so there is more room to see your goodness, allowing you to move into a more balanced energy within; not overwhelmed by feelings of exaggerated self-worth or lack of it; conscious instead of the purity of your heart, guided and directed more closely by the soul. Be alert that when this experience of your heart leaves you, you will be tempted yet again to sink into the negativity of self-denigration and may even start to doubt this beautiful experience you now have. But proof will come and you will trust as each experience unfolds: it will build within your aura a seed of the new life and you will open to it.*"

Proof did come and yes, I did sink into the depression again, but I had learnt a lot from this session. I began to see how I had used guilt to punish myself and how I had misused my memories of negative actions performed in negative ways. Guilt began to release as I learned that I needed to forgive myself for my past and to use the Light given in this life to redeem that past.

When we discover incarnations about which we are ashamed, or from which we still carry hurt, we can bring forth the quality of forgiveness and send it deeply into that past. If we look at our past to learn the needed lessons, we come to know the consequences of wrong thought, wrong speech and wrong action and can make new choices based on that learning. We can find faith that we will learn from our mistakes and, to the best of our ability, can decide to walk in truth, choosing appropriate and balanced thought, speech and action. When we do this we can begin to live in trust of ourselves and those around us. In the excerpt below we see movement from blame and shame into forgiveness.

Meeting the Father

"There are some situations you don't want to happen, and some you have no control over. Often they are not as bad as they seem. They are part of the soul's plan and you must learn to trust it even though you may not understand it or want it."

I had for some time known there was much in my past that I needed to forgive; specific events that I had become aware of in this and other lifetimes, but it seemed to be an intellectual knowing rather than a state of total awareness.

"Look deeply in your heart."

As I looked, I saw a beautiful scene where love pervaded my past.

"In Christ's Light there is only love."

My heart opened and I could feel within me the Light of forgiveness surging through. I felt lifted for a moment, into a Light which understood all. It had compassion and understanding for every aspect of human existence. Many scenes followed, scenes of former lifetimes where I had, from the perspective of this lifetime, judged

myself, for my actions; times when I had seen myself leave the path and walk in darkness.

"It is a karmic process; a path that needed to be walked, so that you would know the suffering. You shouldn't see those lifetimes as failures, because they have given you courage and strength and have helped to give you the ability to discriminate, to know and see the difference in energies of Light and dark. The pain of the separation from God's Light has helped prepare you to a point in your development where your heart is ready to open. If it weren't for those lifetimes you wouldn't be in that

position. Sometimes movement comes from walking in the desert and spending time in the wilderness. Without that, the suffering of the heart couldn't be experienced and the heart would not be ready for the Light of Christ, the Lord of Love. These periods of pain and moments when you touch on pain are therefore of great significance for they mark the stages at which the heart petals can begin to open. They are like seeds that are planted in the life path to act as a trigger for the opening of the heart. These events may seem unfair and unkind because the personality does not understand them but they are actually great gifts from God for us to learn from. So you see, there is a reason, there is a rhyme, and each time you feel the pain of life on Earth be grateful and know it is serving to open your heart just a little bit more. When you see experiences from the past, you often judge the personality of your past as being either good or bad, right or wrong, and forget that, given that they were who they were, there was no other way they could react or respond because they acted from the personality they were just as you do now. God never sees them as wrong for making mistakes. Those personalities persevered to the end of each lifetime, through every test and trial. Stop judging them. Let them be. Let them rest and develop the personality you have now. Call on the personalities of the past for the strength and love they can give, the lessons they have learned and the wisdom they contain. Don't call on them to punish yourself with guilt. Make the motive pure. Let it be only to know and to grow from the knowing."

I began to see an end to the cycle, to the pattern of guilt and shame for past actions. I could see that I could now walk with beings of Light, not having to walk in the darkness any more.

"You have returned to the fold, my child, and I welcome you with open arms. You walked in darkness and felt the pain, but know that in our hearts you always remained with us. You went knowing you would lose consciousness of the Light and what you set out to do you have achieved. You can lift into the Light of Christ, into the Heart and, over the next five hundred years, the heart petals will unfold as they should."

The Father came close once again, His arms outstretched in Love. I could feel a deep pleasure that I had released the pain that had been sitting there for so long.

"Walk with head held high. Forget the past and look to the Light, reunited with those who knew you were of Light, even then, when others could not see this and you yourself doubted."

People often have a series of incarnations where they are paying back a particular karma, for example, someone who was an oppressor in the Spanish Inquisition, responsible for many deaths, may incarnate quickly after that to pay back the karma of that lifetime. The next time around he or she is in the role of victim, in the same inquisition. Perhaps the next time to continue paying off this karma he or she would be at the mercy of people who are torturing him or her in some way, maybe in another war such as World War II. The soul has the memory of the events of these lives and personalities. As we move towards the soul, we move towards that memory, and sometimes we awaken the memory in us. It is through that awakening that we become conscious of reincarnation as an established fact. It becomes something that we know has occurred and we know it because our brain is beginning to sense that very subtle vibration and the higher soul memory of those lifetimes.

It is important that we look through Light always, otherwise we can cast shadows upon ourselves and others. To God in our human form we are faceless: we can take off the personas that are our personalities. They are like coats. To find the truth of ourselves and our existence we must go more deeply within and find our soul.

Using memory wisely

We can use our memory of our past, in this life, in a positive way. However, some of us punish ourselves for what we have done, and try to prove our lack of worth. We use our apparent lack of worth as an excuse not to work for the Light. If we wish to use the memory for its correct purpose, that is, to see who we are, where we have come from, where we are going and what it is we need to learn now, we begin to move into the Light with integrity. We realise that the understanding of reincarnation balances us. The memory of these incarnations reminds us that we are not perfect and beyond error. The knowledge that comes through the understanding of reincarnation and its process can give us compassion for our fellow beings who grapple with their learning lessons. Through our memory we have a unity with them, instead of a separateness, giving us an ability to empathise.

A new attitude to death

The personality and body we now occupy is a temporary house in which the Self lives. Death is a change, or transition to a new form, or lack of form. When we see death this way we can more easily accept it, approach it with less fear, less panic and less need for grief, although we may still feel the need for grief. When people die, we miss that particular personality and know that in that form they will not return, yet their Spirit lives on. We are comforted when we stop and consider "What are we but Spirit?" There is, from the higher perspective, no loss. The following story illustrates this.

Eternal Love

I had been experiencing a lot of grief soon after the death of someone very close to me. So I booked a healing to deal with it. As the healing began a scene came of a public execution. There was a man awaiting the guillotine. I could feel his state of being within me and I could sense an incredible peace inside. The peace came from knowing that the punishment was just. The crime was one of passion for a lady loved, committed in jealousy. The man had killed another unintentionally. However, he had sought to harm the other. I explored the scene further and saw a woman in the crowd. I felt the enormous love the man felt for her and she for him. Nothing could disturb it, not even the threat of death. The closer it came to the moment of the falling of the guillotine, the more deeply the peace and the strength of the love was felt. The blade of the guillotine fell. In me I felt a strange, fearful and confusing feeling that was quite momentary but very strong. I began to feel that I was the man. I felt suspended in the air observing the scene below. I could see the woman below in the crowd. Her face expressed a deep anguish and cry; simultaneously, her Spirit arose and met with mine and we danced on the inner together in great freedom and joy. We were Spirits together dancing in the Light. I could sense that this was Reality and I knew in every cell of my being that love outlived death. The thread of it remained unbroken and the union of Spirit in love was felt.

The scene changed. I saw a young man with dark hair in Bethany, listening to Lord Jesus speak. He then travelled for some time until he came to some caves near Masada, where many of the Essenes were living. He went into a cave where he met with an older man, with white hair, and modest robes. They sat together and an incredible peace was shared, not by conversation as yet, though that followed, but by a deep love between them. When they spoke they shared about the Master's teaching, and shared the wisdom the older man had discovered in his meditation and experience. I felt the peace and love the men shared within me. The old man spoke; I knew he had shared the soul of the person I was grieving, just as I had shared the soul of the young man. "When you remember me, no matter what is happening in the outside world around you, remember this peace and this love - this is what we share." I knew this peace and love to be the Peace and Love of the Lord Maitreya, the Unifier, and I knew that this Peace and this Love came from an eternal well where Spirit abides. I knew that there was no need for grief; rather, I could choose the memory of the union of Spirit.

Why don't I remember?

Sometimes we ask, "Why do I not remember my past lives?" According to Annie Besant (1985b), in her book *Reincarnation*, the true "I" does remember. The true "I" is the part of us that is not yet conscious, not yet fully awake. It is the part of us that is in responsive union with the true Self. Through our union with the true Self, which is the soul, we can begin to know the reality of immortality. By becoming sensitive to delicate and subtle vibrations sent down by the Light we can begin to know the truth of reincarnation. However, a person's ability to remember his or her past lives is not a criterion for a more developed soul. Many factors, such as karma and the need in this life to know such things, contribute to the awakening of the memory.

Questions about reincarnation are very common, and much confusion exists about the subject. It is often not until people reach that place in themselves where they awaken the memory and become sensitive to it, through the brain's receptivity, that people lose their confusion. It is difficult to tell those who do not remember lifetimes that incarnation is a truth. Occasionally people have the knowledge of reincarnation but until that point it can only stand as a theory. H.P. Blavatsky explains it scientifically. However, if your faith is such that it does not allow comprehension of reincarnation, then it is difficult to really be in touch with and reach the subtleties of reincarnation.

A person may access the capacity to find out about particular past lifetimes. He or she may see particular instances and lessons that were learned or not learned. This capacity to review past lessons becomes an extremely valuable tool that we can work with to facilitate spiritual development. It is no use to us if we remain caught in the glamour of who we think we might have been, or if we do not look to find the lessons we needed to learn and how they relate to us now.

Thousands upon thousands of human beings are awakening to the knowledge of previous lifetimes. There is a growing understanding about this constancy of Spirit that remains, regardless of the physical form and the current life personality. It is today a system of understanding that is becoming more and more accepted in the western world through the emergence of the new energies of this present age and of healing and therapy systems. Reincarnation has for many years been recognised in the East in certain religions like Buddhism and Hinduism. Now the western world is starting to incorporate this understanding into its belief systems. The level of vibration of human beings is increasing. People are becoming aware of their past and of the help they can gain by looking into it. We can recognise the benefit of going back into childhood and releasing traumas experienced then. We can do the same with past lives. We can release the traumas of the past and move forward progressing and developing higher qualities in this life and lives to come.

Exploring our past

To get the true picture in our memory of previous incarnations, we need to increase our vibration of Light. The truth, as we perceive it, is only as true as our consciousness allows us to perceive it. Every day as our consciousness grows we come to know more of the truth. What we hold as true on one day may the next day appear not true, but it was the truth as far as we could perceive it then. With the broadening of consciousness we gain a greater capacity for perceiving truth.

It is important for us to remember to look beyond to the world of Spirit; to remember what is Real and what is unreal and not become caught in the form aspect. When we attempt to judge ourselves or others for past actions from previous incarnations we need to acknowledge that neither they nor we are the former people. We may, however, still carry karma from those lifetimes with us. We need to get on with life and be enthusiastic for the great gifts given, use our freedom, express ourselves, "be" and serve.

Karma

What is karma?

Karma is one of the Divine Laws which is called the Law of Cause and Effect or the Law or Retribution. It is a Law that exists under the Law of Divine Justice. It is sometimes explained by the phrase, 'as you sow, so shall you reap.' Unfortunately, karma is not well understood. If it were, it would not carry with it the threat of punishment as it does for so many. Karma is not a punishment or something to be afraid of. It has embedded within it the Love of God and the Divine Law of Justice, which are at work to protect us and help us grow. H. P. Blavatsky (1990, p. 174), in *The Theosophical Glossary*, refers to karma as

> the power that controls all things, the resultant of moral action ... or the moral effect of an act committed for the attainment of something which gratifies a personal desire. There is the karma of merit and karma of demerit. Karma neither punishes nor rewards. It is simply the one Universal Law which guides unerringly..."

In Blavatsky's definition we see that karma is the result or effect created by our acts. The action of karma can give to us, or can take away, in order to restore balance. People have a tendency to look at the karma of merit as good karma, and the karma of demerit as bad karma. Essentially karma is not good or bad, it is simply given according to Divine Justice. We need to learn to embrace karma in a new way. Karma is all essentially good, as it helps us to learn and grow, keeping the Universe in a state of balance and making us all responsible for our actions. It is neutral and does not judge us for our actions. It restores the balance. When we come to see karma in this way a new attitude is born within, which assists us to accept the Universal Plan and our part in it. We begin to see that we are co-creators with the Divine when it comes to creating our own lives. When we deny the existence of karma, we tend to go through life feeling everything is unfair, or without consideration of how others may feel. We may even become resentful and bitter about life experiences that we deem to be negative. Such a view, which is not accepting of the Law of Karma, often means we suffer unnecessarily. It becomes more difficult for us to see our errors and make changes. Instead we bathe in blame, shame and self-pity. Karma actually helps us to become free. Through it we can repay our debts morally. Karma is in effect on all levels of our existence - physically, emotionally, mentally and spiritually. When we transgress a Law, karma helps us to make amends.

The role of motive

The motive behind our actions determines our karma. For example, if we were to decide to do a loving act for another, one day that loving act would return to us in some form, perhaps from the person towards whom we were loving, perhaps from another. If the motive for the loving act is selfless, where we are truly giving with no thought of return, then when we need it, we would be the recipient of a loving act from another. However, if the motive for performing the loving act was to gain others' attention, or to manipulate circumstances to our advantage, we may neutralise the karma for the loving act and even create a karma of demerit for ourselves where instead of gaining, we lose. Often as human beings, in our actions, we have a mixture of motives in operation. Some are positive and some are not so positive. We must dare to look honestly at ourselves if we wish to tell what our driving motive is. Human nature can be changed. New habits can be cultivated. To strengthen our character and thus the virtues of character we must dare to look at our vices and unconscious agendas and work to change them. Simultaneously we must put effort into creating new and better habits that can take the place of negative habits and attitudes that keep us attracting karma of demerit. As we cultivate these better habits, we attract karma of merit and so create better lives for ourselves. If our motive is "I will do better so that better things can happen to me," we know we are not yet enlightened. When we give selflessly ("I will do better so that I may serve others better"), with trust in the universe, and do not count the cost, we are coming closer to enlightenment and to being at peace with the Law of Karma.

Karma is our teacher

In life we have karmic lessons which we must learn in order to evolve. Karma *encourages* us to learn. It does not punish us so that we will learn. The karma we have in a particular life comes from the summation of all the lives that have gone before. In each incarnation, the soul embodies knowing that certain karma is to be repaid in that life. The soul knows that in order for the personality to learn how to live or not live according to the Divine Laws, he or she must balance the karma. It knows too that in order for the individual to learn the splendour of the universe and how it works, the person must also reap the karma for his or her good efforts.

Exactly how and when karma will be repaid, or reaped, can vary according to the nature of the karma. This possibility for variation depends upon what the soul wishes the personality to learn, and the decision of the Lords of Karma. The Lords of Karma are great Beings who reside on the inner levels. It is their job to oversee the Law of Divine Justice, always taking the whole into account whilst also looking into the nature of the soul's needs for the individual concerned.

As we make our choices in life and act upon them, we are creating karma for ourselves. Be it karma of merit or demerit, the choice is ours. This is where the notion of free will comes in. We have the capacity, through our choices, to create, or better, to co-create our lives with the assistance of the Divine forces. How we create it, for better or for worse, is up to us. Karma teaches us the consequences of our thoughts, our feelings and our actions. If we are sensitive and open to it, it can help us learn how to shape our lives in such a way that we develop spiritually, mentally, emotionally and physically, and benefit the growth of the soul.

Karma helps us to see the world and our part in it from a higher perspective. It lifts us beyond the judgement, suffering, pain and hurt in which we are so easily enmeshed. It helps us see that ultimately we are responsible for our spiritual destiny. All the choices we make have consequences; we must learn to take our time and choose carefully - to stop and think before we act and to take responsibility for our decisions. We can let go of the tendency to go into blame or self pity and see that we create our reality. If we wish that reality to be different, we need simply change ourselves and make new choices, the ones our soul would have us make.

When we do not understand the Law of Karma, we also do not understand that the pain and the suffering we experience at times may be necessary for our growth, to help us open our hearts, and to develop compassion for ourselves and those around us. If we could open to trust in karma and its influence on us, which is evident through the events in our lives, we could spend less time worrying or angry that events do not go as we plan. We would come to see that a Higher Plan is in operation, one that we do not need to understand, one that we can open to one step at a time, in trust and love. To live in hope and faith of a better life, a better world where we do not count the cost of suffering, is to open to love. Karma is a vehicle for the Love of God and it guides us with a firm, steady hand.

Types of karma

A record of our karma is kept in the causal body. This record is kept in karmic seeds which are planted in the etheric double as we incarnate. Some of the seeds will come to fruition in the present life. Others will remain as seeds, to be paid or reaped at a future time, depending on the needs of the soul and the choices the personality makes as it maps its way through life.

The activation of some of the karmic seeds is inevitable. It cannot be avoided or offset.

> There are cases where the force of the karma of the past is so strong that no effort of the present can suffice to overbear it (Besant, 1987, p. 47).

Not all karma is inevitable. Karma which is in the process of being made can be offset, particularly if we choose to look for and learn the associated lesson. We cannot avoid or escape the karma. It must be paid, but we can have impact upon its nature by our decision to accept it and let it work within us.

Karma brings us opportunity. The power of its force can be just what we need to push us to a great height, or it may oppose our desires and challenge us to deal with a negative aspect of our past which needs redemption. It helps us to see where we have strengths we can draw on and where we must work to purify and transmute our lower nature. The karmic force may help us and propel us forwards, for example through giving an increased energy of vitality which makes it possible to achieve a task that we need to achieve. It may restrain or hinder us, for example, by denying us money we may need to fulfil our aim. In either case, it is Justice in action and is given to us because we are ready for it, even if the personality may resist it. As we open to it, karma helps to restore balance and equilibrium to our lives. In some lifetimes the soul decides to pay off a large amount of karma quickly - perhaps through illness. This will enable the soul to create better conditions in a future time when better conditions are needed for the unfoldment of the Plan. Paying off karma quickly can speed up the soul's development.

Karma and the healer

When a healer understands the Divine Laws, such as the Law of Reincarnation and the Law of Karma, he or she can help clients to find understanding of life. Knowledge of the Laws also makes a proper diagnosis possible, as it enables us to look at the whole, considering the pattern of our lives, the result of our actions and realistic possibilities for change. It is easier to tolerate and accept others, rather than judge them, when we acknowledge that we too have been like them. The healer can assist the client to move through blame, shame and self-pity into an attitude of personal responsibility. The awareness of karma helps us to become aware of conditions that are given to us to learn. Instead of wasting our time being angry about these conditions, we can get on with taking responsibility for them and learn to live with them. The healer also becomes aware of his or her responsibility in healing work. See chapter: *The Healer*. Understanding karma helps us to understand life.

Creating better lives

Knowledge and understanding of the Divine Laws, such as the Law of Karma, gives us the possibility of looking at our lives and our karmic patterns, and, if we wish, to do something about them. Rather than being angry and self-pitying, we can put our energy to understanding how we have created our life and how we can change it, if we are unhappy with what we have created. It inspires us to become better people. Through it we can learn to be more considerate of others and become more alert to our responsibilities in life. We learn about the nature of the Universe and in so doing we come to understand our place in and ability to create within, our Universe. Our consciousness expands as a result. When we understand karma, we see that to create better lives we must learn to think before we act. Ananda Tara Shan (1993, p. 36), in *The Living Word of the Hierarchy*, expands this point:

> Many foolish and incorrect actions (according to the Law of Karma) derive from not using your ability as a thinking and reasoning person. If you spend some thought on the actions you are about to take and put your experiences as a human being to work for you, then you would avoid making so many mistakes, and surely would not take so many wrong turns in life.
>
> Be aware of the many unholy desires that you harbour within your desire body, for they help you to make many wrong moves in your life. Instead, if you put to good use your mind, and send a thought and prayer to your Lighted Brothers and Sisters (the Masters) Who have gone before you and Who now live to serve, to assist, and to teach you to walk the way of the righteous, then with certainty you shall make better decisions, that in themselves shall result in better actions. Trust in Those Who already have passed through the human kingdom and have through lessons well learned become Souls in flesh and in pure lighted garments.

The choice is yours and yours only. Before you act, be thus silent for as long as it takes to make a good action through wise thinking. Involve the angels, the Masters, involve God in your decision making, and become a person others will look up to and respect.

Below is a story which reveals a time in my life where I came to feel the truth of the Law of Karma and its existence in my life. It reveals how karma returns with impeccable timing and helps us to learn and grow. It was at this time in my life that I understood karma as a living reality. This knowledge has helped me to develop and understand the part I play in co-creating my life with our Creator.

Meeting Ishwara

Singapore, December 24, 1984

It was good to be amongst the hustle and bustle of Asian life once again, with all the smells of Asian life. The exotic foods and flavours, intermingled with the humidity, came into my being at every breath. It was Christmas and I wanted to call home. There being no telephone in my hotel, as I was staying at the cheaper end of town, meant I had to travel to the city exchange. It was a warm evening and the prospect of encountering the night life drew me. Singapore seemed so clean and the clothes of the people very well tailored; everything had its place. I found the exchange and made the call home. I was just about to enter back into the city streets when a very humble looking Indian fellow came across my path. He was wearing a white sari cloth wrapped around his middle with a white business shirt above it. It was a dress typical of Indian men in that climate.

"I am happy to have the pleasure of meeting you."

His face beamed, his teeth, broad and white, showed as he smiled at me and his eyes shone with the light of a sun-filled smile. I could do little but respond in an equally enthusiastic manner for he appealed to the love of life within me.

"It's a pleasure for me to meet you, too." I found myself replying.

"You must come to my temple. There is a wedding being performed tomorrow evening and I would like you to be my honoured guest."

This man was a Brahmin by the name of Ishwara. At that time he was running a Hindu temple. He had been called there from India, to lecture and share his wealth of knowledge with the temple monks. He had spent his life translating Sanskrit into Tamil and English and much time studying comparative religions and philosophies. None of this I knew. I simply felt an immediate trust and felt honoured by the invitation. I accepted and asked for the details of where I was to go the following evening. The interaction was short and clearly spirited. It put me in a sprightly mood for my walk back to the hotel.

I prepared for the wedding the next evening and felt clumsy with my dress. It always seemed difficult to know what to wear in Asia. I felt huge in contrast with the size of the people, especially the women who have tiny waists and petite bodies.

I called for a taxi from the pavement. I would normally have caught a bus, but felt that as I was to be an esteemed guest, a taxi was in order. Within minutes I was at my destination. I walked down the end of the street to the temple and entered.

Everyone was dressed in Indian attire, saris and Punjabi suits. There was a great deal of colour and ceremony. Ishwara greeted me and bade me welcome. I sat amidst all the guests with eyes fixed upon the splendour and simplicity that lay before them. There were many gifts of fruit and flowers, everywhere colour and life. Everything was in readiness for the couple to enter. I could hear in the distance the sound of a horn and the clanging of bells. The smell of incense permeated the room. Flames flickered on the idols around the temple. There were many idols and each, it seemed, had a special significance. It was so unlike any wedding I had ever attended. The couple appeared. She was dressed in gold and wore a veil. He wore white and red and seemed just as colourful as she did. They looked like king and queen. Their beauty was quite marked. I learned later that they were betrothed and had not set eyes upon each other before this ritual. It was something I found difficult to comprehend, but it explained the look of fear on her face, an explanation which may well have been my projection. The ceremony took some hours and the words used were in a language I didn't understand. There followed an enormous feast: beautiful Indian foods, dhal and vegetables and sweets I had never seen the likes of, all delectable in flavour.

Ishwara approached.

"I hope you have enjoyed yourself. I would like to meet you after, if you have the time."

He assigned a boy to show me around and to make me feel at home. He had to wash off the ceremonial paint, the ash which a Hindu priest wears upon the body for the ceremony. I waited in the vestry with the boy. Ishwara entered. His eyes looked more serious than I had seen them. He came straight to the point.

"I am going to ask you for money. There is a family in Sri Lanka, I have a picture of the daughter. They have been hard hit by the war which has been going on for some years. They are a family of ten. The father and older brothers have been killed and there is little they can do to support themselves in that situation. They cannot pay the payments on their house and are in a position where they may lose it. They only need $35 per month to be able to remain in the house. Something tells me to ask you for help. So I am asking."

Floods of memories filled my consciousness as I remembered horrific scenes of Sri Lanka and the war of which I had been a part in 1983. I wondered how he could know this about me, and I realised he didn't.

"Just think about it. Go home and think about it and do what you feel is right for you. I only know that I must tell you of this problem for that is what God guides me to do."

Many fears and voices began to enter my consciousness - "Watch out for con-artists." "People will try to take your money." "It's not true, it's just a story. He's using their plight to get money for himself."

We talked for some time before I left that evening. Not about money but about religion and the heart, about people and God. Ishwara through all his translation and study of religions all over the world had decided that there was one God for all people. It is just the language we use to talk about God that varies.

When it was time to leave he would not hear of me walking alone to the taxi. Instead he came with me to make sure I was returned safely and he offered to buy me a dress, which I could not think of accepting. As we stood at the temple gate I looked into his eyes that were huge and brown and felt the presence of God. I knew there was something to this man, and as I felt that presence, he acknowledged it by saying,

"It is an honour for me to meet someone who is filled with God's Love and I am grateful that God has allowed us to meet."

It was late and the night seemed infinite. Everything had a clarity and oneness. The sense of oneness permeated my consciousness and I felt excitement at being alive. It seemed every cell in my body was vibrating with life itself....

I did not have a lot of money and I had hoped I would be away for several months. This request for money came as quite a surprise but it was something I could not ignore and I had to find the right line of approach. I had to find out what was just and right in this situation. At least I could feel that I was capable of giving from a pure heart. I felt if I gave all the money I had I would feel resentment, for I would not be able to travel which I felt I was meant to do. I felt too that I would like to help the family stay in that home. My own experiences in the war helped me to know the truth of Ishwara's plea, yet he knew nothing of that. He had simply trusted God in his asking.

I decided to pay the monthly interest that would enable the family to stay in their house, and the next day I told Ishwara of my decision. We had many meetings from then on where we shared and exchanged views, ate meals together and cherished the company of each other until the time came to move on. I was grateful for the meeting for it had been a reminder of the plight of others in the world. It had made me look at my boundaries and limits, my levels of faith and trust, and it had made me question my motivation for travel. I felt that I could continue, having been realigned somewhat to my heart....

Penang, Malaysia, January 1985

I opened my eyes and I looked out of the small slat in the ceiling above the bed. I could hear the pigeons squawking and squabbling. There were several of them on the landing outside my room. It was an odd little bungalow, and I was on the top floor in a room that seemingly had once been a pigeons' nest. It was painted blue and the pigeons squabbled outside. There was evidence of their droppings in a few places around the room. I could smell the dampness of the blankets, a musty smell, and I sneezed as I awoke, from the dust. I had arrived quite late the night before with little ability to pick and choose where I might rest my weary bones, and the woman who owned this abode seemed very open to my staying. I went downstairs for breakfast and I could see a French fellow looking suspiciously in my direction. I felt a little uneasy under his gaze and decided that this was not a place where I should be staying.

I decided I would look for another place that morning. I went upstairs to collect my things and the French fellow followed me.

"Maurice." He introduced himself and put out his hand, which seemed feeble to my grasp.

"I need money," he said, "I have been robbed and I need your help."

I had heard many stories of drug users in Malaysia, and the insipidness of Maurice's skin along with the hippy-like appearance of his clothes made all my mistrust and doubt loom large in my consciousness.

"I need money to pay my bills and call for money from France. I need enough to travel to Georgetown. You don't have to answer now. Think about it, feel what is the right thing to do and let me know."

I went out that day looking for a place to stay and the weight of what I had been asked preyed on my mind for I had little money and could rapidly see it being used more quickly than I had anticipated. I asked within what was the right thing to do and searched my conscience. I did not come up with a new place to stay, for everywhere was full and the pigeon hole I stayed in that night was above Maurice's room. I hardly slept a wink, my mind rife with the many judgements I had placed on Maurice. I considered seriously what I could afford to give of the $900 I had left. I gave him $100. I told him that morning. He was grateful and I was unsure whether I could trust him.

I spent the next few months travelling in India and reconnecting with aspects of my former journeys, until I finally travelled to England where I found work and a house at the seaside in Devon. For some months I became part of the English work force and the English way of life. I was living on the breadline, my resources at a minimum, my wages paying the cost of day-to-day living. I had no ticket home, just a return ticket to Bangkok, and in my own way I was learning about survival in the world. I felt I could return to the East, and I could see ways of making money by playing with the differences in the economy between the East and the West. I had no thoughts of going home, but I knew that I should leave England and decided to spend the last weeks in a very English town called Chester, a place to which I had travelled on my first journey, where I felt at home along the River Dee.

Chester, England, September 16, 1985

I was travelling with a good and close friend, and it would be here that we would part ways. In our love for each other we decided we should make that last evening a special occasion and so booked a place at the vegetarian restaurant for dinner. We spent the last of our free money on a special bottle of red wine from the local wine merchant. We had been camping by the river on the tennis court at the YMCA. It was the first time I had dressed in a dress for months. We carefully placed all our goods in the tent and locked it up, preparing for our evening, and made our way to the restaurant. Greeted by waiters in tuxedos and treated with a great deal of respect, we sat by the fire for hors d'oeuvres and moved to a table for the remainder of our meal. We shared the memories of our time together with much fondness and joy. It was a good evening, and it felt as we walked back through the streets that we were satiated with all of life's joys. We had met a humorous English couple in the restaurant and they had offered us coffee at their house. We accepted the offer and stayed the night, grateful for the hospitality and a good bed. The following morning they drove us back home and we approached the tennis courts and our tent, which had been our home for the past two weeks. Something strange began to happen. As we approached, I almost could not believe my eyes. Time seemed to move quickly and space took on a new meaning. I felt a wave of shock come through my body.

"It's not there, the tent's not there." As I spoke I was aware of all it represented. All my worldly possessions. All I held dear. I had illustrated seventy poems, poems and art work. There were photographs of the

places I had been, the people I had met, not to mention my clothing and diary and all of my friend's possessions - all his memories. There had been three thousand pounds' worth of cameras, jewellery, which was to be my means of living for the coming months, and my medication, my means of life support. I could not believe my eyes. My head started to spin. I felt light-headed and sick and could feel a gut wrenching cry emanate from my solar plexus. The severing of the cords that connected me to those attachments, a pit of grief, and tears began to flow down my cheeks. My breath became short. Simultaneously a wave of peace entered my being and a voice spoke in my head.

"Thank goodness you won't have to carry that pack around any more."

I became aware of the weight my lifestyle had become to me, of how trapped I felt in it and my consciousness moved intermittently between these two states of understanding. One feeling, the pain and the grief; the other, the freedom and the perfection of the plan. As I approached the tent site I found some articles on the ground which immediately stilled any pain I had. Somehow they must have fallen out. There on the ground was a picture of Ishwara, the Brahmin I had met in Singapore. My mind went immediately to the family in Sri Lanka, who's father and eldest son had been killed. I remembered, too, the many children I had seen running frightened in the war... the homeless... the starving. In comparison I could see that nothing had happened to me. I was alive and I was free to think and feel as I pleased. I felt the comfort of Ishwara and I knew that God was indeed with me.

Also on the ground there was a mirror, a small compact mirror I had carried. It was cracked and the message was clear "Look at yourself, change the reflection you see." In the confusion of the pain and the joy of freedom I felt a lesson of great significance was being given to me, and in the days that followed its import sank deeper and deeper into my being.

Bangkok, Thailand, October 5, 1985

I sat on the sidewalk with Aung, a little weary from the Bangkok sun and the perennial intake of pollution. My lungs felt tight, my skin full of grit and I was thirsty. Aung had fast become my friend. I had known him for some days, and he was a welcome respite from the loneliness and pain that I had been feeling. I had been in Bangkok for two weeks now without money for shelter or food. I was waiting on money to be wired from Australia that would help me return home, but it had not yet arrived. Aung passed me a coconut. The hole was nicely cut and I took a drink.

I remembered our meeting. He spoke little English and the communication came from the light in his eyes. That particular night I had found my way up the fire escape of a middle range hotel and found a nice spot on the roof where I could curl on the warm concrete, still hot from the day's sun. It was quite a spot that I found, for although it was lower than some of the larger hotels, from that vantage point I could see quite a lot of Bangkok and I could see, too, the night sky and the stars. The moon was full and there was something very peaceful in being here. I heard someone coming up the fire escape and my body had frozen in fear of who it might be. I didn't want anyone to deny me this place to sleep as it had served me well and I was growing to love it. I could see the glint in Aung's eyes as he approached - it was as if the moonlight shone from them. His teeth glimmered in the dark. A rather small impish Thai man, he ambled up beside me. He asked no questions about why I was there or who I was. He simply sat down and looked at the beauty I had been observing. The stillness of the night, the sense of unity in all things seemed to pervade everything. It was not often that I made connection with another human being in such a way. We sat still, sharing the space for some hours.

After some time we began to talk. It was the first time in the two weeks I had been here that anyone was interested in my story, and I felt great relief in being able to express what I had been through. I told him how I had left England, not a penny to my name, no baggage to check in, no toothbrush or hairbrush, just the dress I had on, which I was still wearing. I told him about the French man I had met in Malaysia. How, when he asked me for money, I had mistrusted him and how now, being in the same position, I was placed at the mercy of my own judgements. I had seen others look at me as though I were a drug addict, simply because circumstances, or fate, had put me in such a position. He smiled knowingly as I spoke. I spoke for hours. With every sentence, I could feel my pain unravelling. It had been choking me tightly and in the simple expression of it, I could feel great release. I had been to the Australian Embassy in England where they would not give money for people in my position any more because so many had cried wolf when there was not one. Some hours later in Australia House, a girl passing by had heard my tale as I told it to another and passed me fifty pounds, the exact amount I had given to the French man in Malaysia.

I had been relying on the generosity of others for food. My situation had certainly called upon every ounce of courage. I had to keep my integrity in the process. It had not been easy, for I was open to influences at levels of society to which I was unaccustomed. I rapidly became accustomed to and learned the demeanour necessary to survive. I was so grateful to find this hotel roof for here I was left alone, and it was as if the heart of the concrete embraced me, giving me the hug of which I was in desperate need. Aung served me in that way, too, on the mental and emotional levels, though he never touched me physically; he had enough sensitivity for that.

"I see you have one possession" he said, looking at the letter I was clutching in my hand. I felt warm as he acknowledged it, and though I did not tell him what it contained, I felt the fullness of its contents. It had been waiting for me in Bangkok when I had arrived. I had been to the American Express Mail service and begged them to give me the letter, even though I had no travellers' cheques left. The clerk seemed to see the pain in my eyes as she passed it through the window. It was

from Ishwara, who I had met in Singapore. I recalled the words he had written,

"You are so rich, so wealthy. You are full with God's love."

Though I had no money, as I read the words I felt deeply the truth in his wisdom. I was indeed loved.

As I looked into Aung's eyes, I could see something of Ishwara, and what Ishwara saw in me. It was love. There was no condition, just a simple sharing of life in the moment and I felt gratitude to God for sending me that company, giving me the sense of unity I could feel at one with.

I passed the coconut shell back to Aung. It was half empty and we stood up again from the street where we sat. Across the road I could see the huge black doors of the bank. The building, huge in front of me, cast shadow upon me as I walked towards it. Aung was leaving that day and I was collecting my money; we would perhaps never meet again.

"Sawasdee." We bowed towards each other, our hands in prayer position in front of our hearts. We then turned, walking in opposite directions. The money had come through. Some days after, I left Thailand.

The Unconscious

In this chapter we will look at the psychological impact of healing using the Light of the Holy Spirit on the healer and the client. What happens when we begin to work with the healing Light of the Holy Spirit? How does it affect us? What can we expect? We will look at the role of the shadow and the inner development which comes when we open to the Light.

Working with Light 'shines the light' onto our inherent psychological patterns so that we may discover them and, if needed, re-align them to work for our benefit. Let us consider these psychological patterns and see how they work. A psychological pattern is a recurring process in our mind or emotions that continues to occur as a result of our belief systems, whether conscious or unconscious. These psychological patterns create the circumstances of our lives and help to determine the ways in which we behave. This creates another pattern which we call a life pattern, that is the recurring circumstances in our lives. Our life patterns are what our soul has designed for us to learn and grow from. If we are to live our life in alignment with our soul, we need to be prepared to evolve as the soul would have us do. To do that we must come to know ourselves - body, emotions, mind and soul.

Coming to know self

How do we come to know ourselves?

To come to know ourselves we need to begin to work to make what is unconscious in us conscious, to try to discover our psychological patterns and our life patterns. Some of these we are conscious of, and we need to acknowledge and recognise these. Others we are unconscious of and we need to work towards bringing these patterns to the surface so that we can, in essence, be more conscious and aware of ourselves, how we work, what makes us tick. Thus we have to:

1. Recognise the psychological and life patterns of which we are conscious.
2. Work to make the unconscious conscious.
3. Be prepared to work with both the conscious and unconscious aspects of ourselves.

As the unconscious mind becomes conscious it reveals memories.

Methods we can use to make the unconscious conscious

Figure 4 on the following page is a chart which reveals some of the ways in which we can make the unconscious conscious. The methods include spiritual healing, dreams, counselling, regression and roleplay work. This list is not meant to be exhaustive; rather, it is meant to simply provide an idea of the types of methods meant. You may be able to think of many other methods. Such methods assist us to remember experiences and events that have occurred in our past. Through them the unconscious mind reveals certain memories and understandings so we may become conscious of what is sitting there within us. These are often revealed through memories or symbols, which when looked into reveal the patterns that we need to see.

You will notice in figure 4 that past memories are divided into good and bad, pleasant and unpleasant and that these memories are passed from the subconscious mind to the conscious mind, becoming conscious memories. Let us think about what that means. We have a basic tendency to divide up our experience as good or bad, pleasant or unpleasant. Is this a helpful thing to do? When we decide a memory or experience is unpleasant we try to avoid similar experiences or suppress the memory. This is how some of our patterns are formed.

Figure 4: Making the unconscious conscious

       conscious mind
      conscious memories

       ↑ ↑

       unconscious mind

       past memories
        good / bad
      pleasant / unpleasant

spiritual healing	↗	↖	life experience
dreamwork	↗	↖	regression
counselling	↗	↖	roleplay work
guided imagery	↗	↖	body work

Patterns - formation and effect

In figure 5 the person has decided that he or she no longer wants to have any bad experiences. He or she therefore does not accept life as it comes. He or she responds with a 'no!' to the universe every time an experience comes along which he or she has deemed to be "bad" or "unpleasant." The person no longer responds to what the universe brings in a balanced and open way. Rather, he or she reacts with a conditioned response, which is 'no!' The reality of the present moment is lost as the conditioned reaction immediately puts the person on the defensive against life rather than being in a position of acceptance of life. In this way we sabotage ourselves and stop experiencing the universe effectively, contentedly and lovingly. We do not allow ourselves to see the universal reality of love. The way we respond and our distorted perceptions of the world take us out of alignment with truth.

Let us look at an example. Mary has had a number of experiences with men in her life where she has felt taken advantage of by them in a way that has caused her to suffer financially. She meets a man who has noticed that Mary is an independent woman and though he would quite like to give to her by taking her to dinner he lets her pay when she offers because he does not want to appear sexist. Immediately her past boyfriends flood to mind and she reacts by closing up and begins to feel that she should not see this man again. Mary has projected the nature of her past on to her current situation and she does not see the reality of her current male friend. Her male friend will also have his past which will colour how he sees Mary. Because of our tendency to divide up our past as "good" or "bad" and our decision not to experience the "bad," we react with conditioned responses which destroy our ability to see and know the truth of our life moment to moment.

From past events, in childhood, birth and past lives, impressions are formed about ourselves and the world, either positive or negative, that control us from a subconscious level and influence all areas of our lives. Locked in our subconscious is the memory of every experience we have ever had as a human being, in this lifetime and others. We suppress (push out of consciousness) our unacceptable thoughts and urges and harbour repressed memories (memories that are unacceptable to the ego that have been rejected and suppressed) of painful early experiences. These thoughts and memories help form the structure of our personality. We use a lot of negative energy and negative thoughts to perpetuate negative conditions and suppress life. The negative thoughts colour our whole attitude. We see the universe as full of suffering and we want to escape from it.

Figure 5: The forming of conditioned reactions

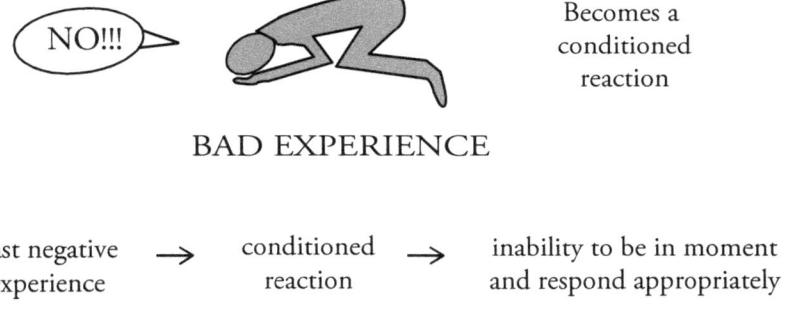

Perpetuating negative beliefs

To perpetuate negative belief patterns we use:

1. self-rejection
2. limiting self labels, such as, "I'm stupid," or "I'm a rotten cook"
3. prejudice
4. anger and resentment

5. guilt and worry
6. jealousy
7. need for security
8. hero worship, that is, lifting others onto pedestals and putting ourselves down
9. procrastination
10. "not fair," that is, self-pity
11. blaming
12. musts/shoulds
13. fear
14. right versus wrong, that is, everything must be black or white, there is no in-between

Changing our life patterns for the better

Through healing, counselling, psychological work and spiritual work we can get in touch with and change our patterns. To find and explore our patterns we can use a range of methods, particularly spiritual healing, regression, counselling, roleplay, contemplation, meditation and guided imagery. We can also question our negative beliefs and, by expressing them and discovering they are not aligned to reality, change them. To move out of these beliefs and destructive behaviours we need to:

1. begin to see the world in a different light
2. change our thoughts about the world's hostility
3. change our duality of right versus wrong
4. be as we are (however it may feel) and raise our awareness
5. find acceptance and relaxation
6. work with forgiveness
7. open ourselves to love and trust

8. take responsibility for ourselves and our lives
9. come to acknowledge and understand our shadow

Working with our shadow in healing

The shadow is a term coined by Carl Jung (1976) and used to cover our negative behaviours, our selfish impulses and drives, and the worst elements of our nature. We usually know many of our faults, and a lot of them we prefer to keep in the unconscious as they are opposed to the social masks we wear; we find it painful to face them and the incongruity in ourselves. The negative tendencies in us take many subtle forms. The shadow reveals itself in many and varied relationships, for example, negative emotions are played out between parents and children, husbands and wives, and work colleagues. We tend to deny such unpleasant things and try to stop others from finding out about them. We also block them from our own awareness and consequently we may think that we are very nice to people while we are actually quite vicious and bad-tempered. The shadow can manifest in a number of ways, for example, through blame, rebellion, resentment, fear, guilt, anger, mistrust, jealousy, pride, ambition, blame, self-pity, depression and possessiveness. These manifestations often form an energy we don't like and want to move away from.

What happens to the shadow once healing commences?

When we open ourselves to be healed and to be a healer working with the Light of Christ, we open to the Will of God in our lives. Through this act we invite change, and the material nature within us that is not of God becomes threatened. We are made up of shadow and of Light. The shadow self, sometimes referred to as "the little self," has the tendency to cling to life as it desires it and manifests as a selfish energy instead of a selfless one. When we invite healing, we open ourselves to become selfless servers of God. The denser matter within us is open to be cleansed and purified, transmuted and transformed. In this process we often become aware of our darkness, which can prove to be a shock to us, particularly if we generally deny its existence, or alternatively, repress it.

Healing leads us from the unreal to the Real. By this it is meant that healing takes us out of the world of glamour and illusion to a world where the Divine Truth and Reality exist. Glamours are formed by our over-attachment to that which we desire. When we desire something too much our perceptions are distorted by that desire. When that happens a glamour is formed. Glamours and illusions are distorted perceptions of reality coloured by our attachments, desires and thoughts that are out of step with reality. When we receive healing and our glamours and illusions are thus exposed, they begin to fall away and our whole worldview changes. We find another perspective on life, the universe and how it works and come to see ourselves as we truly are. In the process we go through stages of seeming imbalance. Sometimes this is necessary in order to find balance again. Before we can reach enlightenment there are many negative energies within us that must be dealt with. It is in the process of dealing with these energies that we may become imbalanced. For more understanding of healing the shadow see chapter: *Spiritual Healing*.

Finding our wounded and conflicting parts

When healing commences it is not only the shadow that we find within ourselves. We also find a lot of unhealed aspects, our deep wounds that need healing, perhaps from past traumas. We find our inner child and parts of ourselves that take us to joy and teach us the good qualities we have lost sight of. We come to know ourselves in new ways. As the personality grows it becomes more complex. New traits and qualities are developed which increase our ability to adapt. These new traits and qualities also cause conflicts within us as the existing systems of the personality compete. Such conflicts are natural. It is interesting to note that many psychologists agree that when a person has a lot of conflicts with others that person is often experiencing conflict within him or herself, between the opposing tendencies or traits (Di Caprio, 1976). As we become more fully aware of ourselves greater control in respect to the conflicts is possible.

Resistance

The responses of rebellion, blame and denial are an expression of our resistance to the Light. When the Light enters the grosser matter of our vibration and the subtle bodies, it stimulates the response of resistance initially. If we can recognise that and dare to look at what in us the Light is revealing of our shadow, we generally find that slowly the aspects of the shadow we can deal with become Light. We are then purified by the experience.

For example, we may come to a period in our lives where a stronger faith is required to move through what life brings us. Our initial response may be to go through a period of more doubt, for a time, in response to that energy of faith. We feel doubt in us until we are ready to take a 'leap of faith.' If we dare to go through the doubt and then take the 'leap of faith,' we will soon discover that the faith in us is strong and immovable. The doubt has been cleansed out of us to the degree we have opened to it, and a new faith and hope are felt in our life experience.

How do we discriminate? What is Light? What is shadow?

Because of our complex nature it is not always easy to tell what is Light and what is shadow. We need to learn not to give the shadow power over us, and to call its bluff. We must discern when to listen to it and when not to. Sometimes it is the key to healing. Sometimes it is merely sabotaging healing. If we do not suppress it and look instead to see the gift it offers, we can see more readily if it is merely sabotaging us - and if so, we can simply choose to walk on. When we explore energies we perceive as negative, such as projection and anger, sometimes we find the key to higher learning. Table 3 gives examples of what can be learned from negative energies. Our shadow teaches a lot about ourselves, and it can teach a lot about life. Its energies can be self-perpetuating and negative, and need to be guarded against. However, within them we may find a gift. In the left-hand column of Table 3 there is a list of the negative psychological processes that often manifest as part of the shadow. These are wilfulness, blame, rebellion, resentment, fear, guilt and anger. In the right-hand column there are a list of positive qualities and traits that can be learned from working through the negative energy and making it positive. In Table 3, I have illustrated the gifts that can come when we recognise the negative psychological process around these negative energies and look to find how we could behave better. To help you understand how you can open to these gifts I have written some explanations in the midsection of the table.

The unconscious can become conscious in a multitude of ways. One way is through the process of guided imagery. For an explanation of guided imagery see chapter: *Guided Imagery*. One day in a guided imagery session I had the experience of discovering some of what lay in my unconscious. Discovering it has helped me enormously. In the short story below I will share this discovery.

Table 3. The Gifts that Negative Processes teach us

Negative process	Explanation	Positive qualities, lessons and traits that can be learned and developed from working through negative processes.
Wilfulness	When we are wilful, we are following the little will and are not caring about the Will of God; we care more about our own self will and what we want. We can learn to overcome this negative quality by aspiring to align our will with the Will of God. By doing so we come into contact with the quality of willingness, through which come humility and gratitude. "Not mine but Thine Will be done," becomes our inner prayer. We become aligned to the spiritual Path.	Alignment to Path Willingness Humility Gratitude
Blame	We can learn to overcome this negative energy by beginning to take responsibility for ourselves. As we stop projecting, we begin to take the energy of blame back off another person, and to feel all the feelings we've been trying to avoid in ourselves, like the anger, the fear and the guilt that we have within us. This gives us the ability to see ourselves and others more clearly and come closer to truth in our lives. Not everything we see in others is there, just because we see it. We need to remember we look through our aura and often see what is in us, thinking that it's in them. Whether it is or isn't part of them is not our business. Here we can adhere to the saying, 'Deal with what is in your own backyard, and don't interfere with others.' When we acknowledge our part, we see that we are not perfect either, and through understanding and acceptance that we are all human, we develop compassion and empathy for others. This in turn helps us find the wisdom of life. We drop our unrealistic expectations of others and ourselves and begin to accept our humanity.	To take responsibility for ourselves To see ourselves and our actions clearly Clear vision Compassion Wisdom

Rebellion	When we are rebellious, not wishing to conform, we have negative thoughts and behaviours that may be harmful. We also have difficulty acknowledging authority. Our programmes with authority figures come to the surface and we get a distorted view of others and the world around us. We can work through our authority programs by accepting the true authority of the Spirit and the soul. We come to see that the true authorities are love and truth which manifest through right action. We learn the value of right thought and harmlessness.	Balanced thought, balanced action, balanced obedience, balanced authority Harmlessness The power of love and truth
Resentment	When we hold on to resentment we are holding a grievance towards another and a feeling that things are somehow unfair. We can become bitter and self-pitying. When we work through resentment we learn the value of forgiveness and unconditional love. We do this by learning not to expect others to live up to our ideals. We become more accepting of life and less bitter. Instead of holding on to our pain and hurt and using it against others, we release it and are relieved of the burden of holding it in. This process helps us open up to the world and others again, let go of self-pity and find instead compassion for others.	Forgiveness Unconditional love The release of hurt and pain Compassion
Fear	When we are in fear, we are holding back from life, find ourselves paralysed and unable to flow freely with life. We are also mistrustful and lacking in confidence. We can work through our fears and find the ability to move forward in our lives again by opening to trust in the true power of love. We find faith, trust and confidence again.	The ability to move into the true power of love The ability to move forward in life Faith, Trust, Confidence

Guilt	When we feel guilty, we have usually acted from the wrong motive and are finding it difficult to forgive ourselves for what we have done. We find it very difficult to accept, trust and love ourselves. We are also put in touch with our conscience. When we explore and work through the guilt, we come to understand about the importance of having the right motive and right conscience. Through forgiveness we come to be less hard on ourselves and find the ability to accept, trust and love ourselves again.	To accept and love the self Right motive Right conscience Trust
Anger	We quickly lose our balance when we are angry and act inappropriately. We often discover that we have held back too much and have not been assertive enough in our daily lives. When we explore anger, we often find that there is pain beneath it, and sometimes that we have been too focused on insuring that our own desires are met. In our anger we become separated from others and quite isolated. We can work through it by cultivating right balance in daily life, in thoughts, feelings and actions, and by learning what it is to be assertive and express in trust the truth of who we are. We learn to accept our pain, move from desire to aspiration, and from separation to union.	Right balance in daily life Appropriate behaviour Acceptance of pain Movement from desire to aspiration Union instead of separation

Daring to dream

I lay down, relaxed and was guided into a quiet place within. It could have been a place I already new or an imaginary place. I went immediately to the backyard of a house I had lived in Aspley in Queensland. In the backyard was a bare garden bed. The earth in it was freshly raked and it had nothing growing in it. It seemed somehow symbolic of something, so I looked further. A number of memories came forward. I remembered the unfinished frame of a cubby house my father had built, the death of a canary my father had given me which had its head bitten off by a butcherbird when I put it outdoors to get some sun, the promise of a horse and land which never came, the dreams of my parents which were never fulfilled, and the story my grandmother told me that if I rubbed pigface on my wart and placed the pigface in the garden and made a wish to have the wart go away that it would - provided I believed. Believing was not an easy thing, especially then.

My father was catatonic in the backyard, suffering from mental illness. The garden bed was indeed symbolic of a life not lived. The only life it seemed came from my brother who put all his efforts into erecting a pigeon cage and collecting pigeons of all different kinds, in pairs, so they could mate and produce new life - he had madenas, fantails, redchecks, blue bars and blue checks - and there was darkie and whity. My brother and I also had fish, and we would go to the creek in the bush nearby and catch whatever life we could find - guppies, neon tetras, snails, penny turtles, tadpoles, even penny frogs. All the life we tried to create seemed to make no difference to the outcome. We had to move and leave our potential heaven- or so was the will of my father's firm. In those days the wishes of the firm were not questioned.

My brother went off to Tasmania on a trip from where he would go straight to a school in Melbourne, the pigeon cage was dismantled and the pigeons sold, the fish returned to the freedom of the creek. My mother was distraught about this decision, and it seemed to embitter her. At the time I could not understand it but as life unfolded, I understood why. Everything was packed into tea chests and the removal van came. My best friend stole the clothes from my favourite doll and with my naked doll, symbolic of my naked self, we left Queensland. I cried for a lot of the time, right from when we began the drive for the last time down that street. I looked into the houses where all my play friends lived and fantasised about what would happen in their lives.

As I drove by I gathered all memory and placed it securely in my heart, and shut the door tight so that I would have the memory safe in my heart. From that time on I learned not to make home anywhere in outer things, it was safer to have home in the heart. That way it could go with you wherever you went. In my mind's eye I could see the drive to Melbourne. My mother was lying down on the back seat; after being distressed for some time she had fallen asleep. My father was driving and having to concentrate as there was a torrential, tropical downpour of rain and hail. I felt he needed company to stay awake so I tried to provide that. To my surprise he began to speak to me and I became aware that he was speaking to me in the current time, even though the scene was one I remember from my childhood.

"You have always had faith in me, even when I was at my worst, you always had faith. Now you must put that faith into your own life and make your life a success. In your unconscious you have carried these memories and the memory my life has given as a model for yourself. My life was my life and is not meant to be yours. Use the energy you have invested in supporting me to make your own life a success."

For a moment I was dumbfounded at the potency of what my father was telling me. As he spoke I felt an enormous shift taking place inside of me.

"But I have learned so much from you, Dad." I replied. "You have taught me so much about love and honesty, and living by your own principles, you have given me so much."

"You always were obstinate," he replied.

I began to comprehend what he was trying to tell me, "Okay, I get the point. Yes I can see how I have stored these memories and the model of your life as proof that I cannot dare to believe or dream, that I cannot dare to be successful, and that needs to change."

"That was my karma, for me to learn by. Yours is to be a different life, according to your karma. Go and make your life a success."

The vision of my father drifted away and I was left feeling very awake and empowered. I could see how much what was stored in my unconscious had been working against me, sabotaging me as I go through life; how I had not dared to dream. I could feel the angels all around me now and I could see that if I did not dare to dream, the angels could not help me to achieve those dreams. I began to see visions of a future filled with hope and faith and I began to see the truth of what my grandmother had told me. It will only happen if you believe.

Regression

What is regression?

Regression is a process that we can use to help us get in touch with our past. It is a process that has been used for many decades whereby the client is guided back in time to a past event for exploration of the event and the emotions and thoughts associated with that event. Through it we may come to know something of our past; perhaps our childhood or a life or experience from our cycle of reincarnation; release old traumas associated with that past and come to learn needed lessons in life. When regression takes place with the help of spiritual healing we are able to help purify, redeem and transmute that past. By sending healing Light into certain chakras the memory of our past is stimulated. Memories arise from the unconscious and become part of our conscious awareness. We are able to get in touch with many underlying anxieties and fears and so get to the cause of many of our recurring problems.

What does regression show us? How do we benefit from it?

Regression assists us to obtain information about our past, present and future. It reveals the path of the soul by giving understanding and insight into our life patterns and our various experiences of reincarnation. Through regression we link into the Divine Memory, as it is reflected in the lower planes, through our intelligence. It enables us to release pain, sorrow and restriction that we may feel physically, emotionally or mentally, and find joy, Light and freedom.

I once had a male client who felt a lot of difficulty feeling at peace with other men in his life. He had noticed that whenever he and other men were alone he felt extremely uncomfortable, so he would avoid such situations. This was beginning to thwart his goals and desires in life. He wanted, for example, to play sport, but had not done so because it meant being alone with men in the sport he wished to play. He decided he needed to know why. What was going on within him? He came for regression. He was clear that something was blocking him from his past and thought regression would be a way to find out exactly what. When the session began he began to smile. When I asked what was happening he told me that he could see himself as a child of about eighteen months of age. He was standing up in his cot, holding on to the bars and jumping up and down. The more he jumped the more excited he became. Within an instant the smile on his face became a look of great pain as he described what then transpired. His father had come in and was angry. His father had begun to beat him and just did not stop. Soon there was blood all over the cot as the young child hit its head on the corner of the cot. Then the child was alone. He did not understand. He had always felt that his father loved him until that moment, and for some time to come in the years that followed he felt he could never trust love. After he had re-experienced the scene fully we contacted his inner adviser and asked why he had re-experienced this now. What did he need to see and learn? His inner adviser advised him that he needed to release the trauma of this experience which was preventing him from bonding with men in his life. It also informed him that the expectations he had of himself and others were too high. People are not always loving. Sometimes they are angry; that is life. Of course it does not excuse the behaviour of his father. But to expect only love from others is to live in illusion. The man was asked to find forgiveness for his father, which he was helped to find by seeing the real pressures that his father was under which led to the unfortunate displacement of anger towards the son. This was a situation with which the son could now truly empathise as he had his own share of pressures now at work. He was then able to begin to develop friendships with men again - without the fear.

Understanding of the Divine Laws comes as we make sense of what is happening to us now. When we go into a regressive process we connect with our soul and find guidance which often assists us to allow the process of inner change and redemption to occur. To find forgiveness and to move on. Guilt, fear, anger, resentment, projection, rebellion, etc., are released and we can move into love. Instead of holding on to our negative emotions we begin to see that there is perfection and love within the Plan.

As we understand the cycle of reincarnation we begin to realise that there is no need to fear death and no need to mourn the passing of an individual. We realise that the Spirit is eternal and that we meet repeatedly. We can acknowledge the need to grieve the person who has left the physical body but only because we will no longer be with our friend or family member in that form. We can also be happy for the person that he or she has moved on.

Regression reveals the Law of Evolution (the process of progressive development towards spiritual perfection) and the Law of Divine Justice (cause and effect). As we come to understand the Law of Divine Justice we gradually learn to live in harmony with the Law of Evolution. As a case example I once had a client who considered herself to be very badly done by as far as the men in her life were concerned. As she explained her story her view on life seemed totally understandable. She had been mistreated, through a series of shocking events. She became quite incensed about life and began to develop an energy of self-pity which did not add to her quality of life. One day she had the sense that there was something in her past which would help her to understand her plight. She came for regression. Within moments of the healing Light being transmitted and being guided back in time she focussed on the memory of a past in which she had been a man and had mistreated many women. I expected she would be quite distressed by this. Instead it came as a great comfort to her. When the session was over she revealed how the knowledge that she had done likewise in the past had helped her to understand and forgive. It was a relief for her not to have to carry around the attitude that she had been badly done by any more. She could see that Divine Justice was in operation. In the years that followed she established quite positive relationships with men where the victim/oppressor dynamic was no longer the strongest common denominator.

Regression shows us that we are responsible for the creation of our opportunities and limitations. We see that from good actions we sow peace and opportunity and that from our negative actions we create sorrow and limitations, as was the case in the example above. If we decide we want to move away from blame and resentment in life, regression can help us to release what needs to be released and see what we need to see to move on. Through regression we see the perfection of the Plan. It gives us time, opportunity and understanding to help us move towards perfection. At times, by the Grace of God, the soul is released from the chains of karma and the person makes new choices from the realisations that occur. We are able to see what the Divine Will is and align ourselves with the good of the whole.

When I was twenty-four, I had a death experience. Both my lungs collapsed. I died physically, and during this time, even though I had cerebral amnesia, a lot happened that I remember. No oxygen went to my brain for a time, and I came back to life and went into a coma for two weeks. The main thing I remember was that I was taken up into the Light. It was a very blinding Light, but there came to me an understanding and knowledge that I had never had before. It was a very different consciousness from my usual one and I was shown a succession of lifetimes that I knew on the inner levels to be my own. There were not just past lives but some future lifetimes. I was shown very clearly what it was in this lifetime I was doing wrongly and what I was needing to learn. I needed to learn how to allow people to be close and to trust people more. In the hospital, the situation I was in was one where I felt totally at the mercy of the doctors and nurses. All I wanted to do was to pull out all the tubes that were there to help keep me alive because they were so uncomfortable. I tried to do this so they gave me drugs to paralyse me. I was in the position of being totally dependent on the people around me. They were calling me by my name, but I did not feel any affinity with the name or the consciousness of the person to whom they were referring. I just had to trust them. I had to trust that what they would tell me about my life was the truth because I had no memory myself. I could not feel any connection to the person that they were talking about. Who was I? All my values and attitudes had gone through a major shift. For a deeper, more detailed account of this experience, see my first book *The Language of the Heart: Is Spoken all Over the World* (1991).

Before this experience I had not meditated or even considered the idea of reincarnation. I had become so disillusioned with religion and the church that I was walking around saying I was an atheist. All of a sudden there was this very spiritual experience which then I had to integrate into my understanding. This meant that I had to de-program my mind from all the beliefs, attitudes and values that I had built up over the years and contact my heart in a new way. I did not talk much about it. I was frightened to talk about it for a very long time as many did not seem to have this consciousness. It took me a number of years before I allowed myself to get to a stage where I could start talking about it to people.

A couple of things happened to help me keep believing in my experience. It's easy to simply dismiss these experiences, if they do not seem to fit in with everything else we have been taught.

First, I went to a person who gave me a past life reading and she told me things I had seen in my own inner experience that I had never told others. I thought, 'there must be something in this!' Furthermore, I kept asking for proof and I started to meet more and more people with this awareness. I went along to a spiritual fair one day and a person there gave me a spiritual healing. During the healing I experienced a great Light, just as I had done in my death experience. Through this I began to see that there was a way to help others experience that great Light. I realised then what I had to do. To help bring that Light and love to people I needed to learn about spiritual healing. During the death experience I had a choice of dying or staying. I chose to stay to bring that Light to people, to let people know that we could experience Heaven on Earth. I discovered that the Light is within us. I started to heal.

As I learned more about healing I learned of other things to do, one of which is regression. I have worked with regression now for thirteen years. Like spiritual healing, regression can enable people to get in touch with the experience of Light without dying. I learned about the chakras and could see that by transmitting Light into certain areas it was possible to stimulate past life recall. I began to see the importance of regression in helping us find our purpose in this lifetime. Through regression we can understand our past, and come to know the lessons we need to learn to further our evolution and development.

There are many different ways to go about regression; the particular method I employ works with spiritual healing. A client came who had been having a terrible time with her children. She was very neurotic and did not want to let them out of her sight. She also kept wearing thick jumpers and wanting the heater on all the time when it was not cold. Within five minutes of beginning the session she went into a rigid state, not like the 'tetany' or numbness that can happen in rebirthing, but stiff like a board.

I had to trust and keep sending Light. I closed my eyes and the word Lucitania came into my mind. It was the name of a ship that sank although I did not know that at the time. Apparently she had died of hypothermia and I could see her clinging to a piece of wood in the ocean. She stayed in this rigid state for twenty minutes, then she cried and affirmed that she had also lost her children at the time of the sinking of the ship: she expressed much grief. The awareness of this experience affected both of us. She came along to more sessions and came to a point where she was able to become more balanced with her children and not wear thick jumpers all the time.

Another instance comes to mind, just one of hundreds. One client had a good job travelling from state to state, but every time he needed to travel by plane he could not. He would sit in the seat and as the plane was about to go he would go into a kind of a fit and have to get off the plane. This had happened three times. It was affecting his job and he had a feeling that he needed to see something from his past to solve his problem, but he did not know what. When he lay down for healing he started to go blue and choke. I could see a flash of light. It turned out that he had been in the British Army and had been in a fighter plane and had crashed in mid air. He parachuted out, but the rip cord had tied around his neck and he had died of very slow strangulation. When in this life he had tried to fly by planes, all these physical sensations and emotional fears had resurfaced. During the regression it seemed as if the Grace of God had descended for this person; by simply re-experiencing the trauma in a relaxed state he was able to let it go. He can now fly wherever his work takes him. I have been given the honour of being witness to many such situations in my work. It has helped me to integrate the experience that I had and helped me to give credit to it, instead of pushing it under the carpet as coincidence.

People obtain information about past lifetime experience in very different ways. Some people, through good karma, will gain a detailed understanding of the past. They may retain the memory of what they felt, knowing what lifetime it was, when it was, what they were doing in that lifetime, and what relevance it has to their current learning. They experience this through words, vision, hearing, knowing and/or feeling. Others may just feel an emotion or physical sensation and not know its relevance to them. That may be enough for them to release the pain. They may not need to know the whole story.

Regression helps us to have greater understanding of our lives. For example: suppose a person sees a vision of a monk. In asking the monk what he has come to show, the monk may answer that the person's life has become too complex. To find peace again, the monk may suggest that the person needs to reconnect with that simple lifetime and bring the simplicity back into his or her current life. There are many things to learn and they change every lifetime. Our paths, our lessons are unique. The person may regress to a memory of the present lifetime. Wherever the person goes to in the session is determined by the Light according to the person's need. Much release and understanding can take place. The person is given individual learning and discovers common universal principles that assist him or her in life.

It is important in regression to query everything you see by asking: how is this image or memory relevant for me today? Why do I need to see it? What can I learn from that lifetime, that memory? You may discover you can heal a wounded relationship through contacting the experience again. Regression does not always go into past lifetimes. Often regression takes us into events from this lifetime, sometimes birth and even conception. Looking at these times can help us understand why we see the world as we do. The process of regression may sometimes not take us into the past and may simply bring forth a symbol which, when explored, gives insight and understanding. Sometimes this happens spontaneously through dream or meditation. The following story gives an example of this.

Coming of age

It was one of those nights when the world seemed limitless. Everything made sense and could be seen. Light was shining everywhere. We were approaching the spring equinox once again and the sense of spring, of new life, new vision, was felt in the air. I could not quite explain the joy I felt within but something was happening. That night I had a dream. I caught a fragment of it the next morning when I awoke to the sun's rays shining through the window. In a moment of time I could see a shield shining as if the sun was shining upon it also. It was made of steel and was full of Light with silver Celtic writing embossed upon it. I didn't know what it meant but seeing it felt like a gift. I could smell the eggs from the kitchen, mingled with the fragrance of toast and I moved into a state of awakeness motivated by my hunger. I got out of bed to greet the new day. It was an ordinary day but I felt I had something to celebrate and also the sense that I needed to look more deeply into the shield and into what it meant. After I ate my eggs I sat with a cup of tea before me. It was steaming. I put on some soft music and went within. The shield came forward with a sense of mystery and of infinite support and strength. The strength came from within it. The words followed:

"You have never needed a shield until now."

With the words came a fear. 'For one to need a shield,' I thought, would suggest a forthcoming battle or a need to protect oneself from something hurtful. I had been given a sword of Light in the past, to give me strength. I could see its purpose, to be a warrior with the energy of truth, but I failed to understand and was fearful of why I might need a shield.

"That gives me fear," I said.

I went deeper within and was given a vision of medieval times. It felt like the time of King Arthur. I could see a knight entering into the battlefield, walking out of the castle, into the world. It looked like Arthur. He had no sword and no shield and I had the sense that without them he was somehow incomplete.

"In those times when a knight reached a certain age and stage of development he was sent to battle with his shield and sword. That time has come for you, now, on the inner."

I could see that I didn't want to go out into the world without the sword and shield. A vision returned of Arthur on his horse, shield and sword in hand. He looked complete now.

"To be open and naive is one thing. To be open and wise is another. One should not go unprepared for then one is open to attack and the opposing forces of nature. To be prepared is enough; to be ready and able to deal with opposing forces should they come your way."

"But I don't like battles," I replied, still a little fearful within of any suggestion of difficulty on my path ahead.

"Become the shield."

I breathed in the shield and became one with it. It was as if I entered it and around me was an infinite source of Light beings - Archangelic forces of Light. All the strength, all the protection, all the love I could ever need.

"We are Michael's army. You will come to know more about us in time. Love is your protection. When you feel fear simply call on us and we will bring it. You don't need to do anything. Simply radiate Love and

Light. Stand steadfast and radiate, no matter what comes your way. Leave the rest to us."

I could see an enormous army of Light beings, there to give support and Love. I felt glad for my shield for it held within it the Life force. I felt that I, like Arthur, could go into the world and do what I had to do, unhindered by darkness, supported by Light.

The beauty of regression is that it works with anyone because it enables people to look into the past within their capacity. The Light guides to the appropriate place and reveals what we need to learn allowing the process of redemption to occur. Sometimes the memory returns over time and pieces are given which ultimately make up the whole picture of the jig-saw puzzle. When we open to regression we must take courage to face what we may find within.

The resistance

I could feel myself becoming more and more agitated. It seemed every situation, every interaction in daily life was irritating me. I felt myself fearful of the future - fearful of life itself. My mind played scenarios of escape. Ways to not be what I had become. I knew something was wrong deep within. I went inward and could see a dark room which badly needed a paint job. It had an oppressive feeling about it. There was a cellar door, a hallway and a lounge room which seemed empty and cold. I was full of fear. I knew it was here I must look if I was to find the answer to my agitation and mistrust of life and those around me. It was very subtle. I could see the room in the distance. Without much effort, the room became all there was and I became aware that I was one of the two women in this room. In the cellar children were kept. It was World War II - and I was part of the Resistance. People had been coming through our house seeking refuge. The threat of invasion was becoming stronger. We had many children to care for. Like us, they were living in fear but keeping quiet. It was hard to keep children quiet but we had to.

It was clear the Germans were getting suspicious as they had made some raids upon the premises to no avail. We managed to avoid breaking down in the interrogations. Without evidence and proof they left us alone. It was only a matter of time. I was very fortunate that I could share my thoughts telepathically with the woman with whom I lived. We were both deeply passionate. I had to keep the passion as an inner knowing, because it could not manifest in the world of which we were a part. The room was quite bare, no ornaments, just bare necessities, for money was tight and we had to feed many on the low income we had. I could feel the terror beginning to grow within me as the scenes became more and more full - they were real.

The footsteps could be heard outside along the concrete streets. The only access to the vision of the street was through tiny windows set in the fibro-cement walls. I could tell by the sound of the footsteps whether the person creating them was a man or a woman, soldier or civilian, by the sound of the thud or the clump that echoed in the stillness of the cold and foggy air. With every footstep, until the owner was identified, an alarm went off within me. My stomach juices arose in fear - not the soldiers, not again. At regular intervals they would come and check the houses. They would bang on the door in an aggressive tone and enter with no consideration or thought that their routine may interrupt the lives of the inhabitants. My fear silenced me. Obediently I opened the doors of the rooms in which they would wish to look. My body was tense, not knowing whether it would be touched in any way or harmed. Silence worked as my protection, hiding my thoughts. I had been here for months now, living on this razor's edge, frightened for every sound, aware that every day more and more of those I knew had been taken away. I would never see them again: friends, close associates, comrades.

Night was coming and I felt I could breathe a little relief at this hour of the evening. I knew the soldiers would be eating, satisfying their stomachs, after the day's work. I could begin the cooking to feed those I had in hiding in my home. As part of the resistance I spent time helping those who sought their freedom through emigration. I worked with false identities, with new passports, and helping people dye their hair, changing appearance to leave behind their life of fear. A strength was growing within me. I felt a purpose and I felt dedicated to the cause. My days were full. I had to appear like an average working woman by day. My wage, along with my friend Eliza's, had to pay for the food of twenty. Eliza was home by day and worked by night. We had split shifts at home, through different jobs on the outside. The house was carefully designed to accommodate its task. The children could be kept in the cellar. The door to the cellar was under the tapestry rug and could be conveniently moved when the soldiers came.

I began to prepare the food. It was important that I prepare only one meal at a time in case the soldiers came. Then they would know. That was the hard part. Every time I took the meal to the children I would see the longing look of need and hunger in their eyes. They would watch the lucky recipient who would quickly eat every morsel as if it was the last meal that would ever be supped.

I spent much of my time in the lounge room, on guard, while people came through the back alleys, on shifts, to help us. There was another room where the adults stayed but their visits to us were more transient. It was a matter of passport, identity change, and go. Some of the children had nowhere else to go. Their parents had to leave them behind.

I myself was 8 months pregnant. I had managed to hide this fact by rugging up in winter clothes, always making it look as if I was carrying my shopping. I was lucky for there was not much show of child even at this late stage. I just seemed to get fatter all over and appeared to be a bigger woman than I was. Women of that size were quite common.

Not much was said between people of the cause. We could not afford to be overheard or seem to be disloyal to the government in any way. The political stance of everyone was a public matter - we were accountable for it at every moment. Communication took place eye to eye, in the seconds of an eye glance where heart to heart connections could be felt.

I had become pregnant after an evening of passion with another of my comrades, Francisco. He was not with me now but I held fond memories of him in my heart. I knew that he, too, was working, dedicated to the task of setting the Jewish people free. That link in purpose was enough to sustain me throughout the pregnancy and to give me the courage to continue on.

Midwives were arranged to help with the birth. I only hoped I could have it in silence and I was aware that, depending on the time of day, I may need to have it on my own. I wasn't sure what I'd do with it afterwards, either. What kind of life would it receive? Why was it coming? My whole attention was given to the cause and I considered the child to be just one more life that may, or may not, be saved. I couldn't understand why a baby would want to come into this world.

I found preparation for the birth difficult. I couldn't open to the joy. The next month passed and I felt myself entering into quite a depression, holding the seed of new life and having to deliver it into a dead and stagnant world full of violence and corruption, of power games without heart, without love. I felt myself devoid of these better qualities. I had been a passionate woman, yet this passion was slowly dying.

When the labour began I had great difficulty. I didn't want to let the baby out. It wasn't safe and I fought hard to keep it in until the time was right. Every sound of every vehicle caused alarm within me. Every footstep caused concern. I had a piece of rubber to use for my mouth, my teeth clenched into it so I would make no sound. I managed to prolong it until the early hours of the morning with Eliza present and an accompanying midwife.

I gave birth to a son. The poor little thing came out with the cord around his neck, his head blue and I began to shake him. I wanted to scream but I could not. He made a cry as the first breath of life was taken. I felt only fear that his cry would bring death. I took him quickly to my breast and tried to help him suckle. For a moment I felt the joy of life, the bonding of mother and son, the link of human beings and the joy of life on earth. I felt this intermittently. I was mostly numb. After a time my son became one of many children who may or may not have further life. It was hard to tell.

My focus shifted once again to the cause of the resistance: to the shunting of the people through the escape route, in the underground, where the watermains were shut down. Paths were made leading to the vans which awaited the people. They were stacked like cargo under the tarpaulins and camouflaged like food and stock deliveries, facing the risk of instant imprisonment or death if found.
The scenes continued to come. My eyes focussed upon a young girl clinging tightly to her doll. She had come out of the cellar aware that she had left it in the lounge earlier when she was playing there. Frightened for the doll's life, she ran towards it. The soldiers were half way up the stairs. She stood fixed in statue position as they entered. They looked at me and at her and I could feel the pull of terror, of grief. Machine guns in hand - threatening uniforms.

"No Jessica." My mouth was tightlipped as I could feel the inner terror racing through my body. Jessica was one of the children from the cellar. Her mother had gone some weeks before to France, with a new identity, in the hope of preparing a new life and sending for her child in time to come. Many had done this - we had seen hundreds of them. They would stay for some hours while we organised their new identities. We kept the tools for this purpose in carefully hidden compartments throughout the house: under the floorboards, behind wall panels, in the roof. It was hoped that the children could be sent for in time and some van loads had already been sent with the destination reached, all in safety. It was getting harder and harder. Roadblocks were more solid and it was becoming too risky to take the children. The adults could travel better on their own. It was so hard to keep the children quiet. Jessica loved the doll. Her mother had left it with her and it was too precious a thing to leave when the Germans were coming. When the others went to the cellar she made a last attempt to save her doll. As a result the tapestry *rug which covered the cellar door lines was not quite covering it as it should. Her presence alerted the Germans to the fact that something was wrong. My terror grew within, my stomach churned and I prayed and prayed that they did not notice the floorboards and the doorway leading down the steps to where the other children were.*

"She's my niece," I blurted out, in the hope to cover up the mistake. "My sister has left her here - just for the afternoon. She's shopping. It's so hard to take children when you shop, they want everything in sight - and when you can't afford it they just keep at you."

I knew as I spoke it was too late. One of the soldiers had noticed the rug and was pushing it aside. Before I knew it the door was opened and they were heading down. "Run Jessica!" I yelled, and she ran out the door. Another soldier grabbed me by the arms. My strength was great for that moment. I ran down the stairs after the soldiers screaming, "no! no!" When I was halfway down the stairs they let fire. The cellar walls were filled with blood and flesh. Pieces of babies and children strewn across it. There was an enormous bloodbath. The horror of what I had seen sent me into hysteria and the soldiers now were taking my arms and pulling me out of the house. I was screaming and kicking, devastated and hysterical. They held my elbows and it was difficult for me to move. The strength I found within myself was enormous. Another German waiting outside in his 3/4 length army coat sunk his boot into the depths of my stomach. I doubled over in the gutter with blood spilling out of my mouth. His kick seemed to bring me back to reality.

I became aware of my friend Eliza, walking along the pavement towards home. With a quick and frightened eye glance I was able to warn her and she walked straight past as if she did not know me. On the inner I screamed at her, "Don't go back to the house whatever you do. Don't go back to the house!" Within seconds I was thrown into the white van with other Jewish people, men and women. All silent, all clearly with their own story to tell. My thoughts were with Eliza. I hoped and prayed she would not re-enter the house but I knew it was only a matter of time before she would and what she would find. I only hoped she would wait long enough for the Germans to leave so they wouldn't get her too. The journey to the train station was silent for everybody. Each had their own pain, their own suffering. And everyone it seemed, was in shock. I guess it was only a matter of time before they got everyone. It had been going on for months now. People would disappear one by one. Friends would not be seen again. Mysterious vanishings were prevalent and many vans were headed towards the railway stations, emptying passengers like myself into the vans of the train. They were like dog boxes, no windows or seats and they were filled with many people. There were no toilets, no possibility for stopping, no light and little air, but somehow that was preferable to be in the dark for it was easier to fantasise that you were somewhere else, though the smells at times made that difficult. I felt completely numb within and the pangs of hunger merged with the numbness that filled my heart like an iceblock, unable to thaw. The pain and the suffering went deep. The train would stop every now and then for soldiers to come in and out and if you did not make room for them, which was impossible with the denseness of the people around you, you were bashed with the rifle end. There was no compassion, much brutality and the horror and terror of it all was clearly written in the eyes of the Jewish people: all in shock at the lengths to which these 'machines' were prepared to go. Occasionally the anger would rise up from some of the people and it would be quickly stamped out by the soldiers who were relentless in their maltreatment of their prisoners. Some Jews were beginning to border on insanity. You could see it in their eyes: the journey seemed to take forever. It was hard to tell how long as there seemed to be no night and day. I only know that when we stopped my body was very weak, as I discovered when I tried to move at the pace the soldiers wanted us to walk. The Germans continued the violence experienced in the dog boxes as we began our walk from the station to the camps. We walked past great lengths of wire fencing. Some people were with partners: I was alone and time came when we entered the gates and they began separating the sexes: some children that were left were taken to different areas of the camps. At this point many protested and with every person who was separated from his or her loved ones I felt the pain. I remembered Eliza and the children, the blood and the flesh. I prayed she didn't go home. It was a constant prayer.

* * *

The whole time I was seeing this, I couldn't understand why children, babies, had to be taken from their mothers and a voice was resonating within me: "It had to happen for people to learn humility. It was as hard for many of the Germans. Everyone thinks they are right and become caught up in the politics of the mind - caught up in negative power. Compassion and suffering are needed to open the heart."

"But why, why!" I asked within. "Why did it have to be so harsh?"

The answer came quickly:

"To show people the necessity of not taking on a role and acting from that role, to alert people to the necessity of not forgetting about Love and God and the Heart." I could see the children again, images flashing through my mind. They all had to remain so silent - they all had things to say but could not. Within them was the seed of new life. I wanted to free them to express themselves, to express joy - to be untainted by the environment of the past. I sent Light and saw the scene change to a group of free and lively children sitting in nature with the sun dancing upon their skin and the sound of laughter echoing in the wind. They could be completely free. I saw then the line of women and men, with fear in their eyes - mainly women, hundreds of them, with grief for loved ones, and found myself saying to them, "God is with you, you have done nothing wrong. In your hearts you have asked God to come and bring love into humanity. God has." I could see I had asked Him to come too. The line of people went on and on. I could sense that I had been given a calmness to see this. I could feel God with me. The scenes grew stronger. I could see resistance amongst the people. The fear was becoming too much and madness was entering their eyes. They tried to fight back in terror. The wire fences were very high. A line of soldiers *were shooting men up against the wall. The line of women, of which I was one, had to pass by. We were placed in little cells with couches. There were doctors. The light in the cells shone directly in our eyes. They wanted information, names - after all this - why? I could see weird things happening in the room. I couldn't understand why they still wanted information. Why they were cutting eyelids, cutting stomachs - the voice resonating within me was saying something about truth.*

"Humanity obtains power from the wrong source within themselves. There is so much love available to them but they choose the wrong power within, manufactured by themselves."

Many awful scenes followed with many of the more private parts of my being sliced. Yet I could sense that finally my values had come into perspective. I could feel the connection to God amidst the pain and suffering of the human condition. I could see that anything less than love is absurd and I could feel myself deciding at that moment that I could never settle for anything less than true love and true friendship with people in any lifetime from then on. The interrogations helped me find the truth within as well as highlighting that our human condition is comparatively insignificant. At this point, nothing could take me from the alignment I was feeling. It didn't matter what happened to my physical body, they could never take away the soul and the Spirit. I could feel myself die, feeling grateful for the release: feeling the Oneness, feeling myself melt together in unity with God.

A sudden pain in the neck thrust me further back in time to a scene of a hanging in a public square. I was out-of-body, looking down on myself with a rope around my neck. Many people witnessed the event. I had been hanged by the Spanish heretics. I had been a Cardinal who signed people away just as the Germans had done. I could see that I should never have done what I did. The Germans came and arrested people because of the forms. I had signed forms - I had done the same thing. I felt so sad for what I had done - I had done it out of arrogance - a very dangerous quality and I felt the importance of learning the lesson of not interfering with the lives of others, with their karma or dharma, no matter what judgments I might make or what self-righteous thoughts I might have about the life they led. I could feel the importance of being careful of thoughts, of words, both written and spoken, and that one should never incriminate others.

The voice began to resonate within me again, "Stay positive, open, loving, be honest and trust that God has good purpose for every test that comes your way."

But I couldn't go yet, not completely. There was something else I needed to do and I felt myself flying over the land, back to the room where the children had been slain. I entered into the room where there now were many rats busy eating the flesh of the children. Eliza was there and was not recognisable. She had put a gun to her mouth. It had been too much for her to bear. She had sat for a long time in that room until she could go on no longer. I gathered the souls of the children and could feel myself now with wings and in the moment of connection with her soul once more I became aware that she had to incarnate again immediately for she had more work to do. I stayed with her on the inner until that task was complete. From the room we travelled to a train - there had been an accident, a woman had been badly hurt and was in a coma. I went with her to the hospital. I helped her enter the body of Lily, a woman who was on the side of the Germans - at least in the outer, but with something of another consciousness now on the inner. It was all part of the Plan. There was much work to do but for my part the payment had been made and I could feel myself being drawn to the inner levels. I took one last look at the life of Francisco, who had begun new endeavours in France. I could go now, my task was complete, and all the scenes grew smaller and smaller as I flew further and further from Earth to where I would reside on the inner levels. On the inner levels there were many angels with mighty wings, preparing to return to Earth and teach what it is to truly love. There I could gather my strength and prepare too for the next incarnation.

Guided Imagery

Guided imagery is a process whereby the imagination is actively employed to help us get in touch with our unconscious psychological, mental and physical awareness. Other names for this process are imaging, directed reverie, creative visualisation, symbolic manipulation and imaginative play. This method of actively imagining is used in psychoanalytic processes, Gestalt and Jungian therapy, psychosynthesis, cognitive behavioural therapy (a psychological model which emphasises the connection between mind and action), and some forms of hypnosis. Guided imagery is a process which is now being used by a variety of practitioners in the psychological, medical, body work and healing fields. Nimrod Sheinman (1987, p. 1) defines guided imagery as:

> Guided imagery is the method of communicating with autonomic processes which occur outside of conscious awareness. In this process, images, symbols and metaphors are explored, while the client is in a state of deep relaxation. The images that are allowed to emerge may be requested to represent symptoms/illness, stress/inner struggle, physical dysfunction/pain, or inner strength/deeper knowledge about oneself and the underlying issues. The images can then be communicated, explored and transformed, in order to mobilise the inner awareness, deeper strengths and personal understandings, toward health and wholeness.

Through guided imagery we gather information about our unconscious processes. We have the opportunity to see how these processes are functioning and come to know whether they may be helping or sabotaging us. Through the process we may also adjust our thoughts, ideas and beliefs to create inner harmony. Guided imagery, through actively employing the imagination, can give us access to higher inspiration, illumination and creativity. We can actively choose to look at issues in our past, present and future, with the possibility of exploring what is hidden around underlying issues that are related to our being. Sometimes the past is activated, and we can see objectively how we have functioned and whether or not that has been a dysfunctional or valuable way of being; we can look and make new choices about how we would like to be. We can also be reminded of past strengths or weaknesses from which we need to learn, and can bring the needed strengths and attributes forward to our consciousness so we may have access to them once again. Similarly, we can look at our current predicaments and see from a higher perspective, "What is my next step? What am I needing to learn from my current struggle? What is it I need to know and understand now in my life?" We can look forward and prepare for possible events, and give energy to decisions we might make about the future.

There are many psychologists, doctors, spiritual healers, masseurs, counsellors, stress management workers and crisis intervention workers who employ guided imagery in their work, in a variety of forms. Martin Rossman (1982; 1987) is one of a number of doctors and other practitioners in the alternative health field who work with imagery, encouraging patients to dialogue with the symptoms of their disease to find the meaning of it, that is, what the symptoms represent, and then to find the steps needed to bring back health and well-being. Dr. Rossman trained with Dr. Irving Oyle, who believes that the power of the visual image to transform life experience is a vital healing tool (Bry, 1978). His work echoes that of many thousands of spiritual people worldwide who, when they come to a problem in life, meditate and look for its message. His work also echoes that of psychotherapists worldwide who work in this way to help people come to know themselves and in so doing increase their consciousness and capacity for choice, helping them to reach their fullest potential.

To rever and respect the inner images we produce through dream and guided imagery has been acknowledged as an invaluable tool to help people move towards wholeness and personal growth by alchemists for hundreds of years.

Guided imagery provides access to understanding the working of the psyche and understanding the nature of the unconscious and our inner life. It is a very empowering and enriching process that helps us to relax and get in touch with ourselves. We can identify our frustrations and fears, and begin to educate ourselves to more functional ways of being. N. Sheinman (1987, p. 1) points out that guided imagery is an

> excellent technique to be used with patients who have chronic pains, cardiovascular disease, depression, asthma, digestive disturbances, skin disorders, medication dependence and a host of other problems, as well as for general health, awareness, and personal growth.

In my experience of working with guided imagery, which spans over ten years, it is also useful for helping us to understand the nature of our shadow (the dark aspects of the personality); for identifying, acknowledging and working towards dealing with the shadow; and for helping us to identify the nature of our resistance to working with it. C. Jung (1976, p. 145) describes the shadow:

> The shadow is a moral problem that challenges the whole ego-personality, for no one can become conscious of the shadow without considerable moral effort. To become conscious of it involves recognising the dark aspects of the personality as present and real. This act is the essential condition for any kind of self knowledge, and it therefore, as a rule, meets with considerable resistance.

Indeed self knowledge as a psycho-therapeutic measure frequently requires much painstaking work extending over a long period. Closer examination of the dark characteristics that is, the inferiorities constituting the shadow reveals that they have an emotional nature, a kind of autonomy, and accordingly an obsessive or, better, possessive quality.

Guided imagery has the potential of helping us come to know many aspects of the self: the inner child, the inner male, the inner female, the shadow, the inner light, the trickster, the helper, the perfectionist, the rebel, the rescuer, the martyr, and the saint, to name only a few.

Guided imagery assists us in finding the parts of ourselves that we can rely upon to help in our growth and development, thus enabling us to find inner friends and guides who can aid us on the way.

In guided imagery the healer or the therapist assists the client, through a process of relaxation and guided visualisation, to contact a quiet and peaceful place within, where the client can relax and contemplate. The healer also assists the client to contact a part of him/herself that knows what the client needs for his or her healing. This part is called the inner adviser. This part usually takes the form of an image or symbol, perhaps of an object an animal or a person. It may also be a sense, a feeling or an impression. Once it is contacted the healer or therapist facilitates communication between the client and his or her image that is representing the inner adviser, thus assisting the client towards his or her healing. The process of guided imagery can also enable a client to get in touch with his or her anger, fear or guilt or the symptoms of an illness. This is done by a healer or therapist assisting the client in guided visualisation to find an image or symbol to represent for example, the symptoms of his or her illness. As with the inner adviser, the healer or therapist works to facilitate communication between the client and his or her image of the symptom to facilitate the needed understanding and growth. (A general guide describing this process in greater detail appears later in this chapter.)

Through guided imagery we seek to strengthen our connection to this help and provide the tools for deepening communication. It gives us a way to come to know ourselves, to better ourselves, to cope with ourselves, to live with ourselves, and to actualise our true potential. It teaches us to learn to identify and discriminate between the higher and lower parts of our nature. We contact the part of ourselves that knows all there is to know about ourselves and our lives, and we open to information from that part that is advantageous to our growth and development. We open also to receive the sense of comfort and support that this part brings. This part of ourselves that knows what we need often makes real its support and comfort by making its presence felt through our senses, impressing us deeply, soothing and satisfying us in a very real and tangible way.

A character or object that presents through the image generated in the guided imagery may represent a part of us that has been forgotten, misunderstood or rejected. These parts of ourselves have dissociated from our conscious awareness. If we wish to reclaim our wholeness, we need to integrate with these parts that have become alienated from us in some way. The first step is to bring these parts to our conscious awareness. The process of guided imagery will help us to do that. Once they are identified we can reconnect to these parts as if meeting a long-lost friend or foe with whom we wish to make amends, change our separated nature and become unified; we can do this through working with our inner parts to create respect, tolerance, acceptance and love. Through guided imagery, we initiate communication between the conscious and the unconscious parts of ourselves.

Through the guided work, a symbol to represent the issue is welcomed, to flow freely to the mind. When the dialogue begins, an inner role-play commences, which allows the hidden, deeper meaning of the symbol to be revealed. The beauty of the symbol is its ever-expanding capacity to reveal all that needs to be revealed. In this way the guided imagery therapy can move into profound psychotherapy. Perhaps the symbol appears as a mythological or archetypal figure, or an object, a sense, an impression, light or a colour. Whatever form it may come in, the symbol communicates with us through dialogue, inner vision or intuitive insight and revelation. We can ask it questions about the issues most pertinent to us, and it will reveal the underlying meaning of what we need to know.

Psychological problems, like physical ones, often appear to suggest imbalance in our lives. If we can acknowledge that and try to comprehend the message the 'problem' brings, and respond to that message, we can generally turn the imbalance around into a deeper understanding of life and its meaning and bring the 'flow' back into our lives. The difficulties we encounter often indicate that we are somehow 'out of touch' with life and ourselves. Somewhere we are holding on too much, or perceiving the world in a distorted way.

Though I had used processes of guided imagery earlier in my practice, I first began to work with it on a regular basis after attending two workshops, *Guided Imagery Workshop for Personal and Professional Growth* and *Guided Imagery for Clinicians* in September, 1987. The workshops were presented by Dr. Nimrod Sheinman, who trained under Dr. Martin Rossman and Dr. David Bresler, leading experts in the field. I found the workshops to be invaluable. Guided imagery has had remarkable effects on my clients, and it has also helped me to access my own inner life in a way I had previously been unable to do. I have continued to work with the process for my own development, as well as using it often as a technique to assist my clients. Guided imagery is a marvellous tool to help us come to know ourselves and to look at our lives from a higher perspective. It helps us to see our blind spots, understand how we work, find direction, find meaning and come to know our next step in life. It helps us open to trusting in the existence and help of our soul, and opens us to the higher forces of assistance that are available to us within. It provides a way through which we can enter the world of our psyche and the world of Spirit, helping us utilise insight and revelation in a constructive and practical way.

In my own personal development, the initial role of guided imagery was to help me come to understand on another level about the asthma I had and the role it played in my life. The images and the process helped me come to find the teacher in the asthma. I had been an asthmatic all my life, and had many hospital admissions for it. On a number of occasions I had asthmaticus paradoxus, where the lungs "invert" because of the difficulty in getting oxygen into lungs filled with carbon dioxide. On one occasion, both lungs collapsed, and after an experience of death, I was placed on a ventilator, remaining in a coma for at least ten days. Suffice to say, I was a severe asthma sufferer. The asthma had always felt like something outside of me that came and took me over when I didn't want it. It felt alien, and when it would come on, I always felt out of control, a complete victim to it. Working with an image of asthma in guided imagery brought enormous relief - just to know I could talk to it, and come to know it, to ask it why it was there, and to gain insights about various aspects and levels of it. I have written about some of these insights in my first book, *The Language of the Heart*. Guided imagery helps us find the teacher within and another way of opening to communicate with the senses of the inner worlds. It helps us to find answers to any question, providing our heart yearns for the answer.

Guided imagery creates strong healing effects. Changes can take place in all of our inner bodies. Once, I had some difficulty in my relationship with my brother; I felt healing immediately when I went to my quiet place. The quiet place was a swing in the backyard of a house I lived in when I was about eight years old. My brother was there pushing me on the swing. As I saw the image I felt great inner joy and a strong sense of being safe and protected with my brother there. It started me thinking of the protection and safety he had offered me in my childhood. Whatever difficulty I had experienced was dissolved in the moment.

At other times guided imagery has helped me to find balance. One particular guided imagery stands out in this regard. I experienced it about four years ago. Through its lessons I learned how to let more joy into my life, and to open more to the way of the heart in life. For reasons of personal privacy and brevity I have not placed the entire guided imagery here. I have simply placed enough to help you see how the process has brought imbalances to my attention and also helped to adjust them to a place of balance. As with many guided imageries, the way was pointed out; it was then up to me to allow the needed changes to be implemented in my life. The problem and the steps out of it were beautifully revealed.

In my quiet place there was a man standing on a beach, on the dunes at the back amongst the grass. He was looking out across the ocean and seemed filled with the energy of dedication, purpose, and steadfastness. There was a sense of freedom and seeing a broader horizon, a feeling of faith, hope and trust in the universe. The man became my inner adviser. When I came to the part of the process where I became one with him, the therapist asked me,

"How does Tara appear?"

I saw two images, the first was a curled up woman, not looking very good, on the ground. The second was a girl doing cartwheels who seemed to radiate the energy of freedom. The first appeared almost dead with no spirit in her, while the second had all the spirit in the world. I was told that the younger (spirited) one represents the older (unspirited) one's potential unmanifested.

The therapist asked the inner adviser, " What can you tell Tara that will most help her at this time?"

"She needs to choose between life and death. She can no longer will off parts of herself to suit the ideal or she'll become like white meat (red meat with blood taken out)."

I asked the dead one, "How did you get into that state?"

She answered, "I let everybody else take over and put them first and this is what happened to me. I gave my power away totally to everybody else. I let everybody else control me because I thought I was worth nothing."

The spirited girl appeared doing cartwheels on the beach like the young girl from the film, "Piano." I asked her,

"What are you doing?"

She answered, "Living life. Being joyful. I have no boundaries. I give myself space and freedom to be. I don't expect anything of myself, except to be."

I could see the two extremes, the two poles of me and could see where the conflict lay. The balance between the two was needed. I could feel that the little girl needed to give some of her life to the dead woman.

The inner adviser stood there.

I asked, "Why are you showing me these two aspects of myself? What can I do to balance or heal them, to integrate them?"

"I am showing you because you need to understand the split in you. It has come as a result of repression of the natural self in favour of the ideal. Explore both - they have things to tell you."

I asked the dead one, "What have you come to tell me?"

"This is what you've done to me - done to yourself."

"What do I have to do to have life again?"

"Follow your heart - trust your heart."

"How do I find my heart? How do I know what is my heart?"

"Right now your heart is crying - listen to the crying voice - to the deep pain. Go into the heart and you will find the heart once again."

"How? I feel like I need help."

I felt the sense of deep pain from the past. I cried deeply and fully.
"Passion is a necessary ingredient to life - many live without it and their lives are a monotone. They are always searching - always feeling as if something is missing. Passion gives enthusiasm and sustains you, so that you can work for Spirit, filled with Spirit. There is a balance always - to be found when one works unflinchingly. You have incarnated on Earth to learn about being human and that is a truth of life which must accompany spiritual evolution."

"How can I achieve the balance?"

"It must be a conscious effort. Your spirit must be brought into the daily life. Passion and enthusiasm are an avenue for the expression of your humanness. You cannot deny these human needs without creating imbalances. Similarly, you cannot let these human needs take precedence over the will of the soul or imbalance will also be created. There is a *balance. If you can acknowledge love and let it live within you, the conflicts and imbalances that are present as a result of its suppression in you can fall away and your earthly life can take its proper course. You will be surprised what happens when you allow love to exist. For in allowing it you will discover your love for all beings and the pressure you have felt will dissipate because the pressure you have felt is the holding in of the love. Love cannot be contained in such a way as you are doing. If it has natural expression, the Will of God can be made manifest through it. You must allow the energy of love to take its own mighty course. You must trust that love is God given. It is a grace sent and, as such, it is an energy which must be allowed for. You are a human being and you cannot impose human rules upon the higher forces. You must, of course, make choices in order to live in the societies and groups you have set up for varying purposes, and in order to cope with your own nature which has been imbued with qualities - jealousy, possessiveness, loyalty, devotion, etc., and must come to terms with the qualities and paradoxes within human existence."*

I could see a lifetime where I went to the extreme of "following my lower passions," and left the Cause (working for the Christ on Earth).

"The Cause demands that a person choose balance in the life - that you have family life, and connection to friends." The image of the dead woman appeared.

"How do I bring life into this dead image?"

"Continue to enter and explore the heart."

"How can I make my relationship with my husband more full of passion?"

"Be yourself and, within reason, do not try to change yourself according to what you think he wants you to be. You have to understand that he has married you because he loves you and your union assists the

263

development of your souls. The personalities might not always like what is placed before them on the path of that development but you can rest assured that the soul revels in the growth that is taking place in you both. You must be prepared to show each other more respect - there are things that are needed to be learned here - such as loyalty, devotion, one-pointedness, determination and steadfastness in relation to the path of the heart. These qualities must be brought into the relationship."

(A lot of very good and valuable insights have been taken out here for the purposes of privacy and brevity.)

"If you truly wish to have the passion re-ignited within the marriage, you must put more focus to it and create space and time together for it to develop, and you must trust each other, but it must be something that both hearts take part in, not one, for one cannot carry the torch. It is the task of two. The wish must be wholehearted; when the wish is wholehearted the Light can help."

I asked the dead one, *"Is there anything else in my heart I have to explore before moving on?"*

"Relationships/partnership is not something decided by the personality but by the soul, and when the personality yields to follow the soul regardless of the thoughts and feelings - then the life can be of great benefit to all humanity and not only a few. Tara - lift your heart to Him - to the Christ. Give it there and work for the Hierarchy; in that way you will be the best example to all around you and you will not get caught in the stumbling traps from previous incarnations. You will have learned and risen in the Christ."

The young girl doing cartwheels on the beach appeared.

"I am your free spirit. I am uncontaminated by social rules and regulations. I have inner rules, however, and they are rules of love that are natural and flow from the Divine. I live in you at times because

you let me in and I fill you with love of life and every cell of your being turns to ecstasy, but my time in you is somewhat limited because of your attendance to social rules and expectations. When I am not needed, I remain here on this beach. I play, I run in the sand and I do cartwheels - I breathe in life and nature, through nature I live. I am the part of you that goes into the backyard when you have the time and sits - feeling the sun on the skin - without me you cannot live. I would like to help you, to inhabit you more often. You tend to turn me on and off like a tap, and I have heeded this because the part of you that is ruled by the social mores is strong and so I get stronger also to compensate, to create balance in you when I come. If you could open to me more often you would find your life filled with enthusiasm - even in your daily tasks. I can help you in your work for the Church, your summer school lectures, for I bring life to all things. Let me in - let me fill your life with love in all its aspects - let me touch all your relationships and bring back the magic of love and life into them."

"I'd like to do that. How do I let you in more?"

"Be alert to me and know that I will help you and not harm you. You will meet others who cannot tolerate me and in the past you have pushed me away so as not to bring discomfort to others but you will find that if you allow me to remain even in the face of others' disdain, that soon their disdain will turn to love, and when it doesn't, it will cause them to see something of themselves and that is not your concern. I am your joy. I am the blood. I am the life force. Let me flow through you and give you life once again. I do not discriminate as you do and there is a balance again that needs to be found, for I open to all and I see myself in all - in everyone's hearts. I am made joyous when I touch hearts and hearts touch me. I am in you, Tara, I am in you now. Just the simple fact of you asking me to come into your life more is enough. I will do it and I will threaten your moral codes - your social rules - your current boundaries in order that you may re-evaluate your life and live it more fully according to the heart. Is that all right?"

"Yes, that is all right as long as you work with me on it and don't push me in a negative way. Show me love and respect during the time it takes me to look at and re-evaluate the space I need - so my life doesn't go too much in the wrong direction, to make up for what I've done, but comes gently back to the middle and is balanced.

Can you do it in that way?"

"Yes, I can - I have the freedom to do that and I have the patience and the will. Tara - I'm very glad you've asked for help. I've always been here - playing on the beach waiting for you to be ready."

"What else do I need to see and know right now?"

A vision came of the inner adviser, the man on the beach, he was now lying down on the grass, ready for Spirit to enter.

"Now just leave it to Spirit, relax and let it happen - let the integration take place - you have set it in motion by asking and looking at each part - let it happen - let the story unfold - let life tell the story - let it be a surprise - an experience, and trust the plan is unfolding as it should. Trust the Christ, as Christ loves each and everyone of us on this path of evolution."

"Is that all?"

"Be at peace - don't try to pre-empt anything - don't think about future - past - just go through life, living each moment in the present. Don't create things with your mind - just let things be. In that way the Light can help you in the work and the work can get done through you."

In the guided imagery work above, it is clear how the symbols unfold and give more meaning as we work with them, and insights are gained that are not always so easy to see at first sight. Usually an overriding sense of logic and common sense is felt about what is shown. Imbalances become obvious when we look

from an objective perspective, as do ways to correct them. It is through practice with guided imagery that we begin to see its incredible capacity for expanding our conscious awareness and its ability to help us let go of many preconceived notions and ideas. It uses imagery, feeling, and the wit of the mental plane to wake us up and help us come to see, know and experience the higher truth. Our inner adviser knows us, and knows exactly what is needed to help us "become enlightened." In many ways it is like an expert psychologist who knows the right words to say, the right images to evoke, the right feelings to be stimulated in order to create a healing effect. When a guided imagery is embarked on, we come to know that we will be changed by the experience. The insights gained, the understandings received, the relaxation given all work together to make us feel more whole. The dialogue given may only be a word or two, the feeling may be momentary, the vision may give just one image, and yet the possibility for insight, understanding, transformation and change is profound.
The following inner dialogue shows how the inner knows and can reveal, through dialogue, feeling and vision, exactly what is needed at any given time in our development. It also shows how through this process deeply ingrained patterns and beliefs can be uprooted to make way for the seeds of new beliefs that are more appropriate for the well-being of the person concerned. In this case it had to do with my learning more about love.

The golden enchantress

"But how can I love two," I asked. "Isn't it so that to love another would be to be disloyal to the one?"

"Not at all," she replied, her golden being appearing before me.

"To love two is to expand the heart and bring forth the fullness of love. Make it three, four, five, there is no limit to what the heart can do, to *how many souls the heart can touch with its essence. You see, love is a sweet and golden nectar that flows from the perennial Source."*

I began to comprehend that it is we who place limits upon love's flow, through our fears and insecurities.

'Yes,' I thought. 'Why not two, three, four or five, perhaps then I would feel more alive.'

I hesitated, beginning to feel life's fullness.

"But you just can't love everyone. You must have to discriminate somewhere. There must be boundaries to consider."

"If you are sure that your love comes through the heart and has awareness in its passage of Divine Principles such as harmlessness, goodwill and justice and if you are sure that its movement is towards manifesting these principles by following the Divine Laws, then there are no boundaries, and the flow of its essence will take you through the river to the ocean. In the ocean, needs as they are felt in human terms are transcended; questioning and analysis cease. Life simply is sustained and nourished by the Divine."

I could sense the beauty of the words that had been spoken and I could feel within some fear. To enter the ocean requires some caution and I was not sure that I was prepared to surrender my control and this appeared to be what the Mother Light was asking of me.

"Yes," she replied, catching my thoughts. "It requires surrender and a step in faith and trust to let the waters of life flow through you and lift you to a place of peace and stillness within. You must overcome your hesitation and fear. The temptation is to close the heart petals, often through fear that others will be hurt by your love, and sometimes through fear of the love itself. The power of love within the heart is enormous and to close down that love, not allowing it an avenue of

expression, could create severe problems with disease or even death. This energy is to be given freely and unconditionally so life can flow. To hold it back causes destruction to the inner being and the life path cannot then manifest. Many are conditioned to think that their joy and love are bad, but they are, in essence, pure and can do a great deal to heal all when they are allowed expression. You see, I am an Enchantress of the Golden Light, and I help you and others to heal - I know how, I understand the Magic. I see the work that needs to be done. I am everywhere and everywhere I look. In all situations where there is lack of Love I bring the Light of the Mother to take away that lack and I go to where that need is greatest. Whether there are two, or three, or four, it does not matter. I will work to bring this Golden Light into manifestation wherever it is lacking. All you have to do is call on me. Do not resist me because of old conditioning or fears. Allow me to come through you as a pure expression of Light and Love. Be true to your heart and allow the Love to flow through that centre to be distributed to where the need is greatest. Always there will be people brought to your door. Minister, tend and care for them as if they were your children. Emphasis must be placed on loving others, not for how they can fulfil your needs or fit in to the pattern you are comfortable with in relation to them, but in such a way that love is given. Focus must not be on the object of desire but upon ensuring the purity of energy from within the heart centre through the intent of goodwill and purity of motive. There is choice to be made, moment by moment, on all levels, in action, thought and deeds."

"That's quite a task and I feel I would go insane knowing I have to monitor it all."

"It does take will and a desire to lift one's energies into the Light of the heart. In time it comes naturally and is no effort at all. Never underestimate the power of life. It can work magic. It is magic and transcends all your limitations."

"But what of suffering?" I asked.

"Will to suffer, will to sacrifice, to serve, and to love. Will to develop compassion for yourself and others and then suffering can take its natural form in your life. It is necessary for the heart petals to unfold, but that does not mean you should create your own suffering. Let it be God-given. Accept the joys and the sorrows, the hills and the valleys, for they all lead us to the path of the heart. Each has his/her own struggle, his/her own mysteries. There is light and shadow within all. Accept this. Accept the pain, for it comes when you least expect it and rightly so, to help your heart expand in consciousness and build within it Love and Compassion in its true form. Don't forget I am here, and do not be overwhelmed by all of this. It's easy, it's like learning to drive: a few things to learn about, then it happens almost without thinking. You may need some idea of the direction in which you are headed, but even that is not always necessary. Let God navigate and always have a seat for God to sit in. Make space in your heart and the journey will be Divine."

Perhaps I could let go of control, I could pass the wheel to God and allow the Divine Will to manifest in my life. That's a scary thought. What would happen then? To open to not only the love in my heart but the Will of God in my life would surely bring many changes. Many of my attitudes, values and beliefs have prevented me previously from doing that. I remembered that as a child I would feel, by giving love to my mother, I was somehow betraying my father, and vice versa. I had felt the same in the spiritual world, in opening to one teacher of the many around me, was I betraying the other? In opening to one aspect of God or quality of divinity, was I betraying another? I thought of the many religions, the many names and languages to speak of God the Divine and its aspects and could see the need to expand my consciousness to incorporate it all, and I thought of the many ways of working with Spirit which are now flooding into life in the West: many faiths, many beliefs and attitudes.

"Is there not room for it all?"

"Aim for the highest. Look for the God in all. The walls of separatism must be dispelled. Respect and honour the path of Righteousness in everyone. Many clothes and personas are taken on in the expression of life but remember they are only clothes and personas. The essence is found more deeply. It is found within the heart of all."

The Golden Enchantress turned into the Mother.

"Here," she said, "I have a set of wings for you to use to help you rise above the stones on your path. The wings will give you the freedom to choose to rise above the form, but be aware, you must still manifest your life in form, for that is how I can enter the Earth and reach the hearts of others on the way. You must respect and honour the form in all its facets and varieties for the form is an expression of God and makes tangible the Love of the Mother which is spirit in action."
I took the wings and rose above the stones on my path. The stones represented my attachments to the Earth.

"How can I love and yet not be attached?" I asked the Mother, as we flew together side by side.

"Let your wings merge with Mine and I'll show you," she said.

We merged and I felt myself heading towards the sun. Its golden light lifted me, helping me transcend all need. The sun and the Mother became One. An explosion of Light ignited my heart. I had no more questions.

Guided imagery is a full experience, not only a mental gymnastic exercise. It acknowledges the role of the mind in affecting our state of being. It also allows space for our intuitive faculties to come into operation, and for our senses to gather impressions, from whatever source they are coming, be it visual, sensual or auditory. We can move freely through space and time, go into memory and recall of the past, move to an anticipated future and plan accordingly. The process utilises the energy of Active Intelligence. Because of this there can be a lighthearted and sometimes humorous energy which makes one laugh. This has the effect of disarming us and opening us up to new ways of thinking and being. We may also be confronted with aspects of ourselves or suggestions from the inner adviser we had not thought about. The process allows us time to find out exactly what is meant, get used to the ideas and ask questions, if we have any, that will help to give us clarity. The story below outlines an experience I once had in a guided imagery session, at a time when I was quite stressed and needed help to relax with all the pressures of life I felt I was under. I will let the story speak for itself. It is amazing what can be revealed.

Finding peace

I pushed the load of psychology books into the shute, returning them to the library. My bag was full of photocopies of the journal articles I needed for my essay. It was 3 o'clock. I had an appointment at four and an hour and a quarter drive ahead. I walked quickly to the car, hoping I didn't have a parking fine, as I had overstayed my welcome at the parking bay by 20 minutes. My pace fastened as I approached my car. The parking fine attendant was two cars away. A sigh of relief expelled from my body when I saw there was no ticket. I threw my bag in the back seat and began to drive. Peak hour started early along these roads, because of the factories. I had to be alert. I tried to think of the ways that would cut down the time of the journey, the many different roads I could take. I didn't like being late, I liked to be on time, and I could feel the pressure building inside my stomach. My mind was focused solely on getting there. It seemed that every set of lights turned red as I approached and the space of my mind began to take up the entire car, along with a tension in the stomach which grew and grew. There was no space for peace. The closer I came to my destination the more out of control I felt.

The appointment I had was for a spiritual healing. It was difficult to find time in my busy life for relaxation and the irony was I had scheduled this healing to help me find peace. The onlooker in myself could only laugh and watch as I became more and more stressed. I screeched to a halt in front of the house where the healing was to take place, went up the drive and pushed the door bell. My healer was waiting. I apologised profusely. In a calm and peaceful manner she told me to relax and assured me my lateness was not an issue for her. I could hardly see her but I managed to find the room, take off my shoes and lie on the couch. My body began to spin and I could hardly utter the words to define my problem.

"Go inside and find a quiet place," she said.

"That's my problem," I replied, "I can't find one. All I can find is stress."

"Create an image to represent the stress," she said.

An image of my trusted diary appeared. It was pocket-size and grey, delivered yearly by my credit union where my account was always "on empty." It was filled every day, every line and the more I looked at it the more ridiculous it became. It started to puff up like a monster about to explode and I began to laugh. As I laughed, it was as though a pressure cooker was being released and the energy of stress started to release from my body.

"Why are you appearing like that?" I said to my diary.

"Because I can't take any more in. I can't fit in any more, yet you seem to find room for more and more, I can't take it."

I smiled because I knew what the diary was telling me was true.

"Sometimes you have to say no," it said. "You can't say yes to everything just because you can do it. Not everything is yours to do, even though *people may ask. You have to understand your limits and the possibilities of creating boundaries and space."*

I could see my diary was not only comical, it also made a lot of sense.

"It's good that you laugh," it said. "Laughter is good for the soul. Sometimes, Tara, you take things far too seriously."

"You look so funny as a pressure cooker. What can I do to prevent you from having to appear like that again?"

"It's your attitude that you need to change. It doesn't matter so much how many things you do; you are capable of doing a lot and sometimes there is a lot that needs to be done. The attitude you take to the things you do is what creates the pressure and the stress. When you think "I have to do this. I have to do that," it creates an energy of stress. If you think, "Now I'm going to do this because I've chosen to do this now," you will create quite a different effect."

"I'm not sure I understand you fully," I replied, hoping for a deeper understanding.

"Here, let me show you." The diary opened itself at a page. The page turned into a basket and inside the basket were many things. There was a set of keys with my parent's address on it, a set of psychology books, a set of scales, a squash racquet, some Theosophical books, and a fish. The list went on.

"Why are you showing me all these things?"

"These are symbols of your burdens. They are not really burdens but you have created them into burdens because of your attitude. You think you `have to' visit your parents, you `have to' read the psychology books, you `have to' stay a balanced weight, you `have to' keep fit and exercise, you `have to' study Theosophy and `have to' eat the foods your body needs."

"But these are all the things I should do, aren't they?" I questioned.

"These are all things you can do if you choose to. You might even be doing them because you want to."

I could feel a shift take place inside, and more of the stress release, as I realised that "yes," I did want to do all these things. I did want to visit my parents, eat well, keep fit, study all these things, and I could feel that these were things I wanted to do from my heart, not because I should do them, or thought I had to. I started to feel that I was capable of much more. I felt for a moment as though I could climb a mountain. All the stress inside disappeared and I felt in its place a bountiful energy in all my bodily cells and organs.

Another basket appeared. In it was a red-checked table cloth, a bottle of wine and a white, French breadstick.

"What's that?" I asked.

"It's a leisure basket. In it are all the things you won't let yourself do. The red-checked table cloth represents the afternoon picnic. The wine and bread represent the nourishment you deserve."

Now I was really confused.

"How can white bread and red wine be nourishing? Aren't they bad for the body?"

"The only thing bad for your body in that leisure basket is your attitude to it. Try to live your life in balance. Have moderation in all things especially in fanaticism with food. Relax."

I was beginning to catch on and began to imagine the green field that the red and white table cloth could be laid out in. When I did this I felt myself lay back in the field and breath in the air. A third basket appeared. In it were paints and crayons and brushes and a harmonium (a musical instrument).

"This basket is your creativity, and when you make space in me for creativity and leisure, you will find that you can come back into balance and stop living the life of stress you have been living. Don't forget diaries are designed to help people, not to stress them. Use me to help you establish balance and peace in your life."

There was still one thing I didn't understand, so I asked:

"Isn't it my job to help others with their burdens?"

"Yes, Tara, that is a part of your job, but understand it is to help people to help themselves. When another comes and shows you their basket of burdens, you can explore the basket with them. Perhaps even make them aware of their leisure and creativity baskets, but when they go out the door you must not keep their burdens. They must take them with them so that they, too, can learn of the joys and sorrows in life and their lives can be enriched as yours is by life's great variety."

With the sense of support and understanding the diary gave me, I gave a big, deep outbreath.

The role of the guide

Though the process of guided imagery is quite simple to learn, and entry to the unconscious is by it easily made, it is important to be aware that it takes skill to learn to guide the client through the aspects of the unconscious that are revealed, and to then bring them into integration with the rest of the personality. Practice and balanced confidence, as well as a few key rules, make it possible for the beginner to make it through and come to learn the skills of guiding. Like any skill, practice makes perfect, and much is learned through trial and error. It is important to be aware of your limitations, the weaknesses as well as your strengths and only take the person to the depths you are capable of dealing with. The process of guided imagery is simple, and sometimes the path of the client is simple. Sometimes the path of the client is complex, however. The steps that are used to deal with the complexity remain simple and follow a pattern of common sense.

When learning to become a guide in this process, a good deal of training comes through experience. Initially I remember being acutely aware of having strengths and weaknesses which both assisted and interfered with the process. In the workshop setting I could explore and experiment with approaches to guiding and was able through this to identify the skills I needed to develop in order to become a better guide. I learned a great deal from being guided as well as guiding. I learned what not to do and what to do to facilitate a helpful flow. The process also helped me to develop certain goals and objectives about my work in this area, which continued to define and redefine themselves as I continued to work in the field. I will endeavour to share briefly the technique, a general guide and points which need to be considered when working with guided imagery. For a more detailed appraisal of the technique I suggest you refer to Rossman and Reman (1982), *Imagine Health*.

The technique

To start the process, the first steps are to define the issue to be worked with, help the client to relax and guide him or her to find his or her inner quiet place. The quiet place is a place where the client can go to relax and to know that he or she is safe. It serves as a place of beginning: a place that can always be returned to during the process, to find the sense of relaxation and centredness again, and a place that can be returned to at the end of the session, to contemplate the learnings and insights given. We all have a quiet place within. We often have many and can go to different ones each time, or the same one as a matter of preference. The quiet place can be a place we know from the vast memory within, or it can be an imaginary place that we come to know as we visualise and explore it.

To activate our ability to use our imagination productively, it is important to be relaxed and alert, with a mind clear of earthly concern. The quiet place helps us in this regard by taking us to a place where we are relatively free of concern. At times when we go to the quiet place, the feeling of struggle may follow. It is possible to acknowledge that the feeling is there and say, "we will return to that feeling in a moment, for now just let yourself experience the beauty of the quiet place," or if the feeling is all pervasive, we can suggest the client form a symbol of the pervasive feeling and we can begin to work with it. Below is a guided imagery exercise to help find the quiet place within. It begins with guidance for relaxation. It is one way in which I work to help clients contact their quiet place. If you wish to look at other approaches to finding the quiet place, you may want to refer to the book by Bresler and Truba (1979), *Free Yourself from Pain*.

Finding a quiet place

Find a comfortable position lying down on your bed or on the floor. Make sure it is at a time and in a place that you will not be disturbed. Close your eyes. Allow yourself to forget about all the cares and concerns of your life and the world, and go within. Become aware of your breath and feel how with every breath you take you become twice as relaxed as the breath before. Mentally affirm, "I go within." Visualise how you breathe in golden light. Allow the golden light to permeate every cell, every organ, every limb, every chakra of your being. (Pause) Feel how, as you begin to become one with the golden light, your mind and emotions are calmed, soothed and at peace. (Pause)

You find yourself now at peace and relaxed. Now you are ready to go to your quiet place. The quiet place is a place where you feel safe. It may be a place you already know, or it may be an imaginary place. It is a quiet place where you feel peaceful and serene - your special place. Just allow yourself to go there now and let yourself be in that place. Allow yourself to explore it. Breathe in the air of your quiet place. Where are you? Sense the beauty and colours of your quiet place. (Pause) When you have been there for a time, try to describe your quiet place. Describe it as fully as you can, for example, what time of day it is, what is around you. Describe all the elements that are present in your quiet place - the water, the fire, the air and the earth. If it is sunny, feel the sun on your skin, the sounds of the nature - whatever is there to see or feel, allow yourself to see and feel it. (Long Pause) Feel how you are rejuvenated and regenerated as you relax in your quiet place. Simply allow yourself to be there and enjoy the space.

Once the quiet place is found, and the person has spent some time relaxing in it, he or she is ready to invite in an image to represent his or her symptoms (if working with an illness or feeling) or to invite in an image to represent his or her inner adviser. In either case, the image that comes is thoroughly explored, and communication with it begins to take place. An exercise is presented below to help you find your inner adviser. For further reading in this area, Rossman and Remen (1982) in *Imagine Health* give details of a technique for "Listening to your symptoms." They also present a technique for "meeting your inner adviser." Martin Rossman (1987) *Healing Yourself: A step by step program for better health through imagery* is also worthwhile reading.

Before beginning this exercise, it is helpful to first go through the process of working out the issue you wish to work with, relaxing and finding the quiet place as outlined above. When you have done this you simply move on to the exercise.

Inviting the inner adviser

Allow an image to form to represent your inner adviser. The inner adviser is a "wise, kind, and compassionate being" that can take any form it chooses. It may be an image, it may be a feeling or simply a sense or impression. Allow it to come forward now and as it does, allow yourself to examine it closely. What is it? What form does it take? Perhaps it's a light or a colour. Let yourself describe it fully. If you need to, ask it to come closer so that you can get a fuller sense of it. What ever it is, simply let yourself explore it and open to its presence. Be aware it has come to help you with the issue with which you wish to deal, and that it knows all that you need to know about that particular issue. Is there anything you would like to say to it or tell it, now that it has come? (A dialogue back and forth is encouraged over some time, until communication is at a point of appropriate completion.) The inner adviser is then thanked for its assistance and a way of meeting it again is established, for example, the image may inform the client that it can be found whenever the client chooses to look for it again.

A general guide of the process

Outlined below is a general procedure which I often use in my practice and which I find very useful. It is a simple set of steps that can be followed.

1. Guide the client into relaxation following his or her breath. There may be gentle music playing to help facilitate this.

2. Go to the quiet place.

- Describe the quiet place. This helps you to develop the technique of imaging and sensing.
- Experience it and come to a point of relaxation.

- Contemplate the issue you are wanting to work on (this step may be omitted if you are really clear about the issue and have discussed it well with the therapist beforehand.)
- Leave when ready.

3. Contact and communicate with the image
(this may be the image of the symptom or the inner adviser).

The image of the symptom or the inner adviser may speak in images or through feelings, rather than in thoughts or words. At all times try to see if you understand what is being said, felt or shown. You may need to explore that. These steps below are a general guideline of procedure which I use once the image of the symptom or the inner adviser reveals itself. Depending on what happens with the client in the session I may, of course, vary it. Sometimes, for example, we may be working with an image of a symptom, then go to the inner adviser and back again, or some other form of variation, depending on the flow that seems to facilitate to the client's process. I may go off on a relevant tangent with a client and will generally return to complete the steps that follow.

- Allow the image to form, it may be an image, it may be a knowing, a sense, an energy or an impression.
- Work out if there is anything you want to say or tell to the image.
- Say it.
- Find out if there is anything it wants to say or tell to you (getting familiar with the image).
- Listen to what it has to say (or see what it has to show you).
- Work out if there is anything you want to ask the image.
- Ask it.
- Listen for its reply (or see what it has to show you).

- If there is anything you are unclear about express that and ask for clarity.
- Find out if there is anything the image wants to ask or show you. Listen or look at what that is.
- Wait for response.
- Become the image and look at (person's name) through the eyes of the image. How does (person's name) appear to you?
- Ask the image to tell (person's name) what you have come to tell or show him or her that will help him or her the most at this time.
- Become yourself again and respond to what has been said, felt, or seen.
- Call the inner adviser forth.
- Is there anything you would like to say to the inner adviser or image, for example, how you feel about what was said?
- Ask the inner adviser if there is anything else that you need to
- know or understand right now.
- Listen or look.
- If there is anything you are unclear about express that and ask for clarity.
- Find out how you can meet the image or adviser again.
- Thank the image or the adviser.
- Say goodbye.
- Return to your quiet place. Be there and allow yourself to integrate what has happened by contemplating what has taken place in the session.
- Points to consider
- Dealing with fear of failure

Points to consider

Dealing with fear of failure

Clients may feel that they cannot do guided imagery because "they are not visual." Guided imagery not only works with images, but also with our other senses, feeling and knowing. It may help to explain this to the client. Clients can also suffer from anxiety about the process itself. They may have fear or even embarassment about what will come up, resistance, a fear of failure related to the process, or a general lack of trust. I have found that such anxiety is quickly dealt with by simply following the processes of the guided imagery. The fear, resistance, or lack of trust can be seen as a symptom for which an image, or impression is found. The guided imagery process then works to deal with that, and a lot of valuable understanding can be found.

What if the client doesn't get an image?

There are a number of ways to deal with this. Patience, perseverance and a loving climate are essential ingredients for this work. If they client doesn't get an image, it is not the end of the world. It may mean that a process of basic relaxation or spiritual healing would better suffice, or it may be that time needs to be spent helping the client relax and learn that an image will eventually come, particularly through continuing to visualise the quiet place. If there is a problem in doing this, which is rare in my experience, it is possible to get the client to think of a quiet place in the physical world where he or she feels safe; and with eyes closed, get the client to describe it to you. For example, his/her bedroom. Through that the client will see that he or she can in fact "do it," and will be more open to allow the process to work as it continues in the session or in future ones.

Allow the process to be the client's

When I first began guided imagery work as a therapist I was amazed how much I learned about life through the wit and intelligence of other people's inner advisers. I found it fascinating and marvellous, especially how meaning and understanding would be revealed through symbol and language. I realised that what was being contacted was actually a higher intelligence than we generally acknowledge in life, an intelligence which has the motive of helping us. I also found that my curiosity, whilst it is a quality which has some merit, was something I needed to watch. I needed to learn to give clients the time and space they needed in their process. My curiosity could affect the questions I would ask - the tone, the content, etc. I needed to learn to relax and simply allow the process to unfold according to the client's need. In the beginning I also needed to get over my own fear of the client not getting an image, to develop my trust and confidence in the process, and to allow time for my skills to develop.

How can I keep in touch with where the client is at?

In guided imagery there is a relationship functioning between the client and his/her symptom and/or inner adviser. There is also a relationship between the therapist or guide and the client. The client has a choice whether or not he or she would like to say out loud what is happening within. Either way the therapist can still stay in touch with what is happening; however, when the client does share, it can help the therapist to know better how to help the client.

I have found that the language of the therapist is of vital importance to the client/therapist relationship and that the client/therapist relationship is important in terms of the possible value of the session for the client. For example, using sentences that allow choice for the client - which respects the client's freedom - helps the client to realise that the guided imagery is his or her process:

Is there something you want to say to the image? (In these examples, if the client answers yes, and then does not say what he or she would like to ask, the therapist needs to ask, 'What would you like to ask it?' As the client says the question, the therapist then can say, 'Ask it, and let it reply in whatever way it chooses.')

Is there something you would like to know?
What does it look like?
Can you describe it to me?
How do you feel towards it?
Is there anything you would like to say to it or tell it?
Is there anything it would like to say to you or tell you?
Is there anything you want to ask it?
Is there anything it wants to ask you?

Some language may be more directive if that is what is needed in the process to move the client on to the next stage. For example, when the person becomes the image and starts looking at him or herself through the eyes of the image, the therapist might say, *Tell (person's name) what you have come to tell him or her*. This could also be said in the following way, *What can you tell her to help her on her path?* As a therapist you need to find a language which works for you, one that you feel comfortable with, and that is suitable to your clients.

This method allows the client to be in his/her own process and lets it be the client's image and answers which determine where the process leads. The therapist simply has to be with the client in his/her process. It is like using a saw on wood: the saw is made to cut wood, you simply apply the saw correctly and it cuts the wood, you don't have to force it. Similarly, guided imagery needs simply to be learned and applied in a given situation. The process does the work; you don't need to force it.

If the client doesn't answer for a long period and you are not sure what is happening, you can simply ask the client, "What is happening (person's name)?" This enables you to stay informed and therefore stay in touch with the process.

What if the client's image is not a positive one?

Sometimes clients get images that are anything but helpful, images that are part of the person's shadow which wish to sabotage the process. These images can be worked with, and when their negative nature is exposed, the client may choose to find another more positive image, or work further with the negative image to find out more about that part of the self. Sometimes a seemingly negative image has gifts of wisdom within it and is not actually negative in intent. That is why it is good to explore the image to find out if it actually is negative. When this occurs, I sometimes ask the client to ask the image directly about its nature, for example, by asking "Are you of the Christ?" (depending on whether such a question is appropriate for the client). This will disarm and expose the saboteur which often then simply disappears. The client can also tell the negative image that it can only stay if it is prepared to lift in vibration and receive some light so that its role will become a positive one instead of a negative one. This elicits a variety of responses from such negative aspects - they may choose to do that, in which case they transform through the power of alchemy and become a useful tool for the client, or they may choose to go, and they simply do just that.

Timing

The guided process must allow the time and space needed in which the experience can take place. The one guiding needs to develop a sensitivity to this and give the client the space he or she needs to do the many steps in the process.

Conclusion

Guided imagery is an amazing tool that helps us to find communication with our own inner nature. So many people on Earth today are searching for ways to do just that. It helps to give us the direction and healing we so need, with the invaluable insight and understanding of our inner advisers. With all the support, comfort and guidance they give, we soon discover that we are no longer alone and that if we should choose it, help is always available.

Alchemy

What is alchemy?

Alchemy is the process of developing from the denseness of lead (the personality) into pure gold, that is, being infused with soul. Essentially it is the process of bringing Spirit into matter. This can only be done by working with the finer forces of nature. H. P. Blavatsky (1990, p. 15) speaks of alchemy as the great mystery which must remain to some degree secret because of the possibility of misuse in a selfish world. She goes on to tell us that alchemy is a process whereby the "Universal Solvent ... possesses the power of removing all the seeds of disease from the human body, of renewing youth and prolonging life." Blavatsky points to patience and purity of heart as being the two essential qualities needed in an alchemist. The object of alchemy is transformation.

Creating alchemy

To transform our personalities and become gold we have to face the dragon in ourselves, the shadow. In the book *Owning Your Own Shadow*, Robert Johnson (1993, p. 4) defines the shadow as "that part of us we fail to see or know." This part of us is made up of all our characteristics which we disown. It has in it energies such as jealousy, pride, aggression, ambition and competition. It also contains the more positive qualities which we may choose to not own. Johnson refers to this as the gold within the shadow. It is the skills, talents and abilities we have which we deny. Rather than identify such qualities as our own we project these qualities to others. For example, we may see others as being successful because we cannot accept success for ourselves. The irony is that then we may become jealous of them.

When we work with alchemy, we identify and separate the negative matter which we wish to transform, transmute and infuse with Light. In this process our lower nature is transformed to become our higher. Often, in the alchemical process, the negative matter to be transmuted is an aspect of our shadow. In the story Ahimsa, which appears in the chapter: *Chakras*, we saw how the negative quality of ambition was identified and worked with until finally, instead of being a thick black snake it became a phoenix, rising from the ashes in flight. The story is alchemy in action. Many experiences of spiritual healing, when seen clairvoyantly, reveal this process of alchemy at work. The matter presenting for transformation will often appear as a black tar-like substance. It may take a form, perhaps a snake or spider or simply be black tar. As the healing work proceeds, the substance changes form, colour and density. It may become grey, then white, change from solid to liquid, from liquid to gas, from gas to air. Sometimes the Universal Solvent will appear as a vibrant, coloured Light, often purple, or perhaps yellow, blue or pink in colour. It will have an etheric appearance and not be in solid form. The fineness of its matter will indicate a high vibrating force that can penetrate and transform even the densest of matter. The healing substance may also appear initially as a golden nectar which can be poured upon the matter to be transformed. The form the healing agent will take varies according to need. In alchemy this agent is referred to as the philosopher's stone. Once the alchemy has taken place, the initial substance of black tar will no longer exist. Perhaps only ashes will remain. When a healer sees these ashes with the inner eye, he or she knows that the work of transmutation is done.

The story that follows is an example of working with grief as a substance needing transformation through the alchemical process of spiritual healing.

Egypt again

Egypt again. "Grief! Don't tell me I'm carrying grief that's centuries old, not again."

The situation was clear. I had been yearning to be with the father of my blood who had chosen not to recognise me as heir to his throne, as I was a girl and not a boy.

I thought I had let that one go, but, no, here it was large as life, and the grief felt as if it had just happened. I could sense it was old, though, by the vinegar-like quality of the energy of grief which appeared like liquid bile.

"Well, this is the year for transformation, isn't it, and I have been travelling to the cave of symbols a lot lately, I'll just take it along and put it in the pot with the rest."

Suddenly I grew wings, first limp and then strong and violet and I flew with all my might to the mouth of the cave and entered enthusiastically to get the job done. I went straight to the laboratory of a little old alchemist, who looked something like Julius Sumner Miller, and presented my grief to him. He took the somewhat transparent yellowish, insipid liquid and placed it in a conical glass flask, already being warmed by the Bunsen burner which emitted a clear violet flame.

As he stirred the liquid, he reached into the drawer beside him and took out a yellow compound which looked like sulphur. I noticed he had many different compounds of different colours. He seemed to know exactly what and how much to put in. But before he placed the yellow compound into the flask he asked me, "What is it you would like the grief transformed into?" I thought for a moment about grief and that it was the yearning to be with my blood father that was the substance of my grief. I pondered, and it came:

"Yearning to be with the father and to serve him. Yearning to be with Christ and to serve God."

"I thought so," the man replied, as if he already knew what I was going to say, and he placed the yellow compound into the flask and began to mix the ingredients. As I watched, it turned into scrambled eggs, just how I like them for breakfast. He looked at me with a glint in his eye. It was symbolic - a fresh start - a new beginning, one that will give great nourishment.

The mixture was a bit too sticky to go back into my heart from whence it had come. The professor turned up the heat and the violet flame turned the eggs into a violet liquid - the purest, richest colour violet I had ever seen. The professor looked very pleased and turned the heat off and poured the violet liquid into a test tube. He placed the test tube in my heart and then took out the tube leaving the violet liquid in my heart.

The job was done and I could feel myself one with Light. As I did this I became aware of a black tar-like substance on me. I could feel that having seen how the alchemy worked I just wanted to give up everything, and I said to the professor "What about this black tar? Can you help me with that?"

And he said, "Well, it won't fit in the flask, come with me, we will need the big pot for that."

We entered a big room where an enormous cauldron sat empty.

"Put it in there," he said. I could feel it was made of anger. Anger that I no longer needed, anger that I had held for my fathers throughout history. I placed the black substance in the pot and it nearly filled it. As the violet fire intensified, the black substance turned grey, then white like marshmallow. As I watched, it slowly began to evaporate and form a violet mist. Shortly afterwards it vanished. I realised that my anger

had no substance and that I could just let it go now. I no longer had to carry it around with me. It didn't have to be turned into anything, it could just be released and indeed it had.

During the time when the substance was turning from black tar to violet mist, I had a deep inner dialogue with my current father, who had recently died, and many misgivings became of no consequence in the Light. Instead, the strength of love that is between us was felt and we were like two souls standing together in the Light of the Great Father, souls searching for our divinity, which through God's grace we were able to find.

Shortly before my father died, I was given a vision of my father and myself as being two blue butterflies, dancing together in the freedom of life. We rested together for a time on a golden chrysanthemum, sharing the love, peace, joy and wisdom that life brings. My vision helped me to go through his death and gave me peace and understanding. Though life may be short, we are transformed by it and like the caterpillar, if we dare to look within and open to Spirit, we are, like the butterfly, set free.

In the story we see that the personality needed to clear things on the emotional and mental levels to help make the alchemical transformation complete. This is a common occurrence. Alchemy is a magical process which works with the inner magician. However, to make transformation total and complete, we must work with our personalities and make efforts to change our habits and attitudes. We must also want to change and must ask for the help of the Light.

One of the main reasons we so often fail to open to healing is because we fail to acknowledge our shadow, and deny that we have negative aspects that need transformation. We often project our shadow onto others (that is, make others at fault or the world generally because our desires and expectations aren't met), perhaps another person or an organisation or group. In doing this we deny ourselves the essential ingredient that will, if owned, reveal to us the way of change and the road to balance. Without owning the shadow, we cannot develop psychologically or spiritually.

We must learn to accept the shadow and learn to love it. Only when we do this can we become whole. The story that follows explores the concept of loving the shadow.

The mudman

The mudman, a dwarf-like being, about three feet high with dark muddied skin and balding head, appeared beside me. I was standing in a cave full of symbols in front of a violet fire. With help, I thought, I could put this little fellow into the fire to be transformed. The mudman was not keen on entering, however.

"Let me take you on a tour of the cave before you go into the fire," I re-assured him.

I could see his fear. He clung to my thigh very tightly and I stretched my arms down to lift him up onto my hip. We went more and more deeply into the cave, to the entrance of another cave. There we met a guardian. As I looked the guardian in the eyes the mudman diminished in size. The fear the mudman had was now in me and I felt afraid to go more deeply into the cave.

I became aware that the mudman was part of my shadow and the cave represented my subconscious. I asked for help to deepen the experience and found myself going into the cave. The mudman had become quite small and sat on my arm. He felt like a friend who could help me because he seemed to know something about what was going on. As we entered the cave I saw many mudmen the size of the original one when we first met. There were at least twenty or thirty, all looking the same. The little mudman on my arm said,

"The shadow is the shadow. The different forms of appearance are simply disguises."

I could feel more trust in this little one and sensed that he truly wanted to help me. I sensed that by my willingness to confront the guardian I was given help in diminishing the shadow. I became more conscious of the little mudman. The roof of the cave in which the many mudmen stood was gone. A worker in the cave passed me a fire hose filled with violet Light. I directed it towards the cave where the many mudmen stood. They all fell down. They had mud all over them and I could feel their ugliness and dirtiness. The Light acted like water and cleansed them. All that was left was mud. The little one on my arm was very excited because he was now on the winning side, the side of the Light. He said he never liked being on the other side - that now he could use his energy for good and could have a sense of higher purpose. He had a lot of energy and was playful. He could help me be light, joyful and clever, to outwit all those men that were only mud. Suddenly, a little man appeared in the mud pile flinging mud at me to get my attention. He appeared like the one on my arm who I had let into my heart. The little man in the mud pile was mischievous and playful. The two looked alike. One I trusted and one I did not trust.

The one in the mud took on a persona like that of the trusted one, but I was alert to its tricks. It wanted me to fight it, but I did not want to. I knew that if I engaged in battle with it, I would lose and would fall into the pit of mud. The mudman I trusted grew again to the height of my thigh; he said,

"Accept me."

I felt quite touched by this and realised I had come to love it on this journey into the cave. I took its hand and walked away from the mud.

I left the more negative shadow behind with less power than when we began. Hand in hand I walked with my little mudman to the guardian where we started. I realised that I could only put this mudman in the violet fire out of love and not because I wanted to get rid of him. I realised that when I could do it out of love he would be quite content to go into the fire. I told him that I would go with him into the fire. We both entered the fire and stood in the centre of the flame. He clung to me. I patted him on the head and told him to let the violet fire do its work. Together we would transform. When it was time to leave the fire I went to take the mudman with me and found there was only pink light. Everything in the cave had turned crimson pink and there was a feeling of love. I felt that the little mudman was my friend and that he had learned something, as I had, in this process. We were sent out to teach about the shadow with humour, compassion, lightness and love. He felt very close to me with an energy that would support me, rather than harm me.

As I left the cave I found myself on top of Mount Shasta. The sky was very clear blue with violet butterflies flying in the air. There was an eagle on top of the mountain. The mudman was gone and in his place there was an eagle. I felt as close to God as I could get. There was an enormous stillness. I felt completely still inside.

We can integrate our shadow into our personality through the process of alchemy where we work towards individuation, self-realisation, and bringing to consciousness the unconscious aspects - coming to know the self. It isn't the shadow itself that is the problem as much as what we do with it and how we refuse to accept and integrate it. When the shadow is left unchecked, it grows as does the power of the negative forces over us, which we feed by our refusal to own our shadow. Yet when we dare to look at it we are often amazed by its deceptive face, and find within us the inner gold or unconscious material that is of great value to our growth. The short story below gives an example of the gold within the shadow which was only found by daring to look into and dialogue with an aspect of the shadow.

The hidden gift

I was terrified. There had been a murder and I was making an attempt to help catch the murderer by acting as a decoy. I was sitting in a room the size of a toilet with four doors around me. One at the front, one at the back and one at each side. At any given moment, the murderer could come to murder me, which I envisaged he would do by piercing me with a large sword-like knife. I checked the doors and was aware I had a little time, but not much. In that time I contemplated whether I should be sitting there at all. Through this contemplation, I discovered that I was doing it for the good of the whole and even though it left me vulnerable and terrified, the motive was right. I should indeed help try to catch the murderer.

The terror and fear of the position I was in began to overwhelm me. The alarm went and I awoke. The terror remained along with a perplexity as I tried to decipher what this dream might have been trying to tell me. I laboured with it for days, trying not to jump to conclusions about it that would invalidate or dismiss it. I tried to find the value of what it was trying to show me. Some days later it became very clear. It had felt like part of me was murdering another part of me. I decided to ask the part that was acting as the decoy what the murderer was murdering.

It replied: "The loving and giving self."

I was astonished for I imagined that the part being murdered, although it may not have needed to be so brutal as murder, needed to die. There was something wrong. The term 'murder' brought many connotations of something grossly out of alignment with my good. The decoy was working for the good of the whole and I trusted it.

"Why are you putting yourself in such a vulnerable position?" I asked it.

"I want to catch the murderer," it replied. "It is time its game was stopped."

"Who is the murderer?" I asked.

"It's the perfectionist part of you that beats me up every time you make a mistake. In fact, it beats me up whether you make a mistake or not."

"Why so many doors?" I asked, aware that these doors could be opened at any time and neither the decoy nor I seemed to have any control over it.

"They represent the levels at which the perfectionist in you attempts sabotage. There are four doors for four levels - the spiritual, the mental, the emotional and the physical."

I remembered that yesterday I had fallen over and grazed my palms. I became aware of my thoughts and I could see how I constantly sabotage myself mentally and emotionally by my beliefs and negative self-talk. I could see that this murderer needed to be caught. At least it was identified and I could begin to work with it. Exposing it in this way I could feel much of the fear of the unknown was released. I began to feel as if I could once again take control over it. I had to be like the decoy and allow myself to become vulnerable, feel the fears and be prepared to confront the murderer when it arrived through whichever door it might come.

As purpose began to grow within me I was ready. In the days that followed, I found many of my behaviours and attitudes beginning to change. I confronted this shadow aspect of the negative perfectionist. I worked with it and gave it a new role in my life, a role of support and co-operation where it could use its energy to work with me instead of against me. This part of me had a lot of energy which could be valuably used for my good. On all levels, changes were being made. I began to eat correctly and exercise, restoring my health, to be kinder to myself in my thoughts, actions and feelings, and nurturing began to take place. The world around me took on a new perspective. Identifying the murderer and embracing it gave me the opportunity to extend love to all parts of my being. The love could also begin to extend to others.

Some time later I was still dealing with my perfectionism. I met the hidden part of myself in full force. She appeared as a dwarf with great strength of character. Her face was square and the jaw bones were set with a sense of purpose and determination as she spoke.

"I don't like to be in public and you keep taking me."

"You are part of me so it is better you come with me."

"But I make so many mistakes and I'm so stupid, ugly and fat. I've got greasy skin and I smell. I'm everything you hate."

I started to feel awful. I knew I hadn't allowed space for her in myself.

"It's your perfectionism, it's become bigger and I've become smaller in the hope that you will notice me. You see, I exist in everyone."

I felt she had a lot of wisdom so I asked her to explain more.

"I am your negative self image and I have a purpose, for without me the seesaw would not balance. I'm needed for balance to keep in check the mighty ego of the little self which if it was given half a chance would see itself as the most fantastic being on Earth. When I come you look at me in horror, but I am necessary for you to stay in balance. I teach true humility, by taking people of the Light into humanity, in all its ugliness, so that they may rejoice that they know the beauty of the Light. I teach gratitude for that Light. In knowing me, you must have gratitude. I teach true compassion for the self and others, for to love me a person must truly open the heart in love, letting go of all judgements of self and others."

The dwarf climbed up and nestled herself in my lap.

"I don't mind being in public as long as I'm not forced to hide and I know I'm loved by you. I'm actually full of Light and Love, so much so that it doesn't matter what I look like, or how I appear to others, I am content. It is when you get upset by my presence that you move out of Light and Love. Do you understand?"

"Yes."

"Good! It's funny, isn't it! We are both working for the Light and yet we see darkness in each other."

"How can I begin to see your Light more often and allow you to come into public with me?"

"You are a seeker of truth - continue to seek to live in truth, and know that you are in your truth when you are prepared to let me be with you in love, whether that be in public or otherwise. If you truly seek truth, then you must find the Light and Love in me for I am That, That I am."

"Give me your heart."

I smiled because I felt much more used to taking others into my heart.

"Yes, you have to be prepared to turn your perceptions upside down and then you may come to know me. I am the Mother and I have many guises. You must learn to love me in all of them. I will always love you, so much so that I will do anything to get your attention, even become a dwarf with pimples. So when you next catch yourself invalidating or putting down an aspect of yourself, remember me and remember that I am that, for I am everything. In sending hatred to that, you send hatred to me and that is all right because I can take that and make it love. I know that one day you will get better at it, for you see, I live in hope and I trust that you will one day become like me, dear daughter. Until that *day I give you my Love and my Compassion. I am your loving mother - I am the Mother Christ. Give me your hands."*

I gave her my hands.

"Now, I have your hands and your heart and I can work through you."

By placing our unconscious parts in the fire of alchemy, their essential fantasy content becomes conscious. Instead of arguing with them, we ask them what they want. They come to our awareness through the process of spiritual healing, guided imagery and the like - and in that way we transmute them. We observe them objectively, look at them and face them. Essentially, we face the dragon. The process of coming to know ourselves cannot be forced but depends on time, balance and patience. Our destructive emotions have to burn themselves out and we have to suffer them in order to integrate the needed understanding and find wisdom. Enduring the suffering is not pleasant; however, we are rewarded when Spirit rises up out of the fire and forms the basis of our future directions and new inspirations. Our transformational process is complete.

The Grail Castle

The green undulating hills stretched in the distance as far as my eyes could see. On the edge of the horizon the Grail Castle stood, a tiny speck in my vision. As I looked more closely, I could see a group of people standing upon a hill not too far away. They were all looking toward the Grail Castle as I was, and I could sense their yearning to be closer to it.

If we could all minimise the distance between us and the Grail Castle we will have come far in the purpose and process of our evolution. I became aware that in order to get there, the yearning in the heart had to be strong. Our teachers can make us aware of the need for transformation within ourselves, but we have to want it and have to take the steps ourselves. If we want help, we have to ask. I asked within to be taken to the Grail Castle, if I could be allowed to be transformed. As I asked I felt myself becoming humble and found myself on my knees on land much closer now to the Grail Castle.

I asked within, "What do I need to do to be transformed?"

"Look inside yourself!"

I could see myself inside the Grail Castle in a chamber surrounded by many riches. There were emeralds, rubies, diamonds and gold unimaginable, fruits of all kinds, grapes, peaches, nectarines from all countries and climates of the earth. I could sense great fulfilment and abundance around me. Before me stood Merlin and Morgaine. I asked then what I should now do.

"Be at peace with yourself and be ready to help the suffering, for they will be led your way. There are many and you must lead them further on."

The path appeared. I became aware that in my work I can take people along it a certain distance until they can be taken on by those further ahead. I am to work with those further ahead in cooperative effort. Just by doing that I will be transformed. I form one of many. As we all work in this way the Higher Plan is fulfilled. Morgaine turned into Madame Blavatsky before my eyes.

"This is the promise you have made in this and many lives, to serve the Christ Buddha. I ask that you don't serve me but you serve Him."

Her role is to point me in the right direction, to show me the way because I must walk there myself. Even Morgaine could only take those to the Grail Castle who were willing to sacrifice and surrender.

"What must I sacrifice?" I asked.

"Your will," the reply came.

As the answer came forward, I could see myself merging with the Will of God and I could see Morgaine again. She told me about a gate ahead and how she would like to help me get through it as I needed to understand something. She says,

"You are free to choose. You choose whether to walk the path or not!"

I was nearing the gate. In my bag on my back I was carrying many old personalities. To get through to the other side of the gate I had to take off the bag and leave it and its contents behind. Morgaine helped me.

"Take it off and leave it there but send a little Light into it. I see other knapsacks there left behind from others who have gone ahead. There are many angels working with them."

I felt a little uncomfortable leaving the bag there for the angels to work with, but I could sense that it was their job and it was all right to do so. I still felt unsure about going through the gate. This let me know that there was more to be done.

"You have to believe in yourself and remember what the Self is. You have to let go of ego for after you walk through the gate, more will be demanded of you. Think and make it a conscious decision. Transmute the fear you have of the promise you have made."

Violet Light filled my being.

"Now you are ready, come with me."

Pink magenta colour was everywhere, the word and energy of Love was resonating.

"Love all others as you love Me. That is what is asked of you, and that you can do. I need disciples who love, who will defend the faith with love and who will follow me. I am the Christ, and I call My legions of angels to work now. There is no time to waste, no time to be caught by the lower self. Rise, rise, rise and follow the higher mind and the true heart."

I could see the love between myself and others everywhere, my eyes now open to it.

Spreading the Light

*Love will make you weep and cry with suffering and pain
and through all that it will never leave you,
but will fill you,
again and again.
Let it live in your heart.
Let it guide your life.
In love you climb the highest mountains
and become Light.
You swim in the deepest rivers
and sail all-weathered seas.
Let your soul guide you
and let your Spirit breathe.
Love it does await you.
Look within your heart.
You will find it there -
ready to help you start to open
to the life that lies ahead,
to a life full of wonder.*

*The Christed One awaits you
- in love -
you will find the Christ.
Together as one you merge with the Sun
- in love -
do you dare?*

When the Light of understanding is available to you, you must use it to help others to see and be illumined also. When you feel the passion inside you for the Light, you must awaken this passion in others, so that the Light can spread and the Earth can become a Flame of Light. At the core of your being is the desire to fill the world with Light and all people in it, so that Earth may rise as a Star and take its place amongst the Lighted Planets of the Universe. That is what is in your heart. Do not be frightened of the power of Love - for it will lift you into your destiny.

References

Spiritual Healing

Ananda Tara Shan (1993). The Living Word of the Hierarchy. Daylesford, Victoria: Maitreya Surya Publishing House.
Ananda Tara Shan (1994). Spiritual Healing. (Booklet in the series, Teachings for the Children of the Heart): Daylesford, Victoria: Maitreya Surya Publishing House.
Bailey, A.A. (1984). Esoteric Psychology, Volume I. New York: Lucis Publishing.
Ferrier, J. Todd (1984). Spiritual Healing. London: Toptown Printers Ltd.
Leadbeater, C.W. (1987). Man Visible and Invisible. Wheaton, Illinois: Quest.
Leadbeater, C.W. (1959). The Masters and the Path. Adyar: Vasanta Press.
Van der Leeuw, J.J. (1987). The Fire of Creation. New York: Quest.

Angelic Helpers

Ananda Tara Shan (1993). The Living Word of the Hierarchy. Daylesford, Victoria: Maitreya Surya Publishing House.
Bailey, A. A. (1982). A Treatise on Cosmic Fire. New York: Lucis Publishing Co.
Davidson, G. (1967). A Dictionary of Angels: including the fallen Angels. New York: The Free Press.
Hodson, G. (1987). The Kingdom of the Gods. Madras: Vasanta Press.
Hodson, G. (1988). The Brotherhood of Angels and Men. Illinois: Theosophical Publishing House.
Hodson, G. Angels and the New Race. Out of print.
Wyllie, T. (1992). Ask your Angels. New York: Ballantine Books.

The Human Structure

Ananda Tara Shan (1993). The Living Word of the Hierarchy. Daylesford, Victoria: Maitreya Surya Publishing House.
Bailey, A.A. (1987a). A Treatise on White Magic. New York: The Lucis Publishing Co.

Bailey, A.A. (1987b). Ponder on This. New York: The Lucis Publishing Co.
Bailey, A.A. (1987c). The Soul and Its Mechanism. New York: The Lucis Publishing Company.
Bailey, A.A. (1990). The Soul, The Quality of Life. New York: The Lucis Publishing Company.
Barbarouka, G.A. (1992). The Divine Plan. Adyar, Madras: The Theosophical Publishing House.
Besant, A. (1985). Reincarnation. Adyar, India: The Theosophical Publishing House.
Besant, A. (1990). Man and His Bodies. Adyar, Madras: Vasanta Press.
Blavatsky, H. P. (1963). The Secret Doctrine Volume 1. Pasadena, California: Theosophical University Press.
Blavatsky, H.P. (1990). Theosophical Glossary. New York: The Theosophical Publishing Company.
Hodson, G. (1981). Basic Theosophy: The Living Wisdom. Adyar, Madras: Theosophical Publishing House.
Hodson, G. (1985). The Miracle of Birth: A clairvoyant study of the human embryo. Wheaton, Illinios: The Theosophical Publishing House.
Leadbeater, C.W. (1977). An Outline of Theosophy. Adyar, Madras: Theosophical Publishing House.
Leadbeater, C.W. (1986). A Textbook of Theosophy. Adyar, Madras: The Theosophical Publishing House.

The Chakras

Ananda Tara Shan (1991). The Last Chakra: From an Open House with Ananda Tara Shan. Daylesford, Victoria.
Bailey, A.A. (1984). Esoteric Healing. New York: Fort Orange Press. Lucis Publishing Company.
Johari, H. (1987). Chakras: Energy Centres of Transformation. Vermont: Destiny.
Landsdowne, Z.F. (1993). The Chakras and Esoteric Healing. York Beach: Samuel Wiser, Inc.
Leadbeater, C.W. (1980). The Chakras. Wheaton, Illinois: Quest.
Powell, A.E. (1987). The Etheric Double. Wheaton, Illinois: Quest.
Powell, A.E. (1992). The Astral Body: and other astral phenomena. Wheaton, Illinois: Quest.

The Aura and its Colours

Ananda Tara Shan (1994). <u>Spiritual Healing</u>. (Booklet in the series, Teachings for the Children of the Heart): Daylesford, Victoria: Maitreya Surya Publishing House.
Bailey, A. A. (1979). <u>Letters on Occult Meditation</u>. New York: Lucis Trust.
Bailey, A. A. (1987). <u>Ponder on This</u>. New York: Lucis Trust.
Besant, A. (1990). <u>Man and His Bodies</u>. Wheaton, Illinois: The Theosophical Publishing House.
Blavatsky, H.P. (1990). <u>The Theosophical Glossary</u>. Los Angeles, California: The Theosophy Company.
De Purucker, G. (1979). <u>Fundamentals of Esoteric Philosophy</u>. Pasadena, California: Theosophical University Press.
Edwards, H. E. (1974). <u>A Guide to the Understanding and Practice of Spiritual Healing</u>. Surrey: The Healer Publishing Company.
Hodson, G. (1981). <u>Basic Theosophy: The Living Wisdom</u>. Madras: The Theosophical Publishing House.
Leadbeater, C. W. (1987). <u>Man Visible and Invisible</u>. Wheaton, Illinois: Quest.
Leadbeater, C.W. (1996). <u>The Inner Life</u>. Wheaton, Illinois: Quest.
Powell, A. E. (1972). <u>The Astral Body</u>. Wheaton, Illinois: Quest.
Sherwood, K. (1994). <u>The Art of Spiritual Healing</u>. St. Paul, Minnesota: Lewellyn Publications.

The Healer

Ananda Tara Shan (1993). <u>The Living Word of the Hierarchy</u>. Daylesford, Victoria: Maitreya Surya Publishing House.
Ananda Tara Shan (1994). <u>Spiritual Healing</u>. (Booklet in the series, Teachings for the Children of the Heart). Daylesford, Victoria: Maitreya Surya Publishing House.
Bailey, A. A. (1979). <u>Letters on Occult Meditation</u>. New York: Lucis Trust.

The Law of Reincarnation

Ananda Tara Shan (1993). <u>The Living Word of the Hierarchy</u>. Daylesford, Victoria: Maitreya Surya Publishing House.
Bailey. A. A. (1987). <u>Ponder on This</u>. New York: Lucis Publishing Co.

Besant, A. (1985a). trans. The Bhagavad Gita.
Besant, A. (1985b). Reincarnation. Adyar: India: The Theosophical Publishing House.
Besant, A. (1987). Death and After. Adyar: India: The Theosophical Publishing House.
Blavatsky, H. P. (1969). An Abridgment of The Secret Doctrine. London: The Theosophical Publishing House.
De Purucker. G. (1979). Fundamentals of the Esoteric Philosophy. Pasadena, California: Theosophical University Press.
Govinda - Rose, T. (1991). The Language of the Heart: Is spoken all over the world. Daylesford, Victoria, Australia: Lotus House.
Hodson, G. (1985). The Miracle of Birth: A clairvoyant study of the human embryo.Wheaton, Illinois: The Theosophical Publishing House.
Leadbeater. C. W. (1977). An Outline of Theosophy. Adyar: India: The Theosophical Publishing House.
Leadbeater. C. W. (1986). A Textbook of Theosophy. Adyar: India: The Theosophical Publishing House.
Rosetti, F. (1992). Psycho Regression: A new system for healing and personal growth. London: Judy Piatkus Publishers.

The Law of Karma

Ananda Tara Shan, (1993). The Living Word of The Hierarchy. Daylesford, Victoria. Maitreya Surya Publishing House.
Besant, A. (1977). The Ancient Wisdom. Adyar, India.The Theosophical Publishing House.
Besant, A. (1987). A Study In Karma. Adyar, India: The Theosophical Publishing House.
Blavatsky, H.P. (1893). The Key To Theosophy. London: The Theosophical Publishing Society.
Blavatsky, H.P. (1990). The Theosophical Glossary. Los Angeles, California: The Theosophy Company.
Hodson, G. (1981). Basic Theosophy. Adyar, India: The Theosophical Publishing House.

The Unconscious

Di Caprio, N.S. (1976). The Good Life: Models for a Healthy Personality. New Jersey: Prentice Hall.
Jung, C. (1976) The Portable Jung. (Edited by Joseph Campbell) New York: Penguin.

Guided Imagery

Bresler, D.E (1979). <u>Free Yourself from Pain</u>. New York: Simon & Schuster.

Bry, A. (1978). <u>Directing the Movies of Your Mind</u>. New York: Harper and Rowe.

Ferrucci, P. (1982). <u>What We May Be</u>. Los Angeles: J.P. Tarcher.

Jaffe, D.T. (1979). <u>Healing From Within</u>. New York: Knopf.

Jung, C.J. (1976). <u>The Portable Jung.</u> (Edited by Joseph Campbell) New York: Penguin.

Rossman, M. and Remen, N. (1982). <u>Imagine Health</u>. Privately published.

Rossman, M. (1987). <u>Healing Yourself: A step by step program for better health through imagery</u>. New York: Walker and Company.

Samuels, M. and Samuels, N. (1975). <u>Seeing with the Mind's Eye</u>. New York: Random House.

Sheinman, N. (1987). <u>The Medicine of the Mind: Guided imagery workshop for personal and professional growth</u>. Class handout. Melbourne, Australia: Paramartha School of Spiritual Education and Development.

Simonton, O.C., Matthews-Simonton, S. and Creighton, J. (1978) <u>Getting Well Again</u>. Los Angeles: J.P. Tarcher.

Thurston, M. A. (1978). <u>How to Interpret Your Dreams.</u> USA: Edgar Cayce Foundation.

Alchemy

Johnson, R. A. (1993). <u>Owning Your Own Shadow</u>. San Francisco: Harper.

Jung, C. (1976). <u>The Portable Jung</u>. Edited by Joseph Campbell: New York: Penguin.

*My heartfelt thanks to all who contributed
to creating this publication, especially
Gregory Govindamurti, Mary Faeth Chenery,
Joana McCutcheon, Joav De Murashkin,
Almut Beringer and Henning Klibo*

Deva Wings Publications

Deva Wings Publications was formed on Right Human Relations Day in 1994. Its purpose and objectives are:

1. to spread the Light by creating literature and other materials that help us to understand Spirit and make the teachings of Theosophy (Divine Wisdom) comprehensible to all.

2. to educate people in the theosophical principles.

3. to educate people in spiritual psychology so that we may come to understand ourselves and become that which we truly are.

Deva is a Sanskrit word meaning shining one or angel. The concept is such that the Light and teachings of Spirit will spread over the Earth on the devas' wings.

TARAJYOTI GOVINDA
(1958-1999)
B.A. Dip. Ed. Grad Dip. Psych. Couns. MAPS

After a spiritual awakening and death experience in 1983, Tara followed an inner calling to establish herself as a professional healer, counsellor, teacher and group facilitator. She became a psychologist whose major focus was the synthesis of spiritual and psychological transformation. Tarajyoti was the founder and director of The Transformational College of Education and co-founder and director of The Theosophical School of Healing.

Her main interests were Theosophy (the study of Divine Wisdom); Jungian psychology; music; native spirituality; being in nature; painting and other creative endeavours.

Tara is also the author of *The Language of the Heart: is spoken all over the world* (1991); *Becoming Whole: the psychology of light* (1998); *The Archangels and the Angels* (1998) and *The Joy of Enlightenment* (1999).

Tarajyoti ascended 5 April 1999 after many years of devoted efforts for the Cause of Love in this world.

Joy to the World

Rejoice

and let heaven and nature sing.

www.ingramcontent.com/pod-product-compliance
Lightning Source LLC
Chambersburg PA
CBHW071315150426
43191CB00007B/632